PHYSICIAN TO THE FLEET

THE LIFE AND TIMES OF THOMAS TROTTER, 1760–1832

Dr Thomas Trotter was a mover and shaker of Georgian medicine. A Scot of humble origin and son of the Enlightenment, he joined the Royal Navy as an assistant surgeon and rose to eminence due to his own abilities, though aided by the occasional piece of patronage. In one period of unemployment in his youth he served as surgeon on the notorious Liverpool slaver *Brookes*. In the Royal Navy, he played a major part in the health improvements that helped turn it into a devastating fighting machine. He was present at the Battle of the Glorious First of June and was acquainted with some of the leading figures of his age such as Howe, St Vincent, Wilberforce, Jenner and Nelson.

Trotter participated in the great maritime events of the day, and a major part of the book is devoted to life in the Georgian navy seen from the medical perspective. He served on numerous warships; worked in the Royal Naval Hospital at Haslar; then, as Physician of the Channel Fleet from 1794 to 1801, was a major player in the control of typhus, the introduction of Jenner's smallpox vaccination, and the conquest of scurvy. The book gives a new interpretation on how scurvy was overcome that shows previous explanations to be flawed.

As well as being a man of action, Trotter was an influential thinker. He was a prolific author and produced important works on scurvy and naval medicine. After 1802, when he retired to marriage and civilian life in Newcastle, he produced the first ever book-length analysis of alcohol dependence, which is widely esteemed today for its prescience. He was also an amateur poet and playwright in the British-Scots tradition

The book reflects the rhythm of his life, records his naval activities on an almost daily basis and offers insights into his thinking through the study of his works. It also covers a range of contextual themes – the Scottish Enlightenment; eighteenth-century medical education; the nature of private practice in Georgian Northumberland; and the organization of the navy and its operations during the Revolutionary War. But beyond the detail this book has, as a central and continuous theme, an attempt to understand Trotter's character – the man, fundamentally, is the story.

BRIAN VALE is a naval historian with degrees from Keele and King's College London. A life-long member of the Society for Nautical Research, he is now Vice President of the Navy Records Society.

GRIFFITH EDWARDS qualified in medicine at Oxford. He is an Emeritus Professor at King's College, London, a Fellow of the Royal College of Physicians and of the Royal College of Psychiatry.

Physician to the Fleet

THE LIFE AND TIMES OF

THOMAS TROTTER

1760–1832

Brian Vale and Griffith Edwards

THE BOYDELL PRESS

First published 2011

The Boydell Press, Woodbridge
ISBN 978 1 84383 604 9

The Boydell Press is an imprint of Boydell & Brewer Ltd
PO Box 9, Woodbridge, Suffolk IP12 3DF, UK

and of Boydell & Brewer Inc.
668 Mount Hope Ave, Rochester, NY 14620, USA

website: www.boydellandbrewer.com

A catalogue record for this book is available
from the British Library

The publisher has no responsibility for the continued existence or accuracy of URLs
for external or third-party internet websites referred to in this book,
and does not guarantee that any content on such websites is,
or will remain, accurate or appropriate.

Papers used by Boydell & Brewer are natural, recyclable products
made from wood grown in sustainable forests

Typeset by Word and Page, Chester, UK

Printed in Great Britain by
CPI Antony Rowe, Chippenham and Eastbourne

To our families

Contents

Illustrations

Abbreviations

NMM   National Maritime Museum
TNN   The National Archives, Kew

Foreword

THIS BOOK has been written to fill a gap. Dr Thomas Trotter MD was an extraordinary man who had a remarkable career. First, as a surgeon in the Royal Navy who reached eminence as Physician to the Channel Fleet under Admiral Lord Howe and Lord St Vincent, he played an important role in bringing about the health improvements that helped turn the Fleet into the devastating fighting machine which routed the French at Trafalgar; then, later in civilian life, he became a forward-looking thinker and a prolific writer on non-naval medical problems. These included the dangers of gas in coal mines, the nervous diseases supposedly caused by social change and the rise of 'luxury' in Georgian society, and alcoholism. Alcohol problems are now a well-established area of medical study, and practitioners look back on Trotter as a pioneer whose work was seminal in establishing that chronic drunkenness was a disease rather than a moral lapse.

Yet Thomas Trotter has never been the subject of a full-scale biography. This may be partly due to the fact that his life had two different phases, the naval and the civilian. But it also reflects the enormous variety of Trotter's career, which, to do it full justice, requires an understanding of a wide range of historical and scientific themes – the Scottish Enlightenment, eighteenth-century medical education, the slave trade, private practice in Georgian Northumberland, the mining industry, the Romantic movement, the organization of the navy, its operations in the English Channel during the Revolutionary War and its determination to improve the health of sailors just as it improved the fabric of its ships. Then, as if that were not enough, Trotter was an amateur poet and playwright in the British-Scots tradition.

In writing of a life as varied as Trotter's, a simple chronological approach cannot do him justice either as a man of action or as a thinker. Before 1802, when the Peace of Amiens and an injury caused his retirement from the navy, Trotter was a participant and observer of some of the great maritime events and issues of the day. In his youth, he had been surgeon on the notorious slaver *Brookes*, a horrifying experience which enabled him to give damning evidence to the Select Committee on the Slave Trade. In his maturity he served as a surgeon on numerous warships, worked in the Royal Naval Hospital at Haslar – then one of the medical wonders of the age – and, as Physician to the Channel Fleet, was a major player in the conquest of scurvy, in the control of typhus and in the rapid introduction of Jenner's vaccination against smallpox. His own journals and the abundance of ships' muster rolls, captains' logs, official dispatches and Admiralty and the Sick and Hurt Board letters to be found in the National Archives make it possible to describe his activities during this period on an almost daily basis.

In 1802, retirement to take up civilian practice in Newcastle brought a change in both his career and the rhythm of his existence. As is the case with most civilians at the time, records and details of his everyday life are difficult to find. Fortunately, this period coincides with Trotter's emergence as a thinker and writer. The final section of the book therefore reflects this change of pace and, while describing the social and professional context in which he lived, draws its insights into his life and thought through a detailed study of his works rather than a daily record of his activities.

In terms of professional achievement Trotter may have been an extraordinary man. But in some ways his career was typical of a man of his time and background – that is, of a Scot of humble origin who obtained medical qualifications in post-Enlightenment Edinburgh, joined the medical service of the navy and rose to eminence on the basis of his own abilities, while benefiting from the occasional piece of useful patronage. However, behind the story of professional success, the fight against disease ashore and afloat, and the background of battles, hurricanes and mutinies, there is the parallel story of Trotter the man. A problem with doing full justice to him as a private man is that he was not an aristocrat. Famous artists did not queue to paint Trotter's portrait. No-one kept his letters or recorded his dinner-table conversation. The plethora of public records and his prolific production of books and pamphlets enable us to establish the details, triumphs and frustrations of his official life; but information on his feelings, likes and dislikes is less easy to find. Fortunately, in the sequence of verses and plays that Trotter produced from his earliest years can be found valuable clues as to the emotional, sensitive and – in his early life – playful side of his personality.

What is clear is that Trotter was a product of the Enlightenment who, throughout his life, combined a passionate enthusiasm for new knowledge and new ideas with a practical ability to do something about it. He was competent and creative, but could also be combative and contentious. It is our hope that this book does full justice to the contribution made by a man who was not only an important public figure, but a complex and engaging private person.

We owe a debt to the many people and institutions who have helped in the composition of this book. Thanks are particularly due to the directors and staff of the National Archives, the National Maritime Museum, the Wellcome Library, the Institute of Psychiatry Library and the Literary and Philosophical Society of Newcastle.

Greenwich
2010

Preface

Visit the Caird Library of the Maritime Museum at Greenwich and the atmosphere is all hushed and quiet with a few scholars sitting at their desks and going through papers. It is not a place to welcome much excitement. Ask for your wanted file and there will be some delay before a mute librarian delivers it to your hand.

So our requested file has been placed before us and we undo its tapes to liberate the contents. Excitement? Here is a letter dated 7 January 1803 in the handwriting of Horatio Nelson, thanking the correspondent for care of an infected eye. A letter dated 18 April 1801 falls open that bears the signature of Edward Jenner, the discoverer of vaccination and heroic benefactor of all mankind: a gift of vaccine had originally been included. Look a little further and we find a note from the famous abolitionist William Wilberforce, acknowledging his correspondent's contribution to the anti-slavery cause. The person to whom each of these letters was written was Dr Thomas Trotter MD, Scottish baker's son made good, sometime Physician to the Fleet, author of various seminal texts, and a mover and shaker of his times. That slim file has echoes of cannon shot and awful naval engagements with young Trotter as a surgeon's mate while still in his teens. The letters bear witness to a life of high endeavour, but not a cough or murmur is heard in the library. There is such a disjunction between the active, complex life that this man led, and the silence of the afternoon and lack of much remembrance.

Then a further letter is uncovered from that file; here we find a fellow guest, who had been enthralled by Trotter's lunchtime conversation encouraging him to start writing his autobiography:

> Dear Sir
> I trust you will pardon what I am going to say – A life so varied as yours has been, a person who has seen so much on board our ships of the line (a scene very new to the literary world itself), a person who can write so well as you can I really do think you should write an autobiography, it only requires a beginning and you will find it the easiest task and most agreeable that ever you took in hand; it will grow upon you imperceptibly. Two or three hours after breakfast will do the business . . . you have seen so much on the great deep and of the great theatre of life.

That importunate letter was written on 2 September 1829; Trotter died on 5 September 1832. If he made any jottings towards an autobiography, no trace of them survives and only a few short biographical essays on him have over the years been published.

Close the file, tie up the tapes again, give the folder back to the librarian. The book we now present aims to repair neglect and tell the story of the life and times of Thomas Trotter, who was a witness of ferocious naval warfare, made crucial contributions to naval medicine and the health of the fleet, published a historically important text on alcoholism, wrote poetry, habitually challenged orthodox views and was never afraid to speak his mind. What we hope to achieve is a full and accurate narrative account of the career and character of a man of large and remarkably varied achievements.

The story is of interest not only because of the intrinsic excitement of one remarkable life, but also because of what it reveals about the world through which this one individual moved. That complex background includes the liberation of thought which constituted the European Enlightenment, Scotland following the Act of Union, the slave trade, the campaigns of the Revolutionary Wars, the strides in naval medicine that enable the fleet to defeat Napoleon and the political and cultural upheaval of the Industrial Revolution. Trotter was a man who was fashioned by and who much engaged with the world around him. See this doctor appalled by the indulgence of a fashionable voluptuousness, and we have an intimate window into luxurious Georgian society.

BACKGROUND

Orme Junʳ sculpt. 1796.

Thoˢ Trotter M.D.

PHYSICIAN to the GRAND FLEET.

Fig. 1. Thomas Trotter MD, Physician to the Grand Fleet.
Wellcome Library, London

The Edinburgh Experience

Family and origins

T HE NAME 'Trotter' is widespread in the border counties of Scotland and in Northumberland and Durham. The family's origins are lost in the mists of mediaeval Scots history, and its emergence was not helped by being on the losing side in many local conflicts. One branch was wiped out at the Battle of Flodden; another suffered the fate of the Covenanters and the marquis of Montrose; a third threw in its lot with Bonny Prince Charlie. Fortunately, however, most Trotters accepted the Hanoverian succession and shared in the prosperity of Georgian Britain. By the middle of the eighteenth century, the family was well established across the border, some becoming influential as landowners and local magnates. There were the Trotters of Morganhall, who had grown rich as Edinburgh merchants and had now become respectable by achieving high office in the state and the army; and the Trotters of Bush, one of whom – Robert – had enough political weight to become post master general of Scotland and have portraits of himself and his wife painted by George Romney. There were also Trotters of Dreghorn, of Cutchelraw and of Prentannan; and, in England, Trotters of Blythe and of Stockton. In addition to providing local worthies, the family was remarkable in producing large numbers of divines and doctors, many with a literary bent and an interest in poetry, history and antiquities.

The hero of our story, Thomas Trotter, was born in Melrose, Roxburghshire, in 1760, the third of five children, and was baptized on 5 August. He did not spring from one of the more distinguished branches of the family. His father was a baker, although one who did well enough to own his own house and to be able to ensure that his sons had a good education. Thomas spent his early years in his birthplace of Melrose, an ancient market town on the bank of the Tweed adjacent to the post road from Edinburgh to Jedburgh. It lay in a picturesque, green and well-watered valley between the crags of the Eildon Hills to the south and the smooth pastoral slopes of the Glatton Hills to the north. Thomas learnt the basics at the local parochial school, then moved to nearby Kelso, a more elegant and fashionable town which boasted a fee-paying grammar school. There, under the direction of the formidable Mr Perry, later founder of the *European Magazine* and editor of the *Morning Chronicle*, he mastered arithmetic, French and geography and developed a lifelong love for the classics and a skill in Latin. In 1777, at the age of seventeen, the young Trotter left school and made the thirty-mile journey from Roxburghshire to Edinburgh, or 'Auld Reekie', as the smoky city was then familiarly known.

The country boy had come to town to pursue the study of medicine. There were no entry requirements. To matriculate all Trotter had to do was sign his name in a book and pay half a crown. His purpose was to acquire the credentials that would allow a baker's son in short time to enter a learned and honourable profession, earn a living and acquire social status. A younger brother, Andrew, was also to become a doctor and practise as a surgeon in North Shields. Trotter was an ambitious young Scot following a well-trodden path to personal advancement.

Trotter stayed at Edinburgh for one year, and during that time attended lectures in anatomy and surgery,[1] while also finding the time to publish his first poems. In 1778, he enrolled as a surgeon's mate in the Royal Navy. But, in 1784, he temporarily left the sea and worked as surgeon and apothecary at Wooler in Northumberland while attending further lectures in Edinburgh, which covered the subjects of clinical medicine, *materia medica* and botany. In 1788 at the age of twenty-eight, he obtained the high accolade of an Edinburgh MD before returning once more to naval service.

This chapter is partly about what the medical education provided by the University of Edinburgh is likely to have given Trotter as a young, and later as a more mature, student. What kind of intellectual experience did a medical training constitute at that time? Besides this exposure to a specific curriculum, Trotter was in Edinburgh to undergo an experience of a broader and astonishingly potent kind. He was to breathe in this city the heady atmosphere of the Scottish Enlightenment:[2] the Edinburgh medical training was an introduction to the ideas and values of what was to be known variously as the Enlightenment, the Age of Reason or the Age of Improvement. To comprehend what the medical school did for Trotter's intellectual development, one needs to understand the nature of the Edinburgh medical training of that time as, in its very essence, a product of its age. Thomas Trotter would have found himself in a city awash with new ideas, and with the sense all around of an old order fading and a new one being born. It was a city where an intellectual elite was setting about a comprehensive remaking of society's understanding of the human condition. That intellectual background needs to be described and the chapter will also give an account of the physical realities of the city whose streets Trotter was now to walk. With the ferment and the physical reality of this remarkable city sketched in, the chapter will then go on to deal with the specifically medical aspect of the experience, issues such as who was likely to become a doctor, the content of Trotter's training and the status of the professors who taught him. We also need to understand what at that period gave an individual the credentials to practise, and the significance of an MD degree when Trotter put on his gown.

---

[1] I. A. Porter, 'Thomas Trotter MD, naval physician', *Medical History* 7 (1963), 155–64
[2] D. E. Daiches, P. Jones and J. Jones (eds), *A Hot Bed of Genius: The Scottish Enlightenment 1730–1790* (Edinburgh, 1986); A. Broadie, *The Cambridge Companion to the Scottish Enlightenment* (Cambridge, 2003)

The Age of Improvement

A witness to the life of eighteenth-century Edinburgh claimed that towards the middle of the century, someone standing in the street was likely before long to have shaken hands with fifty men of genius.[3] That assertion may have been a little flattering, but all witnesses to the life of the city over those years agreed that this was a place and period characterized by extraordinary developments in the range and qualities of academic endeavour. The truly startling nature of this evolution was characterized by Dugald Stewart, the philosopher: 'A sudden burst of genius, which to the foreigners must seem to have sprung up in this country by a sort of enchantment'.[4]

The human mind seemed abruptly to be tasting liberation, and liberty was to be deployed in rational pursuit of every sort of scientific and philosophical question. In 1697 Thomas Aikenhead, an eighteen-year old Edinburgh student, had been tried, condemned and hanged to considerable public satisfaction for having questioned the divinity of Christ: he had the temerity to declare that Christian theology was 'A rapsodie of feigned and ill-invented nonsense',[5] but the constraints on thinking which in any previous century would have been exerted by church and state were at the dawn of the Enlightenment no longer able to block the adventure of the mind. An academic tradition dating from the Middle Ages which required the unthinking acceptance of 'authorities' in the form of classical texts going back to antiquity was overthrown by Francis Bacon. Observation, inductive reasoning and scientific method were, in his view, the way to acquire knowledge and improve the human condition. As the seventeenth century gathered momentum, natural philosophers on the continent and in the newly formed Royal Society of London followed Bacon's lead. From then on, science became a matter of experiment and observation expressed in a new language of measurement. Loose and undisciplined speculation was to be avoided, and too great 'enthusiasm' (religious or otherwise) was profoundly undesirable. The study of philosophy, social science and the physical sciences was transformed, and they were still conjoined as one endeavour: their fragmentation was yet to come. As a consequence, the workings of the physical world were no longer a mystery shrouded in Aristotelian metaphysics or theological dogma. Thinkers like Descartes, Boyle, Hook and Newton now presented the natural world as a machine governed by mathematical laws that could be discovered with the use of new techniques and scientific instruments. In more sensitive areas, Diderot and the encyclopaedists, believing that knowledge would free the individual and society from superstition and irrational social forms, began to plant the seeds which would lead to the French Revolution.

To draw precise boundaries for the dawn and dusk of the project which was the Scottish Enlightenment is difficult, and to an extent arbitrary. The movement was on its way by 1700; by 1750 it was in full swell; and by 1800 it had run

---

[3] W. Smellie, *Literary and Characteristic Lives of Gregory, Kaines, Hume and Smith* (Edinburgh, 1800), 161–2
[4] G. Bryson, *Man and Society: The Scottish Inquiry of the Eighteenth Century* (Princeton, 1945), 5
[5] D. Denby, *Northern Lights* (New York, 2004)

its course. The origins of the movement were in Glasgow, but Edinburgh was soon to become the epicentre. The Scottish Enlightenment was a happening in its own right, but it fed and was fed by the wider European Enlightenment.

A backdrop to the spectacular developments in Scottish intellectual life was the profound changes that took place during those hundred years. In 1700 Scotland was a backward and impoverished country controlled by a landed oligarchy, in thrall to Calvinism and with an economy ruined by its attempt to found a commercial colony in the malodorous swamps of Darien on the Gulf of Panama. By the Act of Union of 1707, the country exchanged political independence for economic opportunity. It lost its own parliament but gained commercial prosperity.

By 1800 Scotland's economy was booming and its agriculture had been revolutionized. After the horrors of the rebellion of 1745, the Highlands began to overcome their extreme isolation and enjoy improved living standards. Scottish politicians began to occupy influential positions in the Westminster Parliament, while growing industrialization and access to the burgeoning British Empire provided opportunities for professional men in Scotland and created a new social class. From that turmoil emerged a wave of philosophers, historians, mathematicians, scientists, academic lawyers and medical doctors of scientific bent. It is evident that the intellectual advances were nurtured by the economic, political and social developments, but it was a two-way trade since an integral part of the Scottish Enlightenment was the idea of 'improvement': in other words, the intellectual and scientific advances should lead to practical benefit for both individuals and society as a whole.[6]

What characterized the Edinburgh endeavour was that the principal actors were on intimate terms with each other. Even street corners saw personal interactions. Here is Adam Smith, the founding father of the science of economics, describing an encounter in 1760 with William Cullen, a physician who crucially helped turn Edinburgh into the leading European centre for medical teaching:

> My friend Dr Cullen took me aside in the street of Edinburgh and told me that he felt it his duty to inform me plainly that if I had any hope of surviving next winter I must ride at least 500 miles before the beginning of September.[7]

As well as revealing the kind of advice that a distinguished physician might casually and confidently hand out to a passer-by, this story captures the quality of intimacy which so characterized the Edinburgh of that period. The Edinburgh elite met together in clubs and societies, disputed and corresponded prodigiously, and all the time it was the warmth of their friendships in a still relatively small city that so characterized the Edinburgh life of the mind. The duke of Hamilton, one of the greatest land owners and the employer of Cullen's father, once attended a meeting of the prestigious Select Society, but was too drunk to make any contribution.[8] There were of course social hierarchies to be negotiated, but Edinburgh society was more open and egalitarian than

---

[6] Daiches *et al.*, *A Hot Bed of Genius*, 32
[7] E. L. Mossner and I. S. Ross (eds), *The Correspondence of Adam Smith* (Oxford, 1987), letter 5
[8] Daiches *et al.*, *A Hot Bed of Genius*, 35

London's. And there was a particularly Scottish emphasis on good manners and politeness.

The undisputed intellectual giants of the Scottish Enlightenment were Adam Smith and David Hume. They both shared membership of the Select Society with Cullen, and all three had a Glasgow training before taking up positions in Edinburgh. But a full chronicling of the men who made this golden age would certainly have to add scores of additional names to the cast list. The social sciences advanced, geology was fathomed, the steam engine invented, chemistry made revolutionary advances, architects and town planners and bridge builders were part of the scene, Scottish painters specialized in portrait painting, antiquarians built up their collections, the Grand Tour attracted Scottish travellers, and a remarkable medical school was born.

Edinburgh: the city in the eighteenth century

Fundamentally, it was the geology of the place that made Edinburgh so extraordinary. The city was built along a volcanic ridge, with steep hills in many places making passage impossible for carriages, and hard-going for pedestrians or sedan chairs. There was a pervasive sense of crowdedness, and a maze of alleyways known as 'wynds' spread out from the main streets. A feature of the domestic architecture, then as now, was the tall tenement blocks rising sometimes to as much as fourteen storeys in height. Rich and poor would share the same staircases and, in the absence of much domestic living space, the taverns and the oyster bars provided favoured meeting places. In 1767 the construction of the New Town was started, with its elegant houses providing accommodation of a markedly improved kind.

What caused horrified comment from visitors was the lack of sanitary provision in the Old Town. After nightfall, the slops would be thrown out from the tenement windows to a cry of 'Gardy Loo', a phrasing derived from 'Gardez l'eau'. Many a periwig was accidentally soiled and the stench in the streets was appalling. During the night, teams of scavengers were employed to clean up the mess. The domestic water supply came from pumps located down at street level, and a hardy breed of water carriers would, for a fee, deliver to tenants even at the fourteenth floor.

Despite the crowding, neither dense areas of deprivation nor lawlessness were features of life. The city prided itself on its peace. The food supply from the surrounding countryside was ample, and there was plenty of fresh fish to be had.

So much for the physical reality of the city where Trotter was to find his lodgings. As regards the social flavour of this place, comments from visitors were favourable, with general agreement that Edinburgh was at its best a cultured and sophisticated city. A sharply observed account of the Edinburgh of that time was given by Captain Edward Topham, an officer in the Coldstream Guards, who during 1775 spent six months in the city.[9] He saw the town as more French than English in its manners:

[9] E. Topham, *Edinburgh Life in the Eighteenth Century* (Edinburgh 1884, repr. 1994)

A man who visits this country, after having been in France, will find in a thousand inſtances the resemblance which there is between these two nations. The air of mirth and vivacity, that quick and penetrating look, that spirit of gaiety which diſtinguishes the French, is equally visible in the Scotch.[10]

Topham, however, went on to describe the Scots as being capable of displaying a characteristically serious cast of mind:

A Scotsman does not relax himself for amusement. His diversions are not calculated to seduce the unwary or recreate the idle, but to unbend the mind without corrupting it.[11]

Topham commentated favourably on the level of education commonly found among Scottish women, whose conversation he found to be well informed.

If this visiting guardsman had any criticism to make of the society on which he commented, it was in relation to the drinking habits. Lawyers would settle to a mutchkin (three-quarters of an imperial pint) of sherry, before discussing any new case. He found here

A convivial age and it was a drinking society. When St Giles bells played out at half paſt eleven in the morning, each citizen went to get a gill (half a pint) of ale, which was known as his 'meridian' although before breakfaſt he had paid a similar visit and in the course of the day he went not seldom with his cuſtomers to drink over their bargains.[12]

When the town guard at night beat the 10 o'clock drum, the streets would fill with young people spilling out of the taverns and singing their drinking songs, and with 'old merchants and unsober judges' mingling in the jostle.

The Edinburgh Medical School as an Enlightenment project

As in other scientific fields, the effect of the Enlightenment was to free medicine from the straight-jacket of authority – in this case, the ancient doctrines going back to Hippocrates and Galen – and open it up as a field for observation and experiment. The body was to be understood in the light of the findings of anatomy, chemistry and physics. At first, the views of the physicists dominated, and the body was seen as a machine and conceived as a set of pipes, pulleys, springs and levers. But the impossibility of explaining its full complexity though this means moved the focus towards chemistry, and the notion that all vital processes which took place in the organs of the body were the result of a particular chemical reaction. Thus it was believed that fermentation was the means through which food was converted into living tissue and that any interruption to the process would lead to putrefaction and debilitating illness.

[10] Ibid., 8
[11] Ibid., 17
[12] Ibid., 44–5

Previous ideas were discarded or extensively adapted. One was the notion that there were four humours, or fluids, within the body that were essential to life – blood, yellow bile, black bile and phlegm. Good health meant they were in balance: illness meant some irregularity or distortion. Belief in the humours did not survive the physical and chemical discoveries of the Enlightenment, though interest in classifying humanity in terms of a quartet of temperaments that derived from them – sanguine, bilious, melancholic or phlegmatic – certainly did. So did the idea that blood, now a vital fluid oxygenated by pure air, was essential to good health and that any defect in its composition needed prompt intervention. Thus, an excess of blood, shown by fever or apoplectic agitation, required bleeding and cold baths; while thin blood, characterized by anaemia and physical weakness, called for rich food and red meat. Another survival from the ancients was a holistic approach which saw the body as an integrated whole and stressed the need for harmony between body and behaviour, the physical and the psychological.

The impact of the Enlightenment on medicine was, however, uneven. In practical fields, such as surgery, where the principles of observation and experimentation could be used, there were advances – although a lack of both anaesthetics and antisepsis limited what was possible. But when applied to infectious disease where the existence of microbes was unknowable, the principles of the enlightenment were difficult to apply and progress was difficult. The treatment of diseases such as malaria and yellow fever continued to be unfathomable; and the cure for scurvy, as we will see in a later chapter, was much disputed.

At the beginning of the eighteenth century medical education at Edinburgh was poorly developed and haphazard. Young men who wanted a Scottish university medical training had a choice between Glasgow, St Andrews, Aberdeen, and Edinburgh. An MD degree could be an award of suspect status. A few Scottish students might have enrolled at Dublin. The only universities in England to offer an MD were Oxford and Cambridge, and these two cities were still home to the only universities in England. Many Scottish students would prefer to travel to one of the well-established continental centres, rather than study in Britain.

The European medical school which was at that time most favoured by aspiring Scots was to be found at Leiden in Holland. That university had been instituted in 1575 by William of Orange and although titually a Protestant foundation, was in reality secular in its outlook and able to attract faculty of high quality from across the continent. The Dutch professor who gave lustre to teaching at this medical school was Herman Boerhaave: he taught medicine as a craft rather than as abstract scholarship. Between 1575 and 1875 a total of 2124 English-speaking medical students graduated from Leiden.[13] Of these, 546 emanated from Scotland, a scholarly flow of such dimensions as to cause economic worries back home about the balance of payments problem.

[13] W. R. O. Goslings, 'Leiden and Edinburgh: The Seed, the Soil and the Climate', in R. W. Anderson and A. D. C. Simpson (eds), *The Early Years of Edinburgh Medical School* (Edinburgh, 1976), 11

The entire first generation of Edinburgh medical professors was trained by Boerhaave: he was their master and inspiration, and a name to be conjured with. He lectured in Latin and respected ancient authority, but developed his own theories and an all-embracing classification of diseases. Clinical teaching was established at a nearby city hospital. Boerhaave was respected for his intellect, but he was also someone whose personal qualities won the lasting affection of the young men from many different countries who flocked to hear him lecture. Jules Offray de la Metrie, one of his French pupils,[14] wrote 'Bon père, bon marie, bon citoyen, bon amie, bon Chrétien, voilà en cinq mots le partout du Boerhaave'.

Despite the Olympian status enjoyed by Boerhaave, and without in any way detracting from his human qualities, such was the primitive state of medical knowledge of that time, that seen in the harsh light of hindsight a great deal of what was taught in Leiden was not well founded, or might even veer towards the absurd. For instance, Boerhaave suggested that the function of the pineal gland was to absorb excess vapour, a sort of dehumidifier. He strove after an empirical basis for medical science and practice but the 'facts' he advanced were often mixed with an element of fantasy.

For Edinburgh, the start of a new deal in medical education came in 1683, when the Royal College of Physicians of Edinburgh appointed three physicians as university professors with a responsibility to teach medicine: these teachers received no salary but they charged fees to the students who came to hear them. That the city fathers instigated this move reflected the close relationship between the city and the university which existed at that time – the nascent medical school was being fostered by the city authorities because they believed it was likely to serve the needs of the community. By the 1720s Edinburgh had developed a recognizable medical school which offered a comprehensive set of lecture series, a curriculum and a formal examination system leading to the MD degree.[15]

What from its earliest days characterized the Edinburgh initiative was the emphasis on practicality. The teaching of medicine was to be developed in aid of better provision of medical care, rather than arcane intellectual delectation or the breeding of doctors as literate gentlemen. Surprisingly, what today might seem to be a sensible philosophy to guide the development of a medical school whatever its location was not at all at that time the guiding principle at Oxford and Cambridge. In those ancient universities, medical training aimed to furnish the minds of gentleman scholars, who might enjoy seven preliminary years of college residence with their studies focusing on literature and the classical world. This had then to be followed by four further years of specifically medical study. One contemporary observer sneeringly remarked that a Scottish medical education was 'good for imparting general knowledge to the middle and lower classes . . . but they are not calculated to educate gentlemen'.[16]

[14]   Ibid., 15
[15]   G. B. Risse, *Hospital Life in Enlightenment Scotland* (New York and Cambridge, 1986), 69
[16]   J. H. Gray, *Autobiography of a Country Gentleman* (privately printed, 1868)

Fig. 2. View of Edinburgh from St Anthony's Chapel. Engraving by W. Miller after Turner

Fig. 3. Benjamin Rush. Stipple engraving by W. S. Leney.
Wellcome Library, London

The Edinburgh medical school would, in contrast, generally require just three years of medical studies for entry to the MD examination, and it attracted a broader class mix than Oxford or Cambridge. Nonetheless, for a student to have a working-class or tradesman father would have been rather unusual. At Edinburgh there were no religious restrictions, whereas the Test Acts restricted entry to English universities to members of the Established Church and excluded Catholics, Jews and dissenting Protestants. Only medical graduates from Oxford and Cambridge could be members of the Royal College of Physicians of London, and until 1808 only graduates from those universities could hold the rank of physician in the army.

Despite the prestige of Oxford and Cambridge, by the middle of the eighteenth century the Edinburgh medical school had, arguably, become the leading school in Europe. And many young Americans were travelling to Edinburgh to study medicine, including the physician and statesman Benjamin Rush. When Trotter arrived there in 1777, he thus enrolled in a school that enjoyed immense prestige. What factors can be identified as contributing to that triumph?

The spirit of the Enlightenment from beginning to end permeated the Scottish experiment in useful medical education. Not only was the training designed to meet practical ends as an exercise in 'improvement', but it was to be soundly based in science with chemistry, botany, physiology and anatomy rigorously taught. Clinical lectures were given at the Royal Infirmary, which opened its doors in 1729 with the specific intention that it would function as a teaching hospital.[17] All instruction was given in the vernacular rather than in Latin.

To enrol as a medical student in Edinburgh required the financial support of parents, but the maintenance costs were likely to be much lower than for the long period of college residence at Oxford or Cambridge. It was possible to live reasonably comfortably as a student in Edinburgh for £1 a month, although wealthier students might spend much more. Here is Thomas Ismay, the son of a clergyman, describing in a 1771 letter to his father what he got for his money:

> Tea twice a day if I chuse; have a hot dinner and supper. The dinner generally consists of a large Tirene of soup, which I like extremely well, a dish of boiled meat and another of roast. There mutton and beef is very good. Veal, I have not seen any yet: Puddings only one. Generally to supper, fish, eggs, beef stakes or what you please. Candles what you have occasion for, and a good fire.[18]

Enrolment fees for lectures could be expensive but poor students might be admitted free.

The records show that during his early stay in Edinburgh, Trotter attended the anatomy lectures that were given by the famous anatomist Alexander Monro Secundus (his father was Primus and his son later held the same chair as Tertius). When Trotter later returned to Edinburgh for his MD studies, he attended lectures given by Dr William Cullen, the most influential Scottish physician of the day, and a champion of modernism. Cullen lectured with the aid only of brief notes, believing that a written text would destroy spontaneity. The following remarks made by Cullen must have sounded like a revolutionary manifesto to his students:

> I allow that we derive much knowledge from the Ancients . . . but they have many deficiencies from their ignorance of Anatomy, Chemistry and natural knowledge. They therefore cannot give us much instruction. The confusion also that prevails in their writings is such that I cannot set them up as models in our studies.[19]

In the event much of Cullen's own theorizing would be consigned to oblivion very quickly. He set up an all-embracing taxonomy of diseases to supplant Boerhaave's system, but this grand scheme did not outlast his own lifetime.

---

[17] Risse, *Hospital Life*, xiii
[18] T. Ismay, 'Letter of Thomas Ismay to his father', *University of Edinburgh Journal* 8 (1936–7), 59
[19] Risse, *Hospital Life*, 37

Fig. 4. Dr William Cullen. Wellcome Library, London

There seem to have been three important ways in which Cullen exerted an influence on Trotter. First, there was the commitment to open-mindedness which characterized Cullen's entire approach to medicine and medical teaching – a style which Trotter was to adopt as his own guiding principle. Second, he put much emphasis on the importance of nervous disorders, and it was he who invented the term 'neurosis', but not with its modern meaning (tetanus was for him a neurosis). Cullen's teaching here fed through directly to Trotter's later interest in 'the nervous temperament'. Third, and of great importance, Cullen's teaching took aboard Hume's thinking on the importance of the association of ideas as basis for habit formation. And it was this that nurtured Trotter's views on 'inebriety'. Here is how Cullen illustrated Hume's ideas on association in his 1773 *Lectures on the Materia Medica*:

> It is very ordinary for a person to make urine when going to bed, and if he has been for any length of time, accuſtomed to do so, he will ever afterwards make urine at that time, though otherwise he would have no such inclination.[20]

[20] W. Cullen, *Lectures on the Materia Medica as Delivered by William Cullen* (London, 1773), 28

We have here identified by name only two of Trotter's professors, and they probably exerted the core influences. Subsequent commentators saw this as having been the golden generation of medical school teachers and feared that the best was over. This is what one witness had to say:

> [He] knew enough of them to make us fear that no other race of men, so tried by time, such friends of each other and learning, all such amiable and such spotless characters, would be expected to arise and again ennoble Scotland.[21]

The Edinburgh Medical School was thus during Trotter's stay a place capable of inspiring in the right man a passionate enthusiasm for the art and science of medicine, and for the advance of medical knowledge as open minded adventure. Trotter was to prove himself one such young man, and the Edinburgh ethic without doubt shaped the entirety of his medical writing.

Besides the inspirational qualities of the appointed teachers, the medical students themselves took a hand in their own education. What was to become the Royal Medical Society was founded in 1774. Its meetings were held each week during term time, with sessions lasting from 4 PM to 11 PM. The Society was run by medical students and for these students, and each member would be expected to present a dissertation for public discussion. Election was a prized distinction and slackness in attendance could lead to a fine. Trotter, when setting out his professional credentials on the front sheets of his various later books, always gave 'Membership of the Royal Medical Society of Edinburgh' due mention.

The Edinburgh MD and other pathways to medical practice

The MD was the pinnacle of medical qualification and the rules for its conferment by the University of Edinburgh were governed by regulations which were first promulgated in 1767. Trotter's MD degree, awarded in 1788, would have been governed by updated regulations which were introduced in 1783.

Strangely, although Edinburgh had broken with Latin as the language of teaching, the authorities still insisted that the examination process should be conducted in Latin. Before taking the degree a prerequisite was attendance at designated lecture courses. The first step along the pathway of examinations which Trotter would have trodden would then have entailed an evening visit by appointment, at the house of a professor who had been nominated for this responsibility by the university. With luck, this would have been a fairly relaxed encounter but it would have been followed later by a more intensive viva with several professors present. The candidate would then be given a case history and was sent away to prepare written comments on it. The records show that Trotter was asked to consider the case of a woman who was suffering intermittent head aches accompanied by low fever.[22] In Cullen's nosology,

[21] Risse, *Hospital Life*, 162
[22] L. Rosner, *Medical Education in the Age of Improvement: Edinburgh Students and Apprentices 1760 to 1826* (Edinburgh, 1991)

the acceptable diagnosis would have been 'apoplexy', an unthinkable response from a medical student of today.

Trotter's discussion of that case presumably satisfied his examiners for he proceeded to the next step in the examination process, and the submission of a thesis written in Latin, followed by its public defence before the professors.[23] The thesis might take one of several possible forms – literature review, case report or experimental work were among the variants. Thus in 1788 Trotter submitted a dissertation entitled 'De ebriatate eiusque effectibus in corpus humanum' ('Of Drunkenness and its Effects on the Human Body'). Some forty pages long, it won him his MD (Edinburgh).[24]

At most only 20 per cent of students attending the Edinburgh medical school would in the eighteenth century have sought to qualify with an MD degree.[25] It was not that the majority dropped out, but rather that they saw no reason to invest time and money in pursuit of this distinction. A year or two at medical school would equip the student to set up anywhere as a surgeon apothecary and earn a reasonable living. In contrast, the MD was the ticket for self-definition as a physician. Physicians were top in the pecking order and could earn huge sums of money. Cullen had an enormously successful consulting practice in Edinburgh, and in addition received fees from an extensive postal-advice service, which would include patients contacting him from abroad. A successful London physician might achieve perhaps £10,000 per year.[26] But establishing a practice was likely to require patronage, much networking and resources to help survive early lean years.

Besides university-based training as a route to a practice, there were several other possible pathways. Many young men would see apprenticeship to a surgeon apothecary as their preferred pathway to a practice. Fees varied but a five-year apprenticeship to a practitioner might necessitate an upfront fee of £50 to £60 or much more for an attachment to a successful surgeon, and there would be later fees for guild membership. An apprentice would live with the family and receive his bed and board. Complaints were, however, sometimes heard from apprentices who felt that they were exploited and treated as servants, rather than being conscientiously taught.

This was also a century during which the London hospitals developed as a teaching base. London could not at that time offer a university medical education, but for a fee students could walk the wards and receive some teaching. The attraction of this kind of experience was that it would teach the frontline realities of medical practice more effectively than did any contemporary university training.

There were in addition some other ways into a career. Private teaching courses existed outside any university aegis. Midwives constituted a profession which was winning increased recognition. If a doctor died his widow might take over

---

[23] Not every student would have had sufficient mastery of the language to compose such a Latin text, but fortunately there were hacks on hand who, for a fee, would run up a translation from English to Latin. These persons were known as 'grinders'. Rumour had it that a complicit grinder might be willing actually to compose a dissertation rather than merely render it into Latin, and there was also dark talk of plagiarism occurring.

[24] T. Trotter, 'De ebriatate eiusque effectibus in corpus humanum' (MD thesis, Edinburgh, 1788)

[25] Rosner, *Medical Education*, 21

[26] Ibid., 26

the practice. Folk healers of every kind abounded, and clergymen too might try their hand. The Scots used the term 'mediciner' to describe this broad array of practitioners.

Medical practice was thus at the time unlicensed and unregulated, with the state taking no hand in determining what counted as a legitimate qualification. Medicine was absolutely a free market. Adam Smith wrote to William Cullen in 1779, arguing at length that medical practice should be left to the market rather than subjected to regulation.[27] He trusted the customer to make informed choices. As to the quality of services offered, he expected to see the better winning out on merit. His opinion of the orthodox medicine of that time was negative, and he referred to 'quackery' and 'exorbitant fees'. These free-market views ran directly against Cullen's proposals for a regulation strategy but Smith ended his challenging letter with a show of personal affection towards his long-time friend:

> Adieu adieu my dear Doctor; after having delayed to write to you I am afraid I should get my lug in my lufe, as we say, for what I have written. But I am ever most affectionately yours.

Trotter, and a medical education as an Enlightenment experience

We have sought in this chapter to put Trotter's medical education in the context of the Scottish Enlightenment which was the rich background to his times. His school education was probably of good quality: when he entered medical school he had some Latin, and in his later books he could quote from classical sources. But whatever his early scholarly training, when he arrived in Edinburgh he was walking into an intellectual experience of an entirely different order.

Perhaps with a little blinkered determination it would have been possible for a young man to take up lodgings in that city without any personal awareness that the Enlightenment was actually afoot. But anyone attending lectures at the medical school would have had the questioning spirit of the Enlightenment made manifest in what was being taught by the gifted teachers who were transmitters of the spirit of that time. What also needs specially to be noted regarding Trotter's overall training is that his two periods at Edinburgh were interspersed with the rigours of naval service and an appointment aboard a slaver. By the time he gained his MD, the academic exposure was thus combined with practical experience of an extraordinarily intense kind.

The fact of the matter is that although Cullen's home-grown nosology had replaced Boerhaave's and although English had replaced Latin in the lecture theatre, much of the actual content of the teaching was still inevitably an obeisance to authority rather than anything based on evidence. The doctors of the Enlightenment may have believed that their subject was advancing sharply but, without the means to investigate the true causes of disease, it was still much

---

[27] J. Thomson, *An Account of the Life, Lectures and Writings of William Cullen, MD* (Edinburgh, 1859), II, 472

in the shadows of ancient tradition. Cullen was a deeply respected teacher but never personally contributed a new description of a single disease, nor did he ever provide substantial ideas on any new treatment. But from the base of that training Trotter acquired the lifelong habit of questioning received opinion.

Whatever the qualifications, experiences and professional attitudes he had acquired in Edinburgh, Trotter still had to make the transition to gainful employment. In 1778 he would not have had the resources or influence easily to set himself up in civilian practice as a physician. The most available career open to him would therefore have been service with the East India Company, a career in army medicine, or a job as a surgeon's mate in the Royal Navy, the pay offered by these various positions varying from £26 to £70 a year. There were, however, pros and cons attached to each. Army pay was the highest but the expenses were formidable since members of the medical branch were commissioned officers – and therefore, by definition, gentlemen – and were expected to maintain this status by meeting the costs of elaborate uniforms and being subject to large deductions for mess bills. East India Company service was attractive since all officers, including surgeons, could make money by private trading on their own account. Numbers were, however, fairly static, and appointments required connections of some kind.

That left the Royal Navy. In prestige and financial terms, this was the least attractive option and offered every expectation of exposure to hideous battle. One doctor disparagingly talked about such an appointment in terms of 'little profit to be gained and the poor plight one's character is in when one wishes to settle in the world'.[28] But for people of Trotter's lowly social and financial status, membership of the naval medical branch offered many advantages. They could live on their pay, there was always the hope of prize money when an enemy ship was captured, and outgoings were low. True, they had to provide their own chest of instruments but, being appointed as warrant officers by the navy's civil arm, the Navy Board, and not as commissioned officers, they did not have to maintain the dignity that went with 'gentlemanly' status. They did not wear uniforms, and surgeon's mates messed in modest style with the midshipmen. And best of all, in war time it was easy to secure an appointment. It was no wonder that Trotter, like so many Scotsmen in his position, chose to opt for a naval career.[29]

---

[28] A. Lessasier, quoted by Rosner, *Medical Education*, 214
[29] When Trotter later gave evidence before the Select Committee on the Slave Trade in 1790, he appeared to claim that between 1774 and 1778 he was serving with Admiral Samuel Graves and Captain Hotham in North America as Cooper on HMS *Preston*, and then entrusted with responsibility for cooperage and brewing for the fleet. There is no truth in this story. No boy of fourteen could possibly have been given such responsibility, and Trotter's name appears neither in the list of Graves's retinue nor in the muster rolls of any of the ships on the station. Indeed, the Cooper of *Preston* during the whole of this time was William Dove. It can only be assumed that the committee clerk muddled the pages and inserted pages at the end of Trotter's evidence which did not belong there.

— 2 —

Medicine at Sea

FOLLOWING IN THE FOOTSTEPS of other aspirants to the navy's medical service, in the winter of 1778 Thomas Trotter visited London to pass the necessary examination and secure an appointment. The first reaction of visitors to the metropolis was often one of amazement. Even to people like Trotter who were used to Edinburgh, the size and scale of London must have been bewildering. Peter Cullen, a compatriot who was visiting for the first time and for the same purpose, described himself as being 'struck with astonishment . . . quite giddy with the noise, confusion, strange sights of wonderful and rare objects . . . for everything was new, strange and surprising'.[1] With a population of over three-quarters of a million, London had long since outgrown its mediaeval boundaries and now stretched from Islington in the north to Lambeth in the south, and along the river from Westminster in the west to Limehouse and Rotherhithe in the east. It was still essentially the London of Dr Johnson, a vibrant mixture of industry and dissipation, riches and poverty, elegance and squalor, vanity and vice. At one extreme were the new squares of Mayfair and Marylebone with their genteel mansions, bow-fronted shops and fashionable coffee houses; at the other, the jumble of apartment houses, workshops, breweries, tanneries and taverns of Whitechapel and Wapping. Between the two, stretching from the white dome of St Paul's as far as London Bridge and Smithfield, lay the commercial heart of the city. Here, in the streets that ran down from Leadenhall Street to the warehouses and wharves that lined the nearby Thames, were the banks, brokers, insurance companies, shipping agents and trading houses that drove Britain's mercantile prosperity. The atmosphere was heavy with the smell of horses and refuse, the rattle of vehicles and the cries of street vendors. The pavements were filled with bustling crowds and the highways with monogrammed coaches, brewers' drays, coal wagons, carts with fruit and vegetables for Covent Garden, and herds of livestock being driven to Smithfield for slaughter.

The Admiralty, as befitted the political hub of the Royal Navy, was to be found in the west, on the corner of Whitehall and Charing Cross, conveniently close to Parliament, Downing Street and the departments of state. When Trotter applied to join the navy, the Board of Admiralty was headed by John Montague, fourth earl of Sandwich, a cabinet minister and leading

---

[1] 'Memoirs of Peter Cullen 1789–1802', in H. G. Thursfield (ed.), *Five Naval Journals 1787–1817*, Navy Records Society 91 (London and Colchester, 1951), 48–50

figure in the government. He was supported by half a dozen other members, two of whom – Vice-Admiral Hugh Palliser and Captain Lord Mulgrave – were serving naval officers, while the rest were political placemen. Far from being the rake and corrupt politician of legend whose only achievement was the invention of the sandwich, the cultivated and urbane Montague was an industrious and improving First Lord.[2] With an influential secretary and a small group of clerks to do its bidding, the Board of Admiralty was responsible for the deployment of fleets and ships, the supervision of the departments that administered a string of dockyards and victualling stations scattered across the globe, and the posting and promotion of commissioned officers. It thus wielded enormous patronage, together with the power to disappoint as well as to please – as Sandwich was to learn to his discomfort.[3] Appointments to the medical branch were not, however, within the Admiralty's remit. To secure one of these, Trotter had to report to the headquarters of the Navy Board.

The Navy Board or, to give it its proper title, 'The Principal Officers and Commissioners of the Navy', ran the civil branch of the service. The principal officers were the comptroller of the navy, a position that was broadly equated with that of rear admiral and was normally occupied by a senior captain on half-pay; the surveyor, who was an experienced shipwright responsible for ship design and construction; the clerk of the acts, who was in charge of the administrative machine; and three controllers for, respectively, the treasurer's, victualling and storekeeper's accounts. In theory, the commissioners of the major dockyards were also members of the Board, but as out-posted officers their attendance at meetings was rare. Individually, each officer had charge of his own department, but together they carried collective responsibility for the Board's activities. The signature of at least three members was needed to validate any decision or instruction.

The Navy Board met daily under the chairmanship of the comptroller of the navy. His position was theoretically first among equals, but Trotter's decision to join the navy coincided with the death of Captain Maurice Suckling, Nelson's uncle, and his replacement as comptroller by a man of a far different stamp. This was Captain Charles Middleton, an ambitious and narrow-minded Scot with a voracious appetite for work, a self-righteous evangelical piety, and a determination to drive the Board down the path of change and efficiency.[4] Hand-picked and encouraged by the diplomatic Sandwich, who was able to harness Middleton's fierce energy while closing his eyes to his irritating and often underhand way of working,[5] the new comptroller immediately applied himself to expanding ship construction, introducing copper sheathing to increase the speed of ships and to resist the attacks of wood-eating insects, and boosting fire power by introducing the carronade, a short-range but heavy-calibre cannon that was deservedly called the 'smasher'.

[2] N. A. M. Rodger, *The Insatiable Earl: A Life of John Montague 4th Earl of Sandwich* (London and New York, 1994)
[3] Ibid., 172–92
[4] J. E. Talbott, *The Pen and Ink Sailor: Charles Middleton and the King's Navy, 1778–1813* (London, 1998)
[5] Rodger, *The Insatiable Earl*, 162–71

The responsibilities of Middleton's Navy Board were vast. They covered the building, maintenance and repair of ships, the management of the royal dockyards, the supply of stores to the fleet, the manning and paying-off of ships, and the appointment of the warrant officers on whose technical skills the navy depended. These included sailing masters, boatswains, carpenters, chaplains and – significantly from Trotter's point of view – surgeons and their mates. A subordinate department, known as the Victualling Board, was responsible for the procurement and supply of rum, beer, pork, beef, biscuit and other foodstuffs, and for the control of supply ships and storehouses in every major port.

Responsibility for naval medical services lay with another subordinate department, called the Commissioners for Sick and Wounded Seamen – known more usually as the Sick and Hurt Board. At the time there were only two commissioners, Walter Farquharson and Vincent Corbett, although their number was normally increased in time of war.[6] Neither was a medical man; their duties were financial and administrative. It was only with the appointment of doctors later in the century that the Board became more involved in strictly medical matters. In 1778, the Board's duties were to post surgeons and their mates, check their accounts, ensure the supply of medicines and special foodstuffs for the sick, and manage naval hospitals. It was also responsible for prisoners of war. Appropriately, the Navy Board and its subsidiary departments were located 2 miles downriver from the Admiralty in the centre of the commercial and shipping district of the city. Occupying a set of plain buildings on three sides of a neatly paved square at the corner of Crutched Friars and Seething Lane, it was a stone's throw from the Tower and from the forest of masts and crowded wharfs of the Pool of London. It was there, in December 1778, that Thomas Trotter went to introduce himself and obtain an order for his examination at Surgeons' Hall.

The headquarters of the Surgeons' Company was located on the other side of St Paul's in the street called Old Bailey, near to St Bartholomew's Hospital and under the shadow of Newgate Gaol. Its surroundings were insalubrious, but inside it consisted of a fine spacious hall supported by pillars, from which opened a number of separate rooms or chambers. In one of these, twice monthly in the evening, leading London surgeons would gather to examine the competence of candidates offering themselves for service in the navy, the army or the East India Company. The procedure which Trotter followed was well established. The examination was an oral one. The candidate would be taken aside by one the examiners, who would assess his qualifications and experience, then pose a series of questions designed to test his knowledge of anatomy, physiology and surgery. If he gave satisfaction on all counts, the candidate was then escorted to a table in the centre of the room and presented to the chairman of the selection panel with words to the effect of 'I find this gentleman fully qualified to be a surgeon's mate in His Majesty's navy'. A fee of a guinea was then paid and a certificate of competence was issued.[7] On 18 December

[6] I. Schomberg, *Naval Chronology or an Historical Summary of Maritime and Naval Events* (London, 1802)
[7] The dates of examination were published by the Admiralty, and printed in *Steels' Navy Lists.*

1778, Trotter successfully passed this examination. Next day, he visited the Navy Board to receive his warrant as a surgeon's mate.

Trotter then had to find a ship. That was no difficulty. The American War of Independence had taken a serious turn. Anxious to make the most of Britain's difficulties, the French had recently joined the conflict, and the Spanish and Dutch were about to do so. Instead of being an internal wrangle, the war had become a global conflict. The Royal Navy was stretched to the limit: ships were being commissioned as a matter of urgency and there were plenty of berths for a newly joined medical officer. Within days Thomas Trotter was appointed as third surgeon's mate to a newly built ship, *Berwick*, then refitting at Portsmouth after a season with the Channel Fleet under Keppel, and the indecisive Battle of Ushant.

Pay and prestige

The Royal Navy offered advancement and a career to young men like Trotter who had served an apprenticeship in surgery but who lacked the social connections needed to gain a more prestigious position or the capital to establish a private practice. But a middle-ranking surgeon's mate received only £26 a year – the same as a midshipman but less than junior medical staff in the army.[8] As a result there were serious shortages of surgeon's mates throughout the period. The quality of recruits varied widely. Some, like Thomas Trotter and Peter Cullen, were idealistic and comparatively well trained; others lacked both ability and literacy. As late as 1800, Surgeon White of *Atlas* complained that his first mate was incompetent, his second was incapable of performing 'a simple operation or . . . making up the common medical preparations', while his third knew no Latin and could not spell the commonest English words.[9] The entrance examination was perfunctory and contained no practical element, and the Company of Surgeons seemed willing to pass anyone for naval service. Former army surgeon Charles Dunne gloomily reflected 'I cannot pass over in silence the absurdity of employing such a number of raw apothecaries' boys as . . . assistant surgeons in His Majesty's army or navy, whose whole education has been acquired in the course of a year or two behind the counter of some obscure apothecary or barber-surgeon, nay in the cockpit of a man of war as a loblolly boy'. Such a background, he added with a shudder, made it impossible to 'acquire the manners of a gentleman, so essential to surgeons in their professional practice, whether in the army, navy or private practice'.[10]

A sore point for many naval surgeons was their low status within the military hierarchy. This was not on the whole surprising. In the medical profession ashore, their historical links with barbers and their lack of the university education combined to give surgeons a modest place in society. Indeed, many naval

For the procedure, see 'Memoirs of Peter Cullen Esq.'

[8] M. Lewis, *A Social History of the Navy 1793–1815* (London, 1960), table VIII

[9] Quoted in C. Lloyd and L. Coulter, *Medicine and the Navy* (Edinburgh, 1961), III, 31–2

[10] C. Dunne, *The Chirurgical Candidate or Reflections on Education indispensable to complete naval, military and other Surgeons* (London, 1808)

surgeons came from the lower rungs of 'respectable' society, had dubious claims to gentility and saw service with the navy as a way of rising in the social scale. Trotter's father, as we have mentioned, was a baker, that of Dr (later Sir) William Beatty who attended the dying Nelson, an Irish revenue officer, and that of Leonard Gillespie, Nelson's Physician of the Fleet, a farmer. The fact that it is impossible to discover the parentage of even Trotter's most senior colleagues confirms this point since people preferred to remain silent about their fathers unless they were members of the aristocracy or the squirearchy. The exception was Gilbert (later Sir Gilbert) Blane FRS. Blane's social connections made him unusual as a member of the naval medical profession and helped take him to the top of the tree as commissioner of the Sick and Hurt Board, physician to King William IV, the government's leading medical adviser and an influential writer. The elevated level of Blane's family background is spoken of with some awe in naval literature, although his father was only a minor member of the Scottish landed gentry. Nevertheless, this meant that Blane had been born a gentleman. Indeed, his first career choice had been that most gentlemanly and undemanding of professions – the church. It was only at university that Blane had changed his mind and opted for medicine.

The modest social status of surgeons in society was therefore accepted and taken for granted. It was not this that caused resentment among naval surgeons: it was their inferior position when compared with colleagues in the army. In the land forces, regimental surgeons and their assistants not only had superior pay and pensions but wore a uniform, possessed the king's commission and enjoyed all the prestige which went with it. In the navy, surgeons received a Navy Board warrant – like carpenters or boatswains – and, unlike sea officers, wore no distinctive clothing or marks of rank.

The rank of surgeon nevertheless brought its own rewards. Average pay in war time was £108 a year – about the same as a senior lieutenant – to which was added various perks and a half-pay pension for the most senior.[11] Within the hierarchy of a warship, a competent surgeon commanded respect and was able to influence strictly non-medical areas like diet and hygiene. Indeed, the journals of many surgeons pay tribute to the willingness of the ship's executive officers to respond to their suggestions. Only a small number of these journals survive, but the picture they paint is a convincing one. A good surgeon also enjoyed the confidence of his captain and had greater independence in the running of his department than any other specialist.

Independence, however, was a double-edged sword. Naval surgeons worked in isolation without professional back-up. The Sick and Hurt Board was an administrative body and gave little guidance. It did not even control entry examinations to the navy or the contents of its medical chests. These were the respective responsibilities of the Company of Surgeons and the Company of Apothecaries. Likewise no formal training in naval medicine was given to recruits, who were expected to learn their profession on the job, or by personal

---

[11] Basic emoluments comprised £5 per lunar month plus a bonus called 'Queen Ann's Bounty' which averaged £43 a year. Lewis, *A Social History of the Navy*, tables VII and VIII; Trotter to St Vincent, 22 February 1801, printed in *Medicina Nautica*, III, 35–7

study of the appropriate books and manuals. An 'Association of the Navy Surgeons of the Royal Navy of Great Britain' had been founded in the middle of the eighteenth century to act as a clearing house for the exchange of ideas, but it is seldom mentioned in documents of the period. In a *Memorial on the Present State of Naval and Military Surgery*, Dr John Bell of Edinburgh painted a dismal picture of the effects of the surgeon's situation, writing

> When a young man enters the Navy, his education is but ill begun and cannot improve. He is put down into a hole, there to remain for years. He is deprived of all communication, all desire for knowledge. To breathe the vital air, he muſt live in the promiscuous conversation of the wardroom. Politics, hiſtory, anecdote, news; everything is heard there but that which intereſts him moſt, his profession. His youthful ambition is dead; his profession is forgotten; his proud feelings . . . are buried there; his mind is vacant and powerless; and all his precious hours are running to waſte. To the life of a naval surgeon there are, God knows, no seduꝗions.[12]

Bell's work has been quoted in naval histories as a generally valid description. In fact it is an exaggeration. Bell himself had never been to sea and felt, like Dr Johnson, that a ship was a less congenial environment than a gaol, and was incapable of producing men of ability whether sea officers or medical men. He was wrong on both counts. Likewise, while a surgeon serving on a frigate or a brig which had only one mate may have felt some sense of isolation, if appointed to the average 74-gun battleship he would have had three colleagues, and if serving on a 100-gun ship like HMS *Victory*, even more. The memoirs of officers like Lieutenant James Anthony Gardener also show that, rather than being overawed by the tone of the mess, surgeons and their mates were often shameless bores, talking incessantly about medical matters.[13]

The surgeon's trade

The popular image of the naval surgeon shows him in battle. He is portrayed as a heroic figure, apron covered in blood, wielding knife and saw in the half-light of the cockpit amid din and chaos as he struggles to keep pace with a mounting pile of wounded and bleeding men. In one way this picture is true. In another it is a distortion since battle was the exception rather than the rule in the life of a warship, and most of the time was spent on routine activities. Life for the surgeon and his mates was no different. Most of their time was spent keeping the crew healthy, dealing with accidents, and combating the diseases that were inevitable in damp and crowded ships. Nevertheless, it was in battle that reputations were made or lost.

Reliant on self-study to master the rudiments of his new profession, where would Trotter have found the guidance he needed? If he had hoped to find the answer in Admiralty orders, he would have been disappointed. The section

---

[12] Bell, Dr John, *A Memorial on the Present State of Naval and Military Surgery Addressed to The Rt Hon. Earl Spencer, First Lord of the Admiralty* (London, 1798)
[13] J. A. Gardner, *Above and below Hatches* (London, 1955)

relating to surgeons in the *Regulations and Instructions Relating to His Majesty's Service at Sea* was largely concerned with administration. It said that he was to supply his own chest of instruments certified and sealed by the Surgeons' Company; to prepare the hold for the treatment of battle casualties; to inspect the special foodstuffs supplied for the sick; to visit his patients twice daily; and to keep the captain fully informed as to the health of the ship. He was required to supply himself with blank sick certificates, to prepare a medical report at the end of each voyage, and to keep two detailed journals for the scrutiny of the Sick and Hurt Board – one dealing with surgical operations, the other with the treatment of disease. The *Additional Instructions* said little more, merely laying down that 15 shillings was to be deducted and paid to the surgeon from the pay of those who had been successfully treated for venereal diseases.

Fortunately there were a number of works specializing in naval medicine for Trotter to consult. A basic text, entitled *The Surgeon's Mate*, had been written as long ago as 1617 by John Woodall, surgeon-general of the East India Company. Another was *The Nature and Cure of Distempers of Seafaring People*, published in 1696 by William Cockburn, physician at Greenwich Hospital. A more recent one was *The Naval Surgeon or a Practical System of Surgery* by John Atkins, first published in 1734. This book had a broad purpose and, in addition to describing surgical techniques, emphasized the importance of hygiene on board ship and of methodical casualty management in action. Atkins recognized that the dirt, overcrowding and bad air that was endemic on warships was closely linked to naval diseases. He also stressed that advanced preparation was as important in battle as surgical skill. Chests should be covered with clean cloths and made ready as operating tables, needles threaded, polished instruments meticulously laid out, dressings and bandages within reach, and clean water and vinegar to hand. Bringing order to the chaos of battle was vital, and Atkins advocated that the wounded should immediately be divided into categories and the order of treatment determined by its urgency.

Trotter would also have used a recent two-volume work entitled *The Marine Practice of Physic and Surgery*, published in 1770 by William Northcote. A former naval surgeon himself, Northcote was entirely practical and sought to establish basic surgical principles and techniques with historical precedents. He followed Atkins in advocating hygiene and method. He also came out strongly in favour of removing foreign matter from wounds and of securing blood vessel by ligature rather than cauterizing with a hot iron. In the debate within medical circles as to whether it was better to operate straight away or to wait until the patient had gathered his strength, he argued that amputation should be carried out immediately as the best way of ensuring a patient's recovery before loss of blood and shock set in.

Battle

When the ship was in action, the surgeon and his mates would be confronted with a mass of frightful wounds. In battle, iron missiles fired into the hull from cannon were probably the greatest destroyers of men and ships. Indeed, the objective of every captain was to cross the undefended stern of an opponent and 'rake' her by firing a broadside that would penetrate the whole length of the ship, overturning guns, igniting powder and causing death and destruction to the men within. For the gun crews, burns were common as a result of the accidental explosion of overloaded or poorly cast guns, or from the ignition of scattered powder and cartridges. Those on the open decks were no better off, being exposed to the telescopic and chain shot that was used to dismember rigging and sails, as well as to musket fire and grape shot. If they found themselves in hand-to-hand combat, wounds from swords, pikes and boarding axes could also be expected.

The greatest cause of injury and mutilation, however, was the showers of splinters released when cannonballs smashed into the masts or the wooden sides of the ship. The amount of damage depended on the velocity of the shot, for a cannonball fired at close range punched a neat hole, while one whose force was nearly spent left a jagged aperture and sprayed the deck with shards of wood as sharp as razors. It was estimated that whereas the ratio of wounds to death was three to one in close actions, it rose to four to one in long-range engagements. These wounds were also more lethal. Not only did splinters cause compound fractures and hideous lacerations, but embedded fragments of wood often led to tetanus.

By the end of the eighteenth century, naval surgeons had well-proven techniques for dealing with battle injuries. Wounds from gunshot or edged weapons were immediately cleansed, foreign bodies removed and the haemorrhage arrested. This was followed by infection and suppuration which, it was hoped, would lead to the discharge of 'laudable' pus and eventual healing. Shock was treated with opiates. Penetration of the abdomen and chest cavities by musket balls and the like was, however, regarded as beyond help and surgeons preferred to leave such wounds alone. Burns were treated by the application of linseed oil, vinegar, lime water or a substance called 'ceruse', which unfortunately contained lead.

Naval surgeons developed considerable expertise in treating fractures, both to the limbs and to the skull, sometimes resorting to trepanning to lift a depressed skull bone, while the incidence of compound fractures and tearing of the limbs made them experts on amputation. Operating without anaesthetics, speed was of the essence. Indeed, a competent surgeon prided himself on being able to cut through the muscle, saw the bone, then locate and apply ligatures to the arteries and blood vessels – all in two or three minutes. After that, the patient would be passed to the surgeon's mate for the preparation of the stump, which would be sutured immediately or left open for a few days to permit the discharge of pus.

In all these procedures, post-operative infections leading to death were frequent. The average mortality rate was one out of three patients. The two most dreaded conditions were gangrene and tetanus. Gangrenous tissue could be cut away, but tetanus was inevitably fatal. The skill and ability of naval surgeons in dealing with battle casualties was remarkable and, indeed, steadily improved. Nevertheless, the conditions in which they worked, the absence of anaesthetics and the general ignorance of asepsis limited what was possible.

Medicine at Sea

Accident and disease

Casualties in action may have been the most dramatic test of a surgeon's skill, but they occupied only a small proportion of his time. Likewise, battle fatalities were small in proportion to the total number of deaths. Statistics for the eighteenth century are incomplete and do not take account of variables such as the number of engagements or the weather, but evidence suggests that battle was the cause of less than a tenth of fatalities. Accidents accounted for between a quarter and a third. This is hardly surprising. Work at sea was hard and physical, whether shifting heavy casks and guns, or handling sails and rigging in all weathers high above a pitching deck. Crushed limbs and bodies, bruises, blisters from handling ropes, falls to the deck or into the sea, strains and ruptures regularly occurred. The great destroyer of men and immobilizer of fleets was not, however, battle or accident, or even shipwreck – it was disease. According to contemporary estimates, at least 50 per cent of fatalities were due to this cause. Gilbert Blane calculated that of the 70,000 men raised for sea service in 1779, 28,592 were temporarily hospitalized, of whom 1858 died.[14] When it is considered that 3619 also died on their own ships, it is clear that the total sick list was much greater, and that almost every man in the navy must have been incapacitated by illness at some time. What this meant in real terms is suggested in figures produced by Blane for the state of the fleet in the West Indies in June 1782 following the Battle of the Saints. In that month, out of a total of 21,608 men, 849 were out of action with wounds but 1850 with fever and violent dysentery, called the flux.[15]

Minor ailments like colds, sore throats, boils and abrasions were commonplace. There were the ever-present cases of venereal disease. And there was also the occasional importation of measles and smallpox from the shore. The list of ailments which were regarded as endemic to shipboard life were printed in a neat table that surgeons were required to complete and attach to their reports on the voyage. It comprised 'Wounds and Accidents, Rheumatism and Lumbago, Pulmonary Infections, Ulcers, Scurvy, Fluxes and Continual and Intermittent Fevers'.

Fevers and flux

Of this list of ailments, it was the fevers – comprising typhus, typhoid, yellow fever and malaria – that were the real threats. The mobilizations of 1739 and 1755 had been undermined by these diseases, and military expeditions to the tropics had often been similarly wrecked. In Britain, the worst example had been the fate of Hosier's Caribbean Squadron from 1726 to 1728, when 4000 out of 4750 seamen, officers, captains and even the admiral himself had perished. Sailors still sang a mournful ditty called 'Admiral Hosier's Ghost'. The problem faced by the medical profession in trying to deal with these ailments is shown

---

[14] Gilbert Blane, *Select Dissertations* (London, 1822), quoted in C. Lloyd (ed.), *The Health of Seamen*, Navy Records Society 107 (London and Colchester, 1965), 198–200 and 205–6
[15] Gilbert Blane, *Observation on the Diseases of Seamen* (London, 1785), 146

vividly in the way they had to be classified. With inadequate techniques for investigation, no awareness of microbes, and theories of the transmission of disease in which the roles of lice or mosquitoes were unknown, it was impossible to establish the nature of these fevers. In the absence of knowledge as to their cause, they could only be classified by their symptoms as 'intermittent' or 'continual'.

Observation may have been inadequate in identifying the nature of these diseases, but it produced insights into the circumstances in which they developed. It was clear, for example, that – unlike scurvy – all were diseases of the land which were imported into ships from the shore. Likewise, although it was originally thought that fevers and fluxes were variants of the same condition, observation began to reveal differences. The symptoms of ague, now called malaria, with high fevers and periodic intervals between attacks, seem to have been the first to be separately identified. It was clearly linked to low-lying swampy areas, and was virulent in the tropics but also present in the temperate zone. In Britain, as Trotter was to find in *Berwick*, Sheerness was well known for it. Yellow fever, or black vomit, was also distinctive enough with its discoloration of the skin, sudden onset of fever, delirium and fatal outcome. A distinction between typhoid fever and typhus was also beginning to be recognized. Indeed, typhus was so clearly related to overcrowding that it was called 'jail', 'camp' or 'ship fever'. It was also contagious. If an infected man were introduced into a warship, the disease spread rapidly. Whether other fevers and fluxes were also contagious was a matter of debate. The flux was predominantly a land disease, and it is not surprising that Britain's leading expert was Sir John Pringle, surgeon general of the army, who had had first-hand experience in Flanders. He noted that flux generally occurred in low-lying areas where the water was bad and the ground replete with excrement and rotting straw.

There were many theories to account for fevers and the flux. One factor in their appearance was thought to be seasonal variations in weather and abrupt changes in climate. Another was unbalanced diet, faulty digestion and internal corruption. Eating a surfeit of fruit, for example, was a common explanation for the flux. Another was that planetary influences made individuals vulnerable.

The single most influential theory, however, came from the idea that pure air was the defining condition of good health. Fevers and fluxes were not therefore caused by filth and bad water as such, but by inhaling the poisonous smells they produced. Hence the origin of the term *malaria*, 'bad air'. It was thought that armies succumbed to fluxes because they breathed in the miasmas emanating from the excrement and corrupted water supplies around their encampments, and that the spread of yellow fever and malaria was due to the effluvia produced by swamps and rotting mudflats. Smell was the way in which disease was transmitted. Infected clothes and bedding were recognized as playing some role, but the main explanation was that typhus was spread by means of the foul smells they produced, and by the breath of those already afflicted.

The fact that there was no understanding of how these maladies could be cured did not mean that the medical profession could not think of any. The Sick and Hurt Board received a regular flow of pills, potions, stomachers and spine pads from doctors and quacks, most of which were referred for outside advice or tested.[16] But if a cure remained a mystery, at least the symptoms could be relieved. This was done by applying the full panoply of contemporary techniques – bleeding to reduce over-heating of the body in fevers; blistering; and the administration of emetics like tartar to empty the stomach, of purgatives to evacuate the bowels, of the miraculous quinine-containing Peruvian Bark to lower the temperature, and of the powder invented by Dr Robert James to induce perspiration.

A cure may have been out of reach, but vigorous attention was paid to prevention. Cleanliness and washing of the decks with sea water became an obsession on British ships. The same principle was applied to the crew. Officers ensured that the men, their clothing and their hammocks were regularly washed, and there was a growing awareness among thoughtful surgeons like Trotter that new recruits – who often arrived in verminous rags after weeks in a receiving ship – were a cause of infection. The pure-air theory was also applied. Attempts were made to remove the bad air and the disease-carrying smells that were inevitably generated by hundreds of men packed together on foetid accommodation decks located above the evil-smelling ballast. Wind sails were rigged to bring air into the bowels of the ship. Dr Hales invented a pump, and Mr Sutton a system of pipes, for the same purpose. When infection occurred, rigorous measures were taken. Ships were emptied of ballast, stripped of fittings, washed with vinegar and fumigated by burning brimstone, gunpowder and a variety of noxious substances. Trotter was later to give a detailed description of these procedures in his *Medicina Nautica*. All this had its effect. Foreigners were astonished at the comparative cleanliness of British warships. French vessels, for example, were notorious for being overcrowded, dirty and disease-ridden. The disadvantage was that the twice-daily soaking with sea water irrespective of the weather or time of the year made British ships even damper than normal and increased the incidence of other categories of disease on the list, namely 'Rheumatism and Lumbago' and 'Pulmonary Infections'.

Scurvy

Scurvy was the scourge of long sea voyages and could be devastating. It was a disease which inevitably attracted Trotter's interest and on which he became an authority. Making its appearance after as little as six weeks at sea, its symptoms were easily recognizable – stinking breath; swollen, bleeding gums; bloated flesh with a rash of bruises; lassitude; and extreme physical weakness leading eventually to death. Scurvy had existed since ancient times, but its incidence had multiplied during the sixteenth century, which had seen a sharp increase in the length of sea voyages in search of new lands and trade. For Trotter's generation, the memory of Commodore Anson's voyage round the world from 1740 to 1744 was still fresh. In the Pacific he had captured the fabled Acapulco galleon loaded with treasure, but the expedition was equally memorable for its casualties. Out of 2000 men who originally set out, 1400 perished, mostly as

---

[16]   P. K. Crimmin, 'The Sick and Hurt Board and the health of seamen', *Journal for Maritime Research* (December, 1999), www.jmr.nmm.ac.uk

the result of scurvy, and of eight ships, only one returned, many of the others having been destroyed for want of manpower.

We now know that scurvy is caused by a deficiency of vitamin C in the diet. Unfortunately, before the beginning of the twentieth century no knowledge of this was possible. Mariners and naval surgeons in earlier times had therefore had to speculate, and came to the conclusion that the disease was linked with salt diet, bad water and the rigours of life at sea. Some saw the answer as lying in the consumption of fresh meat, vinegar, wine, infusions of scurvy grass, spruce beer, and weak acids which would stimulate the digestive system. Others had noticed that citrus fruit seemed to provide a cure. The Elizabethan adventurers Lancaster, Hawkins and Drake in their voyages to Africa and the Spanish Main had all drawn attention to it. John Woodall in his notable book, *The Surgeon's Mate*, had advocated lemons and limes as a cure for scurvy in 1617, but admitted that he had no idea why they worked. The Dutch physician John Bachstrom had also drawn attention to the link between the citrus fruit and the disease in 1734. Unfortunately, all this evidence was seen as anecdotal by medical experts and made no impression on their thinking.

The dominant theory of the time was that scurvy was a disease of putrefaction. The starting point was that while some degree of decay was necessary to the absorption of food, faulty digestion would cause it to rot within the body and cause putrid diseases like scurvy. Boerhaave in Leiden and Cullen in Edinburgh developed the idea further. Both were interested in the new field of chemistry and hypothesized that scurvy was the result of chemical changes in the blood caused by putrefaction brought about by an indigestible diet of salt meat, biscuit and impure water. In England, Dr Huxham of Plymouth and the highly influential Dr Richard Mead, physician to George II and a prominent member of the Royal College of Physicians, took the idea further by promoting what became the standard cure. Writing in the 1740s, they argued that the corrupted blood which underlay scurvy could be cleansed by regularly drinking 'elixir of vitriol', a form of sulphuric acid taken with spirits and barley water and laced with spices.

The next step in the lemon-juice story came in May 1747, when HMS *Salisbury* was afflicted with an outbreak of scurvy. James Lind, a dedicated Scots physician with a scientific turn of mind, was the ship's surgeon and decided to make a scientific trial. He took twelve men, divided them into six pairs and gave each pair a different diet. One was given elixir of vitriol, another cider, another vinegar, another garlic, another sea water and the last, oranges and lemons. After a fortnight the last group had recovered, the rest had not. Lind described the *Salisbury* trial briefly in his 1753 book *Treatise of the Scurvy*.

Lind's experiment has given rise to a number of false assumptions about the oranges and lemons cure for scurvy and the reason why it took sixty years for it to be introduced as a regular item of diet into the navy. Knowing, as we now do, that citrus juice is in fact the answer, and impressed by Lind's visionary use of a controlled trial, writers in the twentieth century came to the conclusion that the publication of the *Salisbury* experiment in the *Treatise* was a defining moment in proving that lemon juice was the cure for scurvy, and that it had as much impact in the eighteenth century as it would have had now. As modern research has shown, neither of these propositions is true. Experts at the time were impressed with the scope of Lind's thinking and by his analysis of past theories on scurvy, but the lemon-juice section in the *Treatise* had little or no impact on medical thinking.

There is no indication than Lind expected anything else. He did not give any emphasis to his lemon-juice experiment in the *Treatise*, and the *Salisbury* episode, though mentioned, was lost in a work that was long, complex and in some areas contradictory.[17] Indeed, Lind never advocated lemon juice as a single answer to scurvy. It was left to another naval surgeon, Nathaniel Hulme, to produce a book in 1763 which did just that. Lind was more interested in the nature of the disease and, since he had to work within the medical concepts of the time, had come to the erroneous conclusion that it was the result of faulty digestion and excretion. He believed that there were multiple causes to the disease – such as salt meat, mouldy biscuit, bad water, foul air, lack of exercise, and a damp atmosphere that blocked perspiration – and that multiple solutions were therefore required. This led him to conclude that the true answer to scurvy lay in changing the whole environment and not in just making a simple addition to the diet.

Lind's position on scurvy was made clear the following year. In 1754, the Admiralty asked him to make recommendations on how the health of a squadron it was about to sent to the East Indies could best be preserved on the voyage. In his reply, Lind made no attempt to push the oranges and lemons treatment that had proved successful on *Salisbury*, but produced a wide-ranging set of proposals that covered the whole environment – salt meat, ventilation, cleanliness, exercise etc.[18] None were particularly novel or controversial. In terms of anti-scorbutics, his major recommendation was to issue a 'rob', or syrup, of boiled citrus juice, which was to be drunk with wine and water and made 'by the means prescribed in my book'. He even recommended the supply of evaporating dishes so it could be made on board. It was ironic that Lind should have moved his ground from lemon juice to 'rob' since, as we now know, the process of boiling needed to produce it destroys the vitamin C. Apart from this 'rob', the only mention of lemon juice was as a substance which could be added to vinegar when washing the sick and their quarters.

Both of the Commissioners on the Sick and Hurt Board were laymen and, as was their custom, they referred Lind's proposals to outside medical experts for evaluation. Two licentiates of the Royal College of Physicians were invited to give their opinion: Dr Schomberg, a physician with social pretensions, and Dr James, the author of many medical articles, compiler of a three-volume *Medical Dictionary* praised by Dr Johnson, and the inventor of the famous fever powder, together with Surgeon Hill of Woolwich dockyard.

Schomberg wrote a brief and unhelpful reply which, in one sentence, pronounced the proposals as being 'ingeniously founded on Reason and Observation' and would be useful. James wrote at greater length. After summarizing the

[17]   M. Bartholomew, 'James Lind and scurvy: a revaluation', *Journal for Maritime Research* (January, 2002), www.jmr.nmm.ac.uk
[18]   Lind to Admiralty, 16 February 1754), NMM, Adm E/13

putrefaction theory, he went through Lind's proposals in a rather perfunctory manner, most of which, he implied, were not novel. Hill, being a working naval surgeon, was more sceptical. He thought that existing treatments were satisfactory and found Lind's proposals either unnecessary or impractical.

The Sick and Hurt Board returned Lind's paper with the three assessments to the Admiralty without comment.[19] In fact, no action was taken. Lind's proposals were too general, offered little that was new, and had received no significant professional support.

Another false proposition put forward by twentieth-century writers was that not only did Lind 'prove' to medical opinion that lemon juice cured scurvy, but that the delay in introducing it into the navy was due to bureaucratic inertia and snobbish obstruction by officials and admirals, and that only when 'disciples' of Lind, notably Gilbert Blane, gained positions of influence in the system, were they able to persuade their naval masters to see reason and issue lemon juice. As the documentary evidence given in this book will show, these assumptions are without foundation. The truth is the reverse. It has been well established that the Sick and Hurt Board was genuinely concerned for the health of seamen throughout the period.[20] Nothing would have pleased it and the Admiralty more than to have received a single answer to the problem of scurvy from the doctors. Alas, it did not come. Instead, there were dozens of different solutions, the most authoritative of which did not work. For years, seafarers had noticed that citrus fruits provided a cure, but the medical establishment, which was dominated by university-educated physicians rather than the humbler and more pragmatic surgeons, would not advocate any solution that did not conform to contemporary theories on the disease.

For the first half of the century, medical thinking on scurvy was dominated by ideas of putrefaction and corruption of the blood. But in 1764, these notions were challenged by a new theory expounded by Dr David McBride in his *Experimental Essays on Medical and Philosophical Subjects*. Building on the ideas of Sir John Pringle, McBride argued that scurvy appeared because the putrefaction caused by imperfect digestion inhibited the production of 'fixed air', or carbon dioxide, which actually held the tissues together. The cure, he explained, could be found in drinking infusions of malt and its derivative, wort, which would then ferment within the body, stimulate digestion and restore the missing gas. Mc Bride's idea attracted support at the highest level and was so persuasive that even Nathaniel Hulme changed his mind and came out in support.

The McBride fermentation theory dominated medical thinking in Britain on the nature of scurvy for more than twenty years. It is no surprise that it monopolized the medical advice received by the Admiralty and the Sick and Hurt Board, relegating citrus juice to the sidelines. Nor is it a surprise that, during Captain Cook's first voyages to the Pacific between 1769 and 1776, malt and wort were top of the list of the cures for scurvy he was ordered to investigate. Others were the use of beer, sauerkraut and the 'rob' that had been suggested

---

[19] Sick and Hurt Board to Admiralty, 6 March 1754, with copies of letters, NMM, Adm F/11
[20] Crimmin, 'The Sick and Hurt Board and the health of seamen'

by Lind.[21] Lemon juice did not appear in the list at all. Cook was highly critical of the 'rob', mildly supportive of sauerkraut, and came down in favour of malt and wort. For his work in preserving the health of his crews, Cook was given a medal by the Royal Society, of which Pringle was now President. The measures Cook had taken on his voyages to maintain health were so wide-ranging that in hindsight it is impossible to isolate any one as the cause of his success. What is clear is that his report did no favours to the cause of citrus juice and reinforced the medical establishment's support for fermentation, malt and wort.

Such was the state of naval medicine when Trotter received his warrant as assistant surgeon in 1779. It was a mixed picture. On the one hand, the causes of the major diseases like typhus and scurvy remained a mystery and the method of treatment uncertain, while on the other, surgeons had developed well-tried procedures for dealing with accidents and battle casualties, even if their success rate was limited. The general level of the profession was, however, rising and the depiction of the drunken, rough-and-ready naval surgeon given in Tobias Smollett's much quoted 1748 satire *Roderick Random* was no longer true. There may have been problems with a minority, but the journals of naval officers and reports on the work of surgeons and their mates during the wars of the last quarter of the eighteenth century paint a picture of competence and skill. The impact of the Enlightenment had improved technique, and the arrival of men like Trotter, who had been trained in the new medical schools of Aberdeen, Glasgow and Edinburgh, was introducing new standards of care and performance. Conditions at sea were difficult, but Trotter's own career would show that surgeons could learn on the job, master the medical literature and, indeed, advance it as well. By the end of the eighteenth century the bulk of works on maritime diseases were coming from serving or former naval surgeons.[22] Indeed, in later life, Thomas Trotter was to establish himself as a leading writer on naval medicine.

———————•———————

[21] B. J. Stubbs, 'Captain Cook's beer: the anti-scorbutic effects of malt and beer in late eighteenth century sea voyages', *Asia and Pacific Journal of Clinical Nutrition* 12, no. 2 (2003), 129–37

[22] For example L. Gillespie, 'Observations on the putrid ulcer', *London Medical Journal* 9 (1785), 373–410; *Observations on the Diseases which Prevailed in HM Squadron in the Leeward Islands* (London, 1792); F. Thompson, *An Essay on the Scurvy showing Effectual and Practical Means for its Prevention at Sea* (London, 1790); R. Robertson, *Observations on Fevers and other Diseases, which Occur on Voyages to Africa and the West Indies* (London, 1792)

FROM SURGEON'S MATE
TO PHYSICIAN TO THE FLEET

⌐ 3 ⌐

HMS Berwick

O N 9 JANUARY 1779, Thomas Trotter reported on board HMS *Berwick* at
Portsmouth to take up his post as third surgeon's mate. It was a blustery
day with a fresh north-easterly wind and a touch of frost in the air. Trotter's first
sight of his new ship floating in the choppy waters of the navy's principal naval
base can hardly have been inspiring. *Berwick* had just emerged from dry dock,
where she had been one of the first vessels to have had her bottom sheathed in
Charles Middleton's new copper plating, and was now a grubby mast-less hulk
tied up at the jetty next to a receiving ship to which her crew had been transferred while the heavy work of preparing her for sea was completed. And heavy
it was. Indeed, on the day of Trotter's arrival, using nothing more than muscle-
power and pulleys, the men loaded on board no less than thirty-one tons of
shingle ballast, twelve cords of timber and a ton and a half of beef and bread.[1]
Two months later, *Berwick* had been transformed. Her stores were complete,
her guns in place, her masts and yards in position and her rigging set up taut
and seamanlike. Newly painted and ready for sea, she sailed out of Portsmouth
Harbour to moor at Spithead in early March. With the ship's officers and men
back on board, the nineteen-year-old Trotter began to get acquainted with his
companions, and to master the daily routines of a man of war.

Officers, men and 'interest'

The crew of a warship in the eighteenth century was a floating community
that contained all the skills needed to sail and navigate the vessel, maintain its
fabric, rigging, sails and guns, feed and care for its inhabitants and, of course,
fight. In terms of authority, the captain was undoubtedly in command but, at
the levels below, the formal hierarchy of rank was complicated by a system of
ratings that had to accommodate a mixture of sea officers, specialists, aspirant
officers, artisans, seamen and landsmen. This was further confused by the fact
that aristocrats and gentlemen were scattered throughout the ship's company
side by side with working men. At the top of the formal hierarchy were the
commissioned officers – the captain and the lieutenants – who were, by definition, gentlemen. Then came the warrant officers, none of whom were gentlemen by rank but some of whom – like the master, the purser, the surgeon and

---

[1] All these details, including the weather, can be found in *Berwick*, Captain's Log, TNA, Adm
51/101; Lieutenants' Logs, NMM, Adm/L/B/80

the chaplain – might be by social origin. Next came the petty officers – a mixed social group that included aspirant officers like midshipmen and masters' mates who were 'young gentlemen'; senior ratings from the lower deck like the coxswain and the quartermaster; and a assortment of inferior tradesmen like the cooper, the caulker, the ropemaker and the armourer. At the bottom were the 'other ranks' – in those days called 'the people' – an amorphous collection of seamen, landsmen, servants and boys. Even at this level nothing was simple. As part of the Georgian network of patronage, entry at the lower levels of the officer corps was in the gift of individual captains and officers of all grades were allowed a complement of 'servants' – a device which enabled them to introduce relatives or the sons of the politically influential into the service as aspirant officers or apprentices. All these young men were randomly rated in the ships books as 'servants' or by any other term that seemed appropriate. Thus, 'the people', which one would have expected to have been a solid working-class group, included the offspring of peers of the realm, of the landed gentry and of admirals, all surprisingly rated as 'able seamen', 'servants' or 'ship's boys'.

The navy in the eighteenth century was a service that demanded technical competence. An inefficient officer was a danger to all and was speedily got rid of, however elevated his social origins. Nevertheless, the patronage system was crucial to the workings of the navy, as it was to every other Georgian institution. Thus, whatever his merits, an individual could only gain employment or promotion if he was the beneficiary of political, aristocratic or naval backing and had friends and sponsors lobbying on his behalf. If he lacked this kind of pull or 'interest', as it was called, his only chance was to show conspicuous gallantry in action. The greatest dispenser of patronage was the Admiralty Board through its power of appointment and its control over promotions. Also important was the power of commanders-in-chief to fill local vacancies caused by death or court martial. But patronage also operated at the level of the individual ship. By the time an officer reached the rank of captain it was common for him to have acquired a group of adherents, or 'followers', of all ranks around him, who gave loyalty and support in return for favours and promotion. And when he moved ship, he took his followers with him. The Admiralty allowed this as part of the patronage system, and in recognition of the fact that a ship with a core of officers and men who had worked together and had confidence in each other was likely to be both happy and efficient. Thus, the captain of a ship of war was able to influence the selection of his officers and, indeed, the composition of the crew. Many used regional connections to ease the problem of recruitment. In the Napoleonic Wars, for example, ships commanded by Sir Edward Pellew and Cuthbert Collingwood had strong contingents of men from their native counties of Cornwall and Northumberland. Other ships were famous for being Irish or 'Scotch'.

HMS *Berwick* did not quite fall into this regional category, but in many ways she typified ships of the period. Her captain, the Hon. Keith Stewart, was a leading Scottish aristocrat, being the second surviving son of the earl of Galloway and grandson of the earl of Dundonald. He was Member of Parliament for Wigtownshire and had briefly represented the Wigtown Burghs. His 'interest' was therefore considerable. He had been promoted to captain in 1762 after only ten years in the service and seems to have had no difficulty in finding a ship. He was highly competent as a seaman, but does not appear to have been overtly ambitious. Lowland Scots were inevitably well represented among the officers. All four members of the medical department were also Scotsmen.[2] Whether the Scottish connection had anything to do with Thomas Trotter's appointment to the *Berwick* is impossible to say. But he would certainly have felt at home.

Berwick was typical of the 74-gun ships that were the workhorses of the Georgian navy and formed the backbone of the line of battle. Launched at Portsmouth in April 1775, she was one of eight 1600-ton vessels built to the design of the famous surveyor, Thomas Slade. All were to serve in the American and Napoleonic Wars and one, the *Defiance*, fought with Nelson at the Battle of Trafalgar. *Berwick* was also present at Trafalgar but, alas, fought on the wrong side, having been captured by the French in 1796. Like all ships of her class, *Berwick* carried her principal armament on two gun decks that stretched the whole length of the vessel, the lower carrying twenty-eight 32-pounder cannons, and the upper an equal number of 18-pounders. Above them was the quarter deck, which occupied the area behind the main mast, and the fore deck which filled the forward part of the ship. It was here that eighteen long 9-pounder guns, the most accurate in the ship's armament, were located. *Berwick* was 168 feet in length, 65 feet in width and 20 feet deep in the hold. Into this space were crowded up to six hundred seamen, marines and officers.[3]

The captain lived in remote grandeur in a sealed-off portion of the quarter deck. His accommodation consisted of a great cabin, which stretched across the full width of the ship and was illuminated by its stern windows, and two smaller cabins for sleep and work. Below was the upper gun deck. The forward part was the location of the ship's galley and the sick bay; the centre, or waist, was open to the elements; and the remainder, stretching from the mainmast to the stern, comprised the wardroom, the area reserved for the ship's senior officers. The wardroom, like the captain's cabin above, was a large space illuminated by the ship's stern windows. Its main feature was a long table in the centre, at which the officers could eat, socialize or work, flanked by two rows of flimsy canvas cabins built against the side of the ship that provided some sort of privacy for eight of the inhabitants. Membership of the wardroom also carried the highly prized privilege of being able to use the closed lavatories in the ship's quarter galleries instead of the open heads in the bow with the rest of the crew. Who was or was not a member of the wardroom was determined by social considerations as well as rank. All five lieutenants and the two marine officers were naturally members. However, only the senior and most respectable of the warrant officers, the master and the purser, were automatically included. The artisans, such as the boatswain, carpenter and gunner, were not, and messed and lived elsewhere in the ship. Whether the surgeon or the chaplain was accepted into the wardroom depended on their educational and social status.

---

[2]   Muster Roll *Berwick*, TNA, Adm 36/8898–8900
[3]   For full constructional and design details and service history of *Berwick*, see P. Goodwin, *The Ships of Trafalgar* (London, 2005), 177–81

Below that was the lower gun deck. This was not only the location of the ship's main battery, but was also the space where the bulk of men slung their hammocks, or gathered round mess tables to socialize or have their food and grog. The part nearest the stern was known as the gunroom, and was where the midshipmen and inferior warrant officers slung their hammocks and had their mess. It was here that Thomas Trotter and the two more senior surgeon's mates, Sam Johnstone and Robert Nevin, would sleep and live.

Immediately under the gun deck was the orlop. It was here that the ship's medical facilities were concentrated. Trotter's chief, Surgeon Alexander Dick, had his own small cabin on the port side near to the stern. Next door was a small dispensary dominated by a large wooden cabinet filled with drawers, bottle racks and recesses for his powders, potions, ointments, drugs and dressings. Immediately outside was the cockpit, which in battle was converted into an operating theatre. The orlop was below the waterline and was the safest part of the vessel in action. It was also relatively tranquil since it was spared the hurly-burly of the accommodation decks above when the watch was changed at four-hourly intervals at sea. Its disadvantage was that it had no natural ventilation or light, save the faint gleam that filtered down through the gratings or was thrown by the occasional lantern.

The lowest level of the ship was devoted to stores. Here was located the ship's magazine and the hold, a vast barn of a space in which the hundreds of casks, puncheons and hogsheads, which carried the vessel's provisions of beef, pork, butter, rum, oatmeal and dried peas, were tightly wedged among the shingle and iron pigs that formed the ballast.

Channel and West Indies: blockade and hurricane

May and June saw *Berwick* cruising the Channel as part of a force commanded by Vice-Admiral George Darby. It then joined the main Channel Fleet off Plymouth. The navy was at this stage in disarray as a consequence of the Battle of Ushant in July 1778. There, during four days of skilful manoeuvring, the French had managed to keep a slightly superior British fleet at bay while inflicting heavy damage aloft by firing high. When Admiral Augustus Keppel had finally tried to attack, the rear squadron under Vice-Admiral Hugh Palliser had been so disabled that it had been unable to comply and the French had escaped. The open public dissatisfaction which resulted had overflowed into mutual recriminations between the irascible Whig Keppel, the Tory Palliser and their respective political allies. Both men successively demanded to be court-martialled and each in turn was acquitted. The political backwash divided the nation and split the navy. Admirals became difficult to find and, when Trotter arrived, command of the Channel Fleet had been vested in the elderly but avuncular and level-headed Sir Charles Hardy. He faced an immediate crisis. In July 1779, the Spanish – with their eyes on Minorca, Florida and Gibraltar, which was soon besieged – declared war on Great Britain. The following month a combined Franco-Spanish fleet of sixty-six ships-of-the-line under Admiral D'Orvilliers entered the English Channel, sweeping British trade before it and coming within sight of Devon. Hardy, with only thirty-nine ships, including

Berwick, had been blown off station and was unable to stop him. An invasion scare swept the south coast and there was panic in Plymouth. Fortunately, the threat came to nothing. The French ships were riddled with disease and short of food and water. In September they withdrew and went home.

Trotter's first cruise on *Berwick* had been dramatic enough, and had given him his first taste of the problems of naval medicine. Scurvy was the main challenge. Although Darby's squadron had been at sea for only six weeks, when it returned to Spithead in September, the disease was already present. Trotter, who had made himself familiar with current medical opinion and knew all about the theories of putrefaction, was struck by the speed with which the symptoms disappeared by reducing the amount of salt meat in the diet, introducing vegetables and fruit, and allowing the crew 'liberty' on the Isle of Wight.[4] He was also scathing about having the ship's sick bay next to the galley. True, the atmosphere was drier and warmer, but Trotter concluded that it had been put there

> more with a view to stifle contagion with the smoke from the fire, than to keep the patients comfortable. Lind's doctrine of fumigation was . . . in full vigour, to which our captain, like all others, bowed with submission. If, however, infection by this means was roasted to a cinder, the poor sick man was often in danger of losing his eyes from the wood smoke in undergoing the fiery ordeal. Lind took it into his head that the situation of the fire place in small vessels between the decks, by affording copious supplies of smoke, was the true cause of these ships being more exempt from infectious diseases.[5]

The strategy of the British government for 1780 was to relieve Gibraltar, then reinforce the fleet in the West Indies, which were believed to be the main French target. The man chosen for this assignment was Admiral Sir George Rodney. Rodney was a snobbish, unpopular but aggressive and successful admiral, who was notorious for the ruthlessness with which he exploited the navy's patronage and financial systems to his own advantage. He was also an ailing and prematurely aged sixty-one-year-old who was a martyr to gout. Rodney therefore took with him as personal physician a socially well-connected doctor called Gilbert Blane. The name of Blane, alongside that of Trotter, was to feature prominently in the navy's fight against scurvy.

Rodney sailed on Christmas Eve 1779, heading first for Gibraltar. Arriving off the Spanish coast he immediately won a minor victory over an enemy force under Admiral Don Juan de Langara, destroying in a midnight battle six of his eleven battleships. Gibraltar was successfully relieved and Rodney pressed on to the West Indies with four ships-of-the-line. Meanwhile in Britain, a second reinforcement of four ships for Jamaica was preparing under Commodore Walsingham. One of these was HMS *Berwick* with the youthful Trotter on board. Walsingham's squadron was held up by contrary winds for three months, but eventually sailed at the end of May, escorting the outward bound West India convoy.

[4] T. Trotter, *Observations on the Scurvy: with a review of the opinions lately advanced on that disease and a new theory defended*, 2nd edn (London, 1792), 107
[5] T. Trotter, *Medicina Nautica: an Essay on the Diseases of Seamen* (London, 1797–1803), III, 441

Apart from the usual hassle of keeping the merchantmen together, Walsingham's ships had an uneventful voyage, sailing south to the coast of Portugal to pick up the south-east trade winds, then heading via Madeira and the Canary Islands to Barbados, where they arrived on 11 July.[6] The weather during the voyage was fine, with blue seas and scarcely a shower of rain, but scurvy, once more, had begun to take its toll. When *Berwick* arrived at Jamaica, Trotter reported that thirty-five men were down with the disease. The naval hospital at Port Royal was full, and could not take the casualties, who had to stay on board to be treated. A reduction in the ration of salt meat and the introduction of vegetables and fruit into the seamen's diet eliminated the scurvy, and within only ten days all *Berwick*'s sick had returned to duty. Both events – the effectiveness of vegetables and fruit, particularly oranges, lemons and limes, and the fact that the disease could be treated without the need for hospitalization – were registered by Trotter, and did much to influence his developing ideas on the subject of scurvy.[7] And Trotter was not the only one. Within months of his arrival, Admiral Rodney, in a typical display of personal patronage, had accelerated young Gilbert Blane's career by appointing him as physician of the fleet in the West Indies. Blane was coming to the same conclusions as Trotter on the value of citrus fruits, and would present them to the Admiralty the following year as part of a special memorandum.

This was Trotter's first experience of the tropics. Young and eager as he was for new experiences, the blue seas, palm-fringed beaches, red soil and richly wooded countryside of Jamaica scattered with white plantation houses would have made a deep impression on him. His interest in professional matters was no less active. In addition to being struck by the beneficial effects of providing oranges and lemons to the crew – a practice they extended themselves by swapping their hard tack for the exotic fruits carried by the market boats that surrounded the ship – Trotter noted that experienced captains in the West Indies habitually supplied cocoa and sugar or molasses in place of oatmeal and cheese. As well as being tasty and popular with the men, Trotter believed that they too had a small but beneficial effect on scurvy.

The contrary winds that had delayed the arrival of Commodore Walsingham in the West Indies also denied Trotter his first experience of battle. Two months before, at the end of April, Rodney with twenty-one battleships engaged the French with twenty-two off Martinique. The result was indecisive, with neither side willing or able to break the line of battle. The signal book inhibited Rodney's attempts to control the engagement, and his aloof personality had prevented his taking his captains into his confidence beforehand. In August, the French fleet returned home to avoid the hurricane season and the British began to disperse their own squadrons. The ships earmarked to remain on station withdrew to secure harbours; Rodney headed for North America, and Walsingham's squadron, reinforced and now under the overall command of Rear Admiral Rowley, sailed for England as escort to the last West India convoy of the season.

[6] *Berwick*, Captain's Log 1780–1, TNA, Adm 51/101
[7] Trotter, *Observations*, 107

Rowley quit the heat of Port Royal at the beginning of September with the 74-gun ships *Grafton, Thunderer, Hector* and *Berwick* and the smaller two-deckers *Ruby, Trident, Stirling Castle* and *Bristol*. The battleships with their convoy took the normal route round the western end of Cuba, then headed east through the Florida Channel and then north-east towards the Azores and Europe. At first, all went well, but on the afternoon of 5 October, 500 miles north of Bermuda, the wind dropped, the sun became obscured by a darkening sky, and the ships were beaten by torrential downpours. By dusk the wind had increased to gale force, driving enormous waves before it. The weather continued to deteriorate until, at midnight, *Berwick* and her consorts were struck by the full force of a hurricane. Even with reduced sails, it was a struggle to keep the ship on course as she reeled in the darkness amid mountainous waves and a shrieking wind. At 2 AM, *Berwick's* foremast was snapped off, taking the bowsprit and maintopmast with it. The crew fought to cut the lines to free the wreckage trailing alongside and to rig storm sails on main and mizzenmasts to keep her before the wind. Then these too went over the side, leaving the ship as a mastless hulk. Tons of sea water crashed over the ship, smashing the stern windows and quarter galleries, tearing guns from their mountings, and sweeping boats and anchors overboard. Below decks, *Berwick* became a shambles, with bread, provisions and water spoiled, and the medical chest swept away.[8]

Working in the blackness, the crew struggled to maintain control, clearing away the worst of the mess and setting scraps of sail to keep the ship manageable. By dawn, the storm began to subside. All that could be seen from *Berwick's* deck in the cold light of day were three dismasted warships wallowing in the foam-flecked sea, one, the *Hector*, flying a signal of distress. Unbeknown to Trotter and his companions, *Stirling Castle* had been driven ashore and wrecked while Walsingham's ship, the *Thunderer*, had foundered, never to be seen again. All along the north coast of Cuba, ships were overwhelmed, dismasted or wrecked.

Over the next five days, in an astonishing display of seamanship, the *Berwick's* crew carried out major repairs at sea. With the ship rolling in the swell, the stumps of the masts were cut short and new ones swayed into position, while the sailmakers toiled to prepare new sails. The ship carried no spare lower masts, so topmasts had to serve in their stead while the smaller upper masts were used to replace the topmasts. That done, new yards were hoisted into position and the standing and running rigging reset.[9] After six days, the crew had carried out all the repairs they could. Stewart, as senior officer, ordered his three consorts back to Jamaica, then, signalling farewell, *Berwick* trimmed her sails to the trade wind and began to head painfully north-east for the Azores and England. *Berwick's* men had done a good job, but the ship could only make 70 miles a day, less than half her normal speed. It was not until 24 November that *Berwick*, with her stunted rig and patched-up hull, dropped anchor at Spithead.

---

[8] *Berwick*, Captain's Log, TNA, Adm 51/101; Lieutenants' Logs, NMM, Adm/L/B/80
[9] *Berwick*, Captain's Log, TNA, Adm 51/101

For Surgeon Dick and Trotter and his colleagues, it had been a grim voyage. In addition to the normal hazards of any long sea passage, the crew had began to succumb to the effects of extreme fatigue, a leaking and damaged ship, spoilt provisions and water-soaked bedding and clothing, and the rapid change of climate as the heat of the Caribbean was replaced by the chill of the North Atlantic. The crew had been healthy when it had left Jamaica but, as the voyage progressed, hundreds of men succumbed to a virulent form of dysentery and delirium. Even Trotter was afflicted by the disease. Scurvy made its inevitable appearance, the hold became filled with the sick, and burials at sea became a regular weekly event. With most of their medicines destroyed, Trotter and his colleagues had little to offer except wine until they reached the English Channel and a passing frigate transferred supplies of opium. By the time *Berwick* reached Spithead, thirty of her men had died and two hundred were on the sick list, of whom sixty were immediately transferred to Haslar Hospital.[10]

The winter of 1780–1 saw *Berwick* moved to Plymouth to be docked and refitted. For the medical team there was the chance of some leisure. Trotter went ashore to enjoy the pleasures of the Devon countryside, picked up his pen once more and produced an *Ode to Winter* in typical Georgian style:

> No soaring lark salutes the morn,
> Or hails the trav'ller with his lay
> But as the season's face forlorn
> He plods his solitary way.
> Chilled with uncomfortable cold,
> How lonely looks the bleating fold.
> How mute the shepherd's love-sick tale,
> That echoed round the list'ning dale.
> The rivers bound in icy chain
> Forget their murmurs as they flow;
> And pendant from the ethereal plains
> The fleecy clouds emit their snow.[11]

In more light-hearted mood he scribbled a short verse for the amusement of his shipmates called *The Origin of Grog*, which celebrated the introduction of this mixture of rum and water by Admiral Vernon on the *Burford* forty years earlier.[12]

The Battle of the Dogger Bank

By the end of February, work on *Berwick* was finished and, commanded now by Captain James Fergusson, she was to join the small squadron based at Leith. The Hon. Keith Stewart was also on board, but he had been promoted to commodore in command of the whole force. On *Berwick*, Alexander Douglas was

---

[10] *Berwick*, Captain's Log, TNA, Adm 51/101; Trotter, *Medicina Nautica*, I, 378
[11] T. Trotter, *Sea Weeds: Poems, Written on Various Occasions, Chiefly During a Naval Life* (London, 1829), 31
[12] Ibid., 39

now first lieutenant and there had been other promotions as well. Among them was Thomas Trotter, who was now first mate to a new surgeon, Jonathan Day.[13]

In July, Stewart's squadron joined a fleet under Vice-Admiral Hyde Parker in the North Sea. The Royal Navy depended on the importation of items like hemp, rope and tar that were carried from the Baltic to British ports in regular convoys of over a hundred ships. The purpose of Parker's squadron was to defend this trade and to harass that of their enemies, which now included Holland. Annoyed at the help they had been giving to the French, and by their threat to join a hostile alliance fostered by Russia and known as the 'Armed Neutrality', Britain had declared war on the Dutch.

August 1781 found Parker off the Dogger Bank escorting a homeward-bound convoy of some 130 sail with seven warships – *Berwick*, *Princess Amelia Fortitude* and *Preston* of 74 guns, and the smaller two-deckers *Bienfaissance*, *Buffalo* and *Dolphin*. At dawn on the 5 August, a Dutch force of equal size was sighted under Vice-Admiral Zoutman, also on escort duty. Both squadrons shed their convoys and turned to fight, Zoutman, who was to leeward, waiting as Parker sailed down to meet him. At first, the British held their fire, but at 200 yards their broadsides erupted in fire and smoke. What followed was a bloody and hard-fought engagement. The British and Dutch had the same temperaments, both were wedded to the line of battle and both used the same brutal tactics in action, firing into hull and rigging alike. Side by side the two squadrons fought it out, the faster copper-sheathed British ships keeping position by occasionally spilling the wind from their topsails. The only drama occurred when damage to her rigging prevented *Berwick*, which was first in the British line, from keeping station so that she shot ahead, became isolated and was threatened by two Dutch vessels. She beat back to regain her position.

The fighting lasted for three and a half hours until Zoutman withdrew from the battle, gathered his convoy and disappeared over the horizon. The British warships were too damaged to be able to follow. Inevitably in such a dogged engagement, the losses were heavy. The British suffered some 450 casualties, the Dutch a hundred more, together with the loss of a two-decker, which sank that night. The fabric, masts and rigging of the *Berwick* were badly damaged, and enemy shot had destroyed all her boats, torn a dozen guns from their fittings and severely injured her crew.[14]

Trotter's first experience of battle must have been traumatic. Working in the half-light of the cockpit, with the deck under their feet and the timbers around shuddering with the crash of every broadside, Surgeon Day, Trotter and his other mates had struggled to bring order to the chaos of battle and to deal with the stream of bleeding men who had been carried below and dumped in every corner of the orlop. Eighteen officers and men had been killed and fifty-eight wounded. There were wounds from cannon shot, from small arms and from wood splinters. Operating in their shirtsleeves with saw and knife, they had worked non-stop, cleaning and binding lacerated flesh and amputating

---

[13] Muster Roll, *Berwick*, TNA, Adm 36/8900
[14] For the battle and its consequences, see *Berwick*, Captain's Log, TNA, Adm 51/101; Lieutenants' Logs, NMM, Adm/L/B/80; Hyde Parker to Stevens, 6 Aug 1781, TNA, Adm 1/519

shattered limbs. It was a task that required skill, strength and speed. No wonder that Trotter later wrote that the ideal surgeon should be no more than forty years old, be physically fit and have perfect eyesight. Trotter nevertheless did well. After the battle, Commodore Stewart's despatch included a tribute to his efforts.[15]

Berwick and her consorts spent two days repairing the worst of the damage and tending to the injured. Stewart then rallied the convoy and headed for Sheerness dockyard at the mouth of the Thames to repair his ships and land his sick. Trotter was struck by the fact that every invalid sent ashore was promptly struck down with ague – that is, malaria. October found *Berwick* again briefly blockading the Dutch coast. In November and December she was moored at the Downs, opposite the town and castle of Deal. Trotter's first experience of battle had given him much to discuss with his medical colleagues, and in October there had been another opportunity to talk about professional issues with the arrival as fifth lieutenant of William Bligh. Bligh's arrival on the ship was not so surprising. Although appointed on the recommendation of Vice-Admiral Robert Roddam, the commander-in-chief at Sheerness who had paid a key role in preparing the blockading squadron for sea, Bligh had originally been a 'follower' of Commodore Stewart, under whose patronage he had joined his first ship in 1763. Although later to achieve fame and notoriety during the mutiny on the *Bounty* and during a military insurrection in New South Wales when he was governor, Bligh was at that stage fairly junior, and had just returned from Captain Cook's third voyage to the Pacific, serving as sailing master on the *Resolution*. Trotter would have been keen to talk with him about the scurvy and the effectiveness of the malt, wort, sauerkraut and 'rob' that Cook had been ordered to try out on the voyage.

As *Berwick* rolled at her moorings in the chilly waters off Deal, the sociable, twenty-year-old Trotter was able to go ashore, meet with local families and mingle with local society in the candlelit elegance of the town's modest Assembly Rooms. Taking up his pen once more, presumably in order to make a name with the young ladies, he produced a whimsical-patriotic *Verse written at Deal* stimulated by an incident in a drawing room – described in the poem's sub-title – when 'a French officer on parole lay down the Violin in Surprise while playing a soft Italian air as a Young Lady struck up "Hearts of Oak" on the Piano Forte'.

In December 1781, Trotter's career on *Berwick* came to an end. Commodore Stewart went on extended leave to take the waters at Bath and her crew were transferred to the *Princess Amelia* and transported to Portsmouth, where they moved once more to the *Cambridge*.[16] Now first mate on a battleship, Trotter was eligible for promotion to full surgeon on an 18-gun sloop or a brig. The Hon. Keith Stewart, who in normal circumstances might have used his

---

[15] Although its existence is confirmed in other documents, Commodore Stewart's report mentioning Trotter's efforts cannot be found in either the admiral's or the captain's official reports on the action (TNA, Adm 1/519, Adm 1/520, Adm 1/1791 Captain's letters (F)). We can only assume that it, and similar accounts, were used to provide the information needed by Admiral Parker to write his dispatch, were then retained in the admiral's papers and subsequently lost.
[16] Muster Rolls of *Berwick, Princess Amelia, Cambridge*, TNA, Adm 36/8904, 9985 and 10475

interest on his behalf, was about to leave the service temporarily in order to get married. Trotter therefore had nothing to lose by saying goodbye to him, and to his erstwhile comrades from the *Berwick*. In April 1782, he transferred as surgeon to the small, three-masted sloop *Bustler*, remaining with her until she was decommissioned four months later. It was an unexciting assignment as the sloop spent most of her time at anchor off Plymouth.[17] Trotter was then transferred to the armed ship *William*, employed as escort for convoys of coasters that plied between Liverpool and Plymouth. Once again the work was routine, the only excitement occurring when she fought off a privateer flying American rebel colours off the Lizard. But in February 1783, making her approach to Liverpool, *William* went aground on a sand bank at the mouth of the Mersey, and was left high and dry by the falling tide. Her damage was too severe to justify repair and, with the American War coming to an end, on 5 April the ship and her crew were demobilized.[18] Thomas Trotter suddenly found himself without a job and, since only the 125 most senior surgeons on the list were entitled to a half-pay or pension, without any form of income.

———————•◆•———————

[17]   Muster Roll and Captain's Log of *Bustler*, TNA, Adm 36/8195 and 51/1044
[18]   Muster Roll and Captain's Log of *William*, TNA, Adm 36/8736 and 51/1060

4

Surgeon of a Slaver

Slavery and the triangular trade

FOR A NAVAL SURGEON to find himself demobilized on the banks of the Mersey was no bad thing. Liverpool was at this time one of Britain's major trading ports. At the beginning of the century, the wealth of London and Bristol had given the merchants of those cities a virtual monopoly over foreign commerce, but within fifty years the pushy upstarts of Liverpool, who cut their costs and paid their captains and agents a fraction of the going rates, had overtaken them. When Trotter began to look for a berth in 1783, three hundred ships were being cleared for foreign trade. And of these, over a quarter were Guineamen – that is, vessels designed to carry slaves from Africa to the booming markets of the Caribbean. For just as Liverpool had become Britain's principal port for overseas commerce, so it had come to dominate the slave trade.

Slavery had been a widely accepted practice since ancient times and had been an integral part of African societies since well before the arrival of the Europeans. Not only was internal slavery common, but slaves had also been an export commodity and part of Africa's trade with the Arab world, where they had been employed as servants, soldiers and in the fields. The development of the plantation-style agriculture in the Americas and the Caribbean in the seventeenth century had, however, stimulated the practice and changed its fundamentals. The development of the production of sugar in Brazil and the West Indies, and of rice and tobacco in British North America, required a labour force that was robust and inured to tropical conditions. Slaves from Africa were the answer. European demand for tropical products soared during the eighteenth century, and no commodity was in greater demand than sugar. By 1750, sugar was no longer regarded as a luxury, but had become a necessity, wanted by the poor to sweeten their tea and put jam on their bread, and by the rich to flavour their coffee, chocolate, puddings and cakes. The sugar plantations of the British, French and Spanish West Indian colonies boomed, and so did the demand for African slaves.

By the eighteenth century, the slave trade became industrial in scale. Statistics are necessarily imperfect, but according to the best estimate some 11 million slaves were shipped out of Africa from the end of the fifteenth century to the nineteenth, of which 9.6 million survived the crossing of the Atlantic.[1] Two-thirds of this number were transported between 1700 and

[1] H. Thomas, *The Slave Trade: The History of the Atlantic Slave Trade 1440–1870* (London, 2006),

1805, with the yearly average growing from 15,000 in 1650–75 to 75,000 in 1797–1807.[2] The flow was by no means uniform. There was a sharp decline in numbers when the European powers were at war or when the kingdoms of West Africa were preoccupied with local conflicts. Nevertheless, the size of the trade, both in terms of the supply of slaves and their transportation across the Atlantic, made it a logistical feat that was as extraordinary at it was reprehensible. The cooperation of local African rulers was of course vital. Indeed, the kings of Dahomey, Ashanti and Loango, who had dealt in slaves for generations, took advantage of the new demand and became major suppliers to the trans-Atlantic trade, becoming richer, better armed with European guns and able to build up powerful empires as a consequence. In 1790, for example, the Ashanti army numbered 80,000 men, of whom half were equipped with firearms.[3] As these rulers preferred to sell their neighbours rather than their own people, prisoners of war taken on the battlefield or from raids on defeated populations formed the major source of slaves. As time went on, the wealth and power to be gained from satisfying the European demand made slave-taking one of the reasons for going to war. There were other sources of supply as well. Local criminal law produced a substantial number of individuals convicted of such offences as theft, adultery or witchcraft. It was possible to sell oneself, or a family member, into slavery as repayment for a debt. Kidnapping by local gangs seems to have been another source of supply – and frequently a more visible one since it often occurred in full view of the European slave ships.[4]

   The Atlantic slave trade was called the 'triangular trade', each of its three legs being expected to make its own profit. The first leg was the voyage from the home port to West Africa where cotton goods, guns, hardware, alcohol and trinkets would be traded for slaves with local African rulers and merchants. The voyage out was unproblematic, though once the ships were lying off the unhealthy coasts and estuaries waiting for a cargo, all kinds of illnesses were likely to break out. There then followed the notorious 'middle passage' from the African coast to points of sale in the Caribbean or Americas. Covering four to five thousand miles, this could take between three weeks and three months depending on the route, the wind and luck. With slaves packed into the holds, the more prolonged the voyage, the worse the conditions became, and the lower the survival rate. The third leg, the return voyage to the home

863; E. Christopher, *Slave Ship Sailors and their Captive Cargoes 1730–1807* (Cambridge, 2006), 6
[2]   Thomas, *The Slave Trade*, 226, 284; P. Curtin, *The Atlantic Slave Trade: A Census* (Madison, 1969), 119
[3]   M. Rediker, *The Slave Ship: A Human History* (London, 2008), 87
[4]   The British authorities were troubled by the actual origins of the slaves carried on the middle passage. How many were prisoners of war, criminals, or victims of man-stealing? In 1721, the Royal Africa Company launched an enquiry. Seventy years later, the Parliamentary Committees on the Slave Trade did the same. The evidence gathered by both was inconclusive and showed different patterns at different periods. It was, however, extensive, and for the later years of the eighteenth century leads to the conclusions given in this paragraph. See Thomas, *The Slave Trade*, especially 368–72; A. A. Boahen, 'The states and culture of the Lower Guinea coast', with references to the work of P. E. H. Hair and P. D. Curtin, in the UNESCO *The General History of Africa* (Berkeley, 1992), V, 408.

port, sometimes in ballast but more often stuffed with cargoes of sugar, tobacco and molasses for the production of rum bought with the proceeds of the sale of the slaves, was likely to be easy and uneventful.

Having reached his American or Caribbean destination, the captain sold off his human cargo, first allowing a few weeks for a rehabilitation and fattening-up. Either a 'scramble' would be organized in which all comers would compete for the more muscular and healthy slaves, or there could be an orderly auction. The sick and less healthy would be knocked down at bargain prices, while the unsaleable human residue could be abandoned to die on the quayside. As for the bottom line of profit, this varied over time and place. A contemporary estimate puts the average sale price of a slave at £40 and the cost of obtaining them in Africa and transporting him across the Atlantic at £35 – giving a profit of 14 per cent on that leg of the voyage.[5]

Conditions on a slave ship during the middle passage were brutal. When a ship was being loaded or was in sight of the African coast, the slaves were kept in strict confinement. Women and children were unrestrained, but the men were shackled closely together, left ankle to right ankle and left wrist to right wrist so as to obviate the risk of a resistance. There was debate between masters as to whether loose or tight packing was the better strategy in terms of economic return: tight packing would entail people being stacked sideways in 'spoon fashion'. The slaves had no clothing and no mats to lie on. Ventilation was inadequate, especially in bad weather when the hatches were covered and the atmosphere in the slave decks was reduced to a suffocating stench. It was said that the smell of a slaver could be detected down-wind for 5 miles. Exercise frequently amounted to little more than grotesque capering in chains on the upper decks stimulated by the lash.

Poor food, bad water, a foetid atmosphere below decks and damp took their toll in terms of ill-health on all overcrowded ships in the age of sail, and were worse when the inmates were confined, as in vessels carrying slaves, convicts or indentured labourers. In Guineamen things were at their worst, since not only was the cargo packed into a stinking slave deck, but they were at risk from a variety of tropical diseases as well. Of the range of maladies reported, the bloody flux, fevers such as malaria and typhus, ophthalmia and smallpox were the most prevalent, complemented by wounds, ulcers and running sores caused by fights, close confinement and whipping. Scurvy too could break out if the voyage became protracted. All this took its toll of human life. The Parliamentary Committee on the Slave Trade later estimated average mortality among slaves on the middle passage at around 15 per cent. In fact, modern estimates put it lower, standing at 10 per cent in 1734, then steadily improving during the eighteenth century to 8.5 per cent between 1769 and 1787 and 4 per cent between 1797 and 1807.[6]

---

[5]   Gower Williams, *History of the Liverpool Privateers and Letters of Marque with an Account of the Liverpool Slave Trade* (London, 1897), 596–8

[6]   Richard B. Sheridan, 'The Guinea surgeons on the middle passage: the provision of medical services in the British slave trade', *The International Journal of African Historical Studies* 14, no. 4 (1981), 601–25; R. Ansley, *The Atlantic Slave Trade and British Abolition* (London, 1975)

Violence was an integral part in the running of a slave ship and, indeed, of the whole system. With a heavily outnumbered crew and an unwilling cargo of agitated captives, brutal enforcement of orders was a daily routine, and the ever-present dread of a slave revolt made beatings the response to the slightest insubordination. And besides the physical brutality there was the despair and emotional strain felt by people who had been torn from their homes and villages, and separated from their families, never to be reunited. Unsurprisingly, 'fixed melancholy' became an observed condition, and attempted suicide and refusal to eat were common.

In some ships at least, it seems that conditions became less harsh once the vessel was at sea. Food became more plentiful, all but the most recalcitrant slaves were occasionally released from their shackles to roam the decks, and those who showed the greatest acceptance of their circumstances and were willing to collaborate were given positions of authority over the rest. Such a relaxation is, however, likely to have been rare in view of the circumstances and the culture of violence which pervaded the slave ship. And brutal treatment was not restricted to the slaves. As one authority has noted, it 'cascaded down' from the captain and officers and was directed as much at the crew as the human cargo.[7] As Thomas Clarkson, the abolitionist, discovered, the degree of ill-usage and brutal floggings and other punishments to which seamen were subjected on slavers was notorious.[8] This, the distasteful nature of the work, poor rations, low wages and the risk of revolt or disease made the Guinea trade one to avoid. For crews, slave ships had to make do with British sailors who had no other choice but to sign on due to debt, the threat of jail, or kidnap by 'crimps' and a motley group of drifters of all colours and national origins. Most – including their captains – looked on them with contempt. Captain Hugh Crow described them as 'the dregs of the community' and Captain John Newton as 'the refuse of the Nation . . . already ruined by some untimely vice'.[9] And they treated them accordingly. Some captains cut their rations, or paid them in West Indian currency of lower real value to save money; others tried to drive them to desert in the Caribbean by ill-treatment so as to reduce the wage bill.[10]

Owners were ambivalent about the violence in the system. In their instructions to captains, they stressed that a slave revolt was one of the greatest dangers to commercial success, alongside shipwreck, fire and a high death rate, and they stressed the need for strict and severe discipline. On the other hand, to avoid the 'contagion of cruelty' and the fact that ill-usage might actually stimulate resistance, discipline was to be exercised with restraint and with all 'the indulgence that Humanity requires'.[11] In the face of numerical reality and the in-built violence of the system, it is unlikely that these sentiments cut much ice with hard-boiled slaver captains.

[7] Rediker, *The Slave Ship*, 10, 239
[8] Christopher, *Slave Ship Sailors*, 97
[9] Rediker, *The Slave Ship*, 227
[10] Ibid., 251; Christopher, *Slave Ship Sailors*, 43–4
[11] Rediker, *The Slave Ship*, 197, quoting instructions from owner Humphrey Morice

There were, however, some anomalies. In the middle of the American War, for example, the *Brookes* arriving in West Indian waters with a full cargo from Africa was attacked by a French privateer. Captain Clement Noble promptly armed fifty of the fittest male slaves and beat the enemy off. After fighting 'with exceeding spirit', they obligingly gave up their arms and returned to the slave decks so the ship could proceeded to Jamaica where they were sold.[12] This was not the only time that slaves were armed and trained to fight the enemy. In April 1781, Captain Stevenson of the *Rose* also gave the male slaves regular musketry practice and used them to help beat off another French privateer.[13]

Almost every European nation was involved in the slave trade at one time or another. In its earliest days, the Portuguese and the Spanish were dominant, but by the middle of the eighteenth century the British had moved into first position, closely followed by the French. The American War, however, caused a sharp reduction in the size and prosperity of the slave trade. Faced with the perils of enemy capture as well as those of disease and the sea, owners gambled that attacking enemy property would be a better investment than carrying slaves, and converted their ships into privateers. Peace in 1783 restored the situation, and inaugurated a decade in which the slave trade reached its zenith. By 1790, some 750,000 more Africans had been taken across the Atlantic. Of these, 270,000 were transported in French ships, the majority from the port of Nantes, closely followed by Bordeaux and La Rochelle, and 350,000 in British vessels. Of these, 60 per cent came from Liverpool, most of the rest coming from London and Bristol.[14]

Liverpool and the slave trade

The business acumen of Liverpool's merchants and their historic links with the West Indies had much to do with this dominance; but it was the city's proximity to the major towns of the Industrial Revolution that tipped the balance. Not only were the cotton checks of Manchester, the guns of Birmingham and the copper and brassware of Sheffield – the very products needed for the first leg of the triangular trade – close at hand, but the costs of transport steadily fell as the inland canal system developed. Benefiting from competitive costs and an average 10 per cent profit, the trade became an integral part of Liverpool's economy. Some sectors were dependent on it. There were docks to provide for the building and repair of the Guineamen; bakeries and brewhouses to provide for their victualling; and warehouses to store the necessities they needed, ranging from canvas, hemp and tar to shackles and chains.

Average profits from the slave trade may have been good, but it was nevertheless a high-risk activity with high entry costs. Those with the capital, the experience and the luck did well. The Liverpool businessmen John Earle

[12] See letter from Noble to his owners, 26 April 1777, detailing the incident in Williams, *History of the Liverpool Privateers*, 560–1
[13] Williams, *History of the Liverpool privateers*, 564–5
[14] Thomas, *The Slave Trade*, 284–5

and Thomas Leyland, for example, were worth £100,000 when they died.[15] To reduce the risk, few dealt exclusively in slaves, but invested in the trade as part of a varied portfolio of activities. John Kennion and Samuel Touchette had substantial interests in Lancashire textiles, Joseph and Jonathan Brookes in building and construction, John Ashton in land, Thomas Leyland in banking, John Blundell in coal and Richard Pennant (later Lord Penryth) in the Welsh slate industry. Some of the more influential families, like the Tarletons and the Kennions, owned sugar plantations as well. Humbler folk too were involved. As a contemporary author noted, 'many of the smaller vessels that import a hundred slaves are fitted out by attorneys, drapers, grocers, tallow merchants, barbers, tailors etc., who have one eighth, some a fifteenth, and some a thirty-second share'.[16] Liverpool's development was fuelled by the trade. The city sprouted streets of elegant Georgian houses, many named after leading slave merchants like Cunliffe, Earle, Tarleton and Bold; a Blue Coat School, a dispensary and a library were endowed by slave-trading benefactors; and the handsome new town hall was decorated with friezes showing crocodiles, elephants and the heads of Africans in acknowledgment of the source of all this wealth.

Liverpool was quick off the mark on the coming of peace in 1783. In one year, the number of ships engaged in foreign trade increased by 40 per cent to reach 293, while the number of Guineamen went up from 47 to 85. Thus when Thomas Trotter arrived in Liverpool, there were plenty of berths on offer. In the event, a personal connection with a local building firm brought an offer of employment on a slaver which was in its ownership, and which carried its name. Trotter found himself appointed surgeon of the *Brookes* under the command of Captain Clement Noble.

Why he chose to serve on a slaver must give pause for thought. There was no embarrassment among the population of Liverpool or anywhere else about slavery at the time. The slave trade was widely seen as an essential part of the economy of all advanced countries. Those who worried about its inhumanity reluctantly accepted it as a necessary evil and comforted themselves with the belief that the lot of a slave was worse in the barbaric kingdoms of Africa than in the brutal regimes of the sugar plantations in the West Indies. The massive popular protest which enabled Thomas Clarkson to launch his 'Committee for Effecting the Abolition of the Slave Trade' four years later was still in its infancy. There was only a distant murmur of dissent from the occasional clergyman questioning the morality of the trade from his pulpit; the soul-searching of Quaker businessmen; the testimony of repentant slave captains like John Newton. Thomas Trotter was one whose conscience was struck. In January 1783, inspired by the distant view of Liverpool from Ladies' Walk, he had penned an uncompromising *Verse* which pondered that all this splendour was based on the suffering of African slaves. It included the lines

---

[15] Rediker, *The Slave Ship*, 47
[16] Elizabeth Donnan, *Documents Illustrative of the Slave Trade to America* (Washington, 1930), II, 49, quoted in Thomas, *The Slave Trade*, 514

> For thee, the negro, robbed of nature's right,
> Bleeds from the lash, and bends, the planter's slave;
> In Christian bondage owns a tyrant's might,
> And stains thy traffic in a shroudless grave.[17]

That Trotter would be treading the deck of a slaver six months after writing this poem seems strange. In fact, it was not so remarkable. Cost-conscious owners of normal merchant ships seldom thought that the services of a surgeon on board were necessary. With Guineamen it was different. Common sense dictated that as many slaves as possible should survive the middle passage and be delivered to the markets of the Americas and the West Indies: yet the slave ships were breeding grounds for disease. To prevent a medical and commercial disaster, surgeons had been employed on slavers from the beginning. Indeed, there was a standard work on the subject in the shape of Dr Thomas Aubrey's 1729 classic *The Sea Surgeon, Or the Guinea Man's Vade Mecum In Which is laid down The Method of Curing such Diseases as usually happen Abroad especially on the Coast of Guinea; with the best way if treating Negroes both in Health and in Sickness* . . . Aubrey advocated a mixture of self-interest and Christian charity when he wrote of the slaves:

> the more you preserve of them for the plantations, the more profit you will have and also the greater reputation and wages another voyage. Besides it is a call of conscience to be careful of them . . . For although they are heathens yet have they a rational soul as well as us, and God knows whether it may not be more tolerable for them in the latter day than for many who profess themselves Christians.[18]

It is therefore no surprise that the majority of sea-going appointments on offer when Thomas Trotter arrived in Liverpool were in Guineamen, nor that he found himself as surgeon on the *Brookes*.

Trotter's choice was not unusual. It was common for surgeons of the Royal Navy to serve on slavers in times of peace. Discharged with little or no half-pay, they needed to earn their living, and to establish a civilian practice would for most of them have been difficult if not impossible. The pay was satisfactory. The going rate for a surgeon averaged £5 a month – the same as he would receive on a man-of-war – but to that would be added the supply of free medicines and instruments, and a variety of bonuses such as 'head money' of one shilling for each slave delivered, or a bonus determined by the percentage of deaths on the voyage.[19] Sir William Dolben's Act of Parliament, which attempted to prevent the worst excesses of the slave trade in 1788, gave this legal form by making the employment of a surgeon compulsory and laying down a payment of £50 for a

[17] Trotter, *Sea Weeds*
[18] T. Aubrey, *The Sea Surgeon, Or the Guinea Man's Vade Mecum In Which is laid down The Method of Curing such Diseases as usually happen Abroad especially on the Coast of Guinea; with the best way if treating Negroes both in Heath and in Sickness* (London, 1729)
[19] For the actual emoluments of Dr Thomas Stephens of *Africa* 1776, see Rediker, *The Slave Ship*, 193–4

mortality rate of below 2 per cent and £25 if less than 3 per cent. Some surgeons would be given a 'privileged' slave to sell on their own account, but whether Trotter benefited from this is unknown.

The role of a surgeon on a slaver was a responsible but delicate one. At best he was someone who would be robustly committed to the care of the slaves. He would be required to carry out medical examination of slaves at their time of purchase. He also carried responsibility for the treatment of the sick with what were probably entirely ineffective medicines, and might contribute to the preservation of health by ensuring an adequate diet aboard and, in particular, the availability of anti-scorbutics. In theory the surgeon enjoyed considerable autonomy, and it was he and not the master who had final responsibility for the welfare of the slaves and also for the health of the crew. And the captains of slavers were not easy men. Long years at sea, the isolation of command and the responsibilities they carried for the safety of the ship, the rigours of the voyage, the security of the slaves, their effective delivery, and the negotiation of prices at both the points of purchase and of sale, took their toll. The experience left many masters stressed, irascible, foul-mouthed, ruthless, and brutal to both crew and slaves alike. Clement Noble of the *Brookes* seemed par for the course, and Trotter was to encounter constant criticism and carping from him during the voyage.

The voyage of the 'Brookes'

The *Brookes* sailed from Liverpool on 3 June 1783 with a crew of forty-nine men and a cargo of trade goods in the hold. Unusually, a great deal is known about this ship and about the voyage. Trotter himself described it, and the medical problems encountered, in his *Observations on the Scurvy*;[20] the conditions were given in graphic evidence to a select committee of the House of Commons in 1790; and it was a plan of the *Brookes*, showing the internal arrangement and the way in which slaves were crammed unto every inch of space, that Clarkson and the abolitionists used with such effect in their campaign against the trade.

After a voyage of four weeks, the *Brookes* reached West African waters. Passing Cape Palmas, she made for her initial port of call – a small settlement set among the white beaches and salt water lagoons of the Ivory Coast, called Cape de la Hou. Using a local agent called Accra, Captain Noble soon took on board his first hundred slaves. They were mostly members of an upland people known to Trotter as the Duncos, a group that had been the victims of more powerful neighbours for years and were fatalistic and morose as a result.[21] That done, the *Brookes* headed east to the more familiar waters of the Gold Coast, where the Dutch, Danes and British maintained a string of forts to act as depots for trade goods, and assembly points for slaves. There, the local rulers were the Fantee people, who were maintaining a precarious resistance in the face of the steady expansion of the mighty Ashanti kingdoms to the north. As

[20] Trotter, *Observations*, 50–72
[21] Trotter was mistaken in the use of this word. These people were in fact members of the inland Chamba people, 'Duncos' being Fante for 'a stupid fellow'; Rediker, *The Slave Ship*, 334

well as controlling the routes to the interior, the Fantee chiefs were careful to restrict foreign trading companies to particular zones. Captain Noble headed for the principal British settlement at Cape Coast, then continued for another 30 miles to a newer fort called Anamabo. Noble's hopes of finding a quick cargo were, however, quickly dashed. Local rulers were distracted by tribal wars, slaves were in short supply, prices were extortionate, and there were ten other slave ships waiting off-shore.

February 1784 came. By that time, the *Brookes* had been rolling at her anchors before Anamabo for six months but had only managed to load two-thirds of her complement of slaves. Many of these were the victims of local kidnap gangs, although Noble had little interest in their origins and took whoever was on offer. Fortunately the roadstead in which the ship anchored was a healthy one, open to the sea and untouched by any land breeze or 'miasma' from the shore. During the six-month wait, nineteen of the *Brookes'* slaves had perished from one cause or another, but Surgeon Trotter had had few serious medical problems to deal with. A crew member had died of smallpox before reaching the coast, and the one slave who contracted it had been isolated in the longboat until the disease ran its course and he recovered. That was all. But the health of the slaves who had been bought at Cape de la Hou now began to deteriorate. Fed on a diet of horse beans boiled with rice and maize with a relish of palm oil and pepper, they had not only put on weight but begun to exhibit soft, bleeding gums, bruised flesh, foul breath and lethargy – the unmistakable signs of scurvy. Trotter immediately recommended to Noble that the intake of food should be reduced and that the male slaves should be released from their chains so that they could exercise by dancing round the deck. Both suggestions were refused.

Relations between the captain and his surgeon were already poor. Trotter found Noble arrogant, obstinate, rude and brutal to slaves and crew alike. Noble saw Trotter as young, uppity and dangerous. Naturally obsessed with security, he found that his surgeon's suggestions were typically naïve – the idea of making slaves thinner when they were about to confront the perils of the middle passage, or of easing their confinement when everyone knew that escapes and slave mutinies were a constant danger while a ship remained in sight of the coast were totally unrealistic.

Trotter keenly observed the course of the scurvy and began to draw conclusions that were to influence his own theories as to its nature and cure. He noticed that the crew remained free of the disease, and put this down to their ability to trade their provisions for local vegetables. He noticed that the women and boys, who were allowed to roam the ship unshackled, were far less affected than the men, who were constantly in irons and had little exercise. He was struck by the fact that the depressed and gloomy Duncos, who had been loaded at Cape de la Hou, were far more susceptible to the disease than the active and cheerful Fantees, who had arrived at Anamabo. Clearly some psychological factor was at work. Last, he became certain that scurvy was not contagious, as some writers had suspected.

In March 1784, Noble managed to complete his cargo and weighed anchor at last to head for the West Indies. The *Brookes* was one of the larger of the

Liverpool Guineamen, displacing 292 tons and being 'frigate built' – that is, square-rigged and carrying sails on three masts. She measured 25 feet in width and 100 feet in length and her bottom was sheathed in copper, which accounted for her speed. Internally, her lower deck was divided into separate compartments for men, women and boys. With each individual allocated little more space than the width and length of a coffin, Noble had been able to cram more that 666 slaves into this space, packing them tightly together in four rows on the deck, and jamming another row onto a narrow platform built against the side of the ship in the space above.

Captain Noble's personality may have been prickly, but he was an experienced seaman who knew his business. This time, the *Brookes* completed the middle passage in only five weeks. The months of waiting off the African coast had, however, taken their toll, and after a week at sea over 160 slaves were showing symptoms of scurvy, some in an advanced state. Trotter's experience as a naval surgeon and his analysis of the writings of Lind and Blane led him to believe that a lack of vegetable and citrus fruit in the diet was the cause. He therefore recommended to Noble that an extra supply of both should be purchased on the Gold Coast to keep scurvy at bay during the voyage. Typically, these proposals were rejected out of hand. The result was that when the *Brookes'* limited supplies of lime juice and oranges ran out, the condition of the slaves deteriorated further. Thirty-three died on the voyage, and another six in Kingston harbour.

Brookes made a quick passage to Antigua, where the process of fattening up the slaves and preparing them for market began. There was fresh air and exercise, and ample supplies of water, food, fruit and vegetables. As Trotter noted, the improvement in health which resulted was so dramatic that in a few weeks the ship was able to continue to Kingston, Jamaica. There, the slaves were sold in the usual 'scramble'. Purchasers rushed among the distraught slaves brandishing tallies and grabbing any they wanted, separating husbands from wives and friends from friends. That done, Noble had his ship cleansed, overhauled and loaded with tropical produce for the return journey to England.

Thomas Trotter was shocked and sickened by what he had seen on the *Brookes* during the middle passage: the packing of shackled slaves into the hold so tightly that it was impossible to walk between them; the brutality of their treatment; the moaning cries from the lower deck at night as the slaves began to realize their true fate; and the suffocating stench when the hatches were covered in bad weather – all left an indelible impression. As soon as the *Brookes* reached the Mersey in August 1784, Trotter quitted the ship a dedicated abolitionist and glad to be alive. In Jamaica, he had been struck down with what he described as rheumatism. Both legs became swollen and inflamed, and he was racked with fever. 'My confinement', he later wrote, 'was long and painful and only a quick passage to Europe in the August following saved me from the grave.'[22]

---

[22] Trotter, *Medicina Nautica*, I, p 392

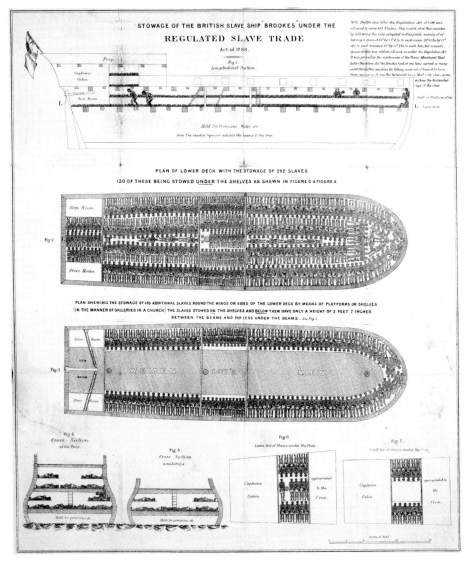

Fig. 5. The abolitionist poster showing the 'packing' of slaves on the *Brookes*.
Courtesy of the Library of Congress, LC-USZ62-34160

The abolitionists

When Thomas Trotter had sailed for West Africa in 1783, the abolitionist movement had been in its infancy. Six years later, it had grown into a powerful and articulate political pressure group. In that short period, opposition to the slave trade had become a national issue espoused by a wave of divines and publicists and organized by a young, and initially naïve, Cambridge graduate, the Rev. Thomas Clarkson. Before this, there had been no mass movement, although theologians had denounced the morality of the trade in their sermons, and the efforts of the Wesleyans and Quakers had been reinforced by those of the Clapham sect, the evangelical wing of the Church of England, whose members, which included Hannah More, the writer, and Sir Charles Middleton, comptroller of the navy, could be found in the highest reaches of the social and political establishment. Then, in 1783, had come the case of the Liverpool slaver *Zong*. The legal issue at stake was a simple one: were the owners of the vessel entitled to receive insurance on a cargo which had had to be jettisoned at sea? The actual circumstances were, however, horrific, for the 'cargo' in question consisted of human beings. Two years before, the *Zong*'s captain, Luke Collingwood, had made a navigational error which delayed his arrival at Jamaica and made him fearful that he would run out of water. Convinced that his insurers would not pay compensation for slaves who died on board, but would do so for any lost overboard, he had deliberately thrown 133 slaves into the sea to drown. The insurers refused to pay: and the case went to court. The *Zong*'s owners were judged negligent and lost their claim, but what horrified the public was not just Collingwood's brutality but the legal realities of the situation. Lawyers found that 'no impropriety' attached to the captain's actions and that the treatment of slaves need be no different from that of horses or any other livestock.

The growing public concern with the evils of the trade was symbolized by the foundation in 1787 of the Committee for Effecting the Abolition of the Slave Trade by Clarkson and his allies. Its first act was to commission Clarkson to visit Bristol, Liverpool and other ports in search of evidence and information on the realities of the trade. Shunned by ship-owners and merchants, he found himself relying on the testimony of ordinary seaman, which led Clarkson to realize not only the day-to-day brutality of the trade but the callous ill-treatment to which the crews themselves were subjected. After exhaustive enquiries, during which he travelled some 7000 miles and visited 320 ships, Clarkson released his findings in two pamphlets published in 1788, and in his 1789 book *The Substance of the Evidence of Sundry Persons connected with the Slave Trade Collected . . . in the Autumn of the Year 1788*. The shocking revelations continued with *The Interesting Narrative of the Life of Olaudah Equiano, or Gustavus Vassa*, and James Field Stanfield's *Observations on a Guinea Voyage, in a Series of Letters addressed to the Rev Thomas Clarkson*, both published in 1789, which respectively described the realities of the trade from the perspectives of a slave and a seaman.

With the movement gathering momentum, William Wilberforce, the youthful Member of Parliament for Hull, embraced the cause and the campaign began to be directed more deliberately at Westminster. Both Lords and Commons were at this time 'unreformed' and were dominated by the landed interest. Commerce and the new industrial towns, where there was support for the slave trade – or at least serious concern about the economic effects of abolition – were underrepresented. Many of the senior members of the House of Commons, like Pitt, the prime minister, and Fox, the leader of the opposition, were therefore sympathetic to the arguments of the abolitionists and were ready to respond to the avalanche of petitions which Clarkson and his followers stimulated.

Trotter's evidence before the select committee

The result was a series of parliamentary enquiries that revealed the true horror of the slave trade. The first of these sat during 1788 under the auspices of the Privy Council committee for trade and plantations. Even during its sittings, the revelations were so disturbing that they stimulated an act sponsored by Sir William Dolben, the elderly member for Oxford University, to regulate the trade by limiting the numbers carried on ships and attempting to improve conditions. In its turn, the Privy Council report stimulated the appointment of a select committee of the House of Commons to look further into the realities of the slave trade. This sat from 1789 to 1792, and received verbal evidence from hundreds of witnesses – ship-owners, merchants, surgeons, naval officers, mayors, manufacturers and slave owners – and was the recipient of scores of petitions from supporters and opponents alike. There were conflicting views on the economic aspects of the trade, but the remorseless accumulation of first-hand evidence left no doubts as to the brutal and horrifying realities of what took place on slave ships and in slave markets. One of the expert witnesses who gave evidence was Thomas Trotter.

Dr Thomas Trotter MD, a Surgeon in the Royal Navy, called and examined.

Have you ever been on the African Slave Trade?
I sailed from Liverpool in 1783, surgeon of the *Brookes*, Clement Noble, master.

Thus began the exchanges between Trotter and the members of the House of Commons Select Committee on the Slave Trade in May 1790.[23] There was a terseness about the questions asked, and Trotter's answers tended to be to the point rather than embroidered. In the forty-page transcript of his three consecutive sessions before the committee on 5–7 May, one may come near to hearing his voice. He was talking about shameful barbarity but it is the objectivity of his answers which gives them their edge.

The transcript of Trotter's evidence runs to twenty-eight quarto pages. The text has here been edited down to about a quarter of the original but with content and tone of those committee-room exchanges well preserved.

How long were you on the coast of Africa?
From the time we made Cape Palmas, till we completed the cargo at Annamaboe, was about ten months.

Did you in that period make any enquiries concerning the methods of procuring slaves?
I made many enquiries concerning that particular part of the trade. Of the slaves themselves, of the traders, and particularly of Accra, a trader at Cape La Hou. Accra particularly had no interest in deceiving me; besides, the man was well known to the English who traded there, as a man of great integrity.

[23]   S. Lambert, *House of Commons Sectional Papers of the Eighteenth Century (HCSP)* (Wilmington, 1875), LXXIII, 81–101

I found him a most intelligent man.

What was the general result of the information on this subject which you received from him, and the other parties you have mentioned?

I found that the natives of Africa were sometimes condemned to slavery for crimes of different kinds; but by far the greater number were what they called 'prisoners of war'. But of all the cargo, I only recollect two for adultery, and one for witchcraft, who, with his whole family, were sold.

Did you learn the circumstances which attended the conviction of the persons for adultery?

One of the men told me that he had been decoyed by the woman, who informed her husband, and was sentenced to pay a slave; but by being a poor man, and unable to pay, he was sold himself.

You have mentioned a man, who, with his family, were sold to you on account of witchcraft; can you relate the circumstances of the case?

The man had been a trader, and spoke a little English; the circumstances of his case are shocking; the women on coming on board (his mother, wife, and two daughters, I think) exhibited every sign of affliction; the man himself had every symptom of a sullen melancholy; he informed me that he had quarrelled with the chief or cabbosheer of Saltpan, who, to be revenged upon him, accused him of witchcraft, for which he and his family were condemned to slavery; after coming on board, he refused all sustenance; early next morning I was called to him and found he had made an attempt to cut his throat, but by only dividing the external jugular vein, he lost little more than a pint of blood; the parts were immediately secured by sutures, but he made a similar attempt on the other side; he declared, he never would go with white men, looked wistfully at the skies, and uttered incoherent sentences. He refused all sustenance, and died in about a week or ten days afterwards of mere want of food.

You have stated that by far the greater part of the slaves consisted of what they called prisoners of war; what meaning did you understand them to affix to the term 'prisoner of war?'

I repeatedly and often asked Accra what he meant by prisoners of war; and I learnt that they had been carried off by a set of desperadoes or marauders, whose business it seemed to be to ravage the country, and carry off the inhabitants in this manner, and to sell them as slaves.

Was this account confirmed to you by any other circumstances?

Yes – by the slaves themselves – many of whom shewed me by gesture or motion how the robbers had come upon them – and during the Middle Passage, some boys in my ship played a sort of game, which they called, Slave-taking, or Bush fighting; and I have seen them perform all the manoeuvres, such as leaping, falling, and retreating, and all other gestures made use of in bush fighting.

In your last answer, you have spoken of boys whom you had on board; can you state whether these were brought to your ship, with or without their parents, or other near relations?

We had many both boys and girls, who had not father, or mother, or any relation on board – many of them told me that they had been kidnapped, particularly a little girl of about eight years of age, who told us she had been carried off from her mother by the man who sold her to our ship.

Did any instances of kidnapping by the natives fall within your own personal knowledge?
Yes; I saw Fat Sam, our gold taker, dispatch his canoe for three fisherman employed in the offing; they were immediately brought on board, put in irons, and about a week afterwards he received payment for them.

Were the slaves much crowded in your ship in the Middle Passage?
Yes; so much so that it was not possible to walk amongst them without treading upon them.

Had they room to turn themselves, or in any sort to lie at ease?
By no means; the slaves that are out of irons are locked spoonways, according to the technical phrase, and closely locked to one another. It is the duty of the first mate to see them stowed in this manner every morning; those which do not get quickly into their places are compelled by the cat, and such was their situation when stowed in this manner, and the ship had much motion at sea, they were often miserably bruised against the deck, and against one another.

Did you find the gratings sufficient for ventilating the slave rooms; and had you any additional means for that purpose, such as ventilators or wind sails?
I am now speaking of the Middle Passage. When the scuttles are obliged to be shut, I do not think the gratings are by any means sufficient for airing the rooms; for I never could myself breathe with freedom, unless I was immediatly below the hatchway. Ventilators I never heard of being used in these ships; we had none; a wind sail was frequently tried while we lay upon the coast, but I remember of none being used in the Middle Passage

Did the slaves appear to suffer from the want of fresh air?
Yes; I have seen their breasts heaving, and observed them draw their breath with all those laborious and anxious efforts of life, which we observe in expiring animals, subjected by experiment to foul air of different kinds, or in the exhausted receiver of air pumps.

6 May 1790, Dr Thomas Trotter called in; and further examined.

Do the slaves appear greatly dejected when they first come on board?
Most of them, at coming on board, shew signs of extreme distress, and some of them even looks of despair; this I attributed to a feeling for their situation, and regret at being torn from their friends and connections; many of them, I believe, are capable of retaining those impressions for a very long time. . . . the slaves in the night were often heard making a howling melancholy kind of noise, something expressive of extreme anguish. I found that it was occasioned by finding themselves in a slave room, after dreaming that they had been in their own country amongst their friends and relations.

How many slaves did you purchase, and can you state how many you lost in the course of the voyage?

To the best of my memory we purchased upwards of 600, and I think lost about 70 in the voyage.

Were there any instances of slaves jumping over-board?

One man jumped over-board while we lay at Annamaboe, and was drowned; another man, in the Middle Passage, jumped over-board, but was taken up again; a woman, after having been taken up, was chained for some time to the mizzen-mast, but being let loose again, made a second attempt, and was taken up and expired under the punishment of flogging for having made these attempts.

Are the slaves, during the Middle Passage, obliged to take exercise, and by what name is this commonly called?

I believe the practice of dancing them is very general in the trade, and in all ships; but in ours it was not practised till their health made it absolutely necessary that they should be allowed some exercise. Some of them, who did not seem to relish the exercise, were compelled to it by a lash of the cat; but many of them refused to do it, even with this mode of punishment in a severe degree.

In what manner was your cargo disposed of in the West Indies?

By what is called a scramble. People who wish for slaves are ready when the signal is given to open the sale to apply their tallies to the slaves they wish to purchase, by rushing all at once among them. On this occasion some husbands and wives were parted, and many other relations.

Did you see any of the seamen ill-treated by the master?

I remember, during the Middle Passage, some of them being most unmercifully flogged by him, so much so, that I saw from the quarter-deck some of the seamen coming aft from the forecastle with the view to rescue the man; on seeing this, he was immediately let go; and I remember, that he never afterwards punished any of them in that manner: he was carrying twelve parroquets to the West Indies; they either all died, or were all killed by somebody; he suspected a seaman of killing them, and ordered the man to be confined or lashed for twelve days to one of the topmast heads, during which time he eat nothing but one of those parroquets, and a pint of water a day; though it was in the Middle Passage, the punishment was rigorously inflicted, and, wonderful to be told the man survived it. I have heard the man who perpetrated this wanton piece of barbarity relate it in a public company, with a degree of triumph and satisfaction that would have disgraced an Indian scalper. The masters of the vessels who were present when he related it applauded his invention for the novelty of the punishment.

What is your opinion of the capacity and disposition of the natives of Africa, so far as you have had an opportunity of judging of them?

From what I have seen, I should suppose their minds very capable of cultivation.

When did you quit the Brookes?
The moment I could get a boat on her arrival in the River Mersey.

You said that you quitted the Brookes as soon as you possibly could after the ship's arrival in the River Mersey, had you had any difference with Captain Noble during the voyage?
I know of no difference but abusive language that he very frequently bestowed upon me as the slaves were dying, which he was pleased to call 'machinations of the doctor and devil'.

Did he ever complain to you of your inattention towards the slaves?
He certainly very frequently accused me of ignorance in my profession.

Did those negroes, in fact, suffer by the scurvy?
Many on our ship died of that disease; and it that was probable that only a very quick Middle Passage saved the half of the cargo, for about betwixt two and three hundred were tainted with this disease, in different degrees, at the time we arrived at Antigua.

Was the nature of their food such as to produce the scurvy?
I do not think the food alone would have done it, had not other causes concurred – these are, the peculiar circumstances of their confinement, and the contaminated atmosphere of the ship, with all those depressing passions which must ever be inseparable from the situation of a human being, torn from all that is to be valued in existence.

Did Captain Noble consent to use every expedient you suggested for securing the slaves from suffering by the scurvy or other disorders?
By no means – I was often thwarted by him in the exercise of my profession, particularly in the medicines I prescribed for those who had the flux, and in violent bursts of anger he swore they fell victims to my medicines – but his contradicting my prescriptions was much more observable when the scurvy made its appearance, and when I urged him to carry a great quantity of fresh fruits, such as limes and oranges, my opinion was treated with contempt, and not one twentieth part of the quantity that ought to have been carried to sea was in the ship when we left the coast – the event fully justified what I had proposed, for when we had a liberal supply of these fruits at Antigua, the recovery of the slaves was rapid beyond example.

End of session

Immediately following the conclusion of Trotter's session on 7 May 1790, the committee continued later on the same day and on 10 May to hear evidence from the master of the *Brookes*, Captain Clement Noble. Here the approximately eleven pages of the original transcript have been shortened by about one quarter.[24]

How many voyages have you been to Africa, and in what capacities?
I have been nine voyages, two as a mate, and seven as master.

---

[24] Ibid., 109–21

Do you remember the voyage when you had Mr Thomas Trotter as surgeon?
Yes. We sailed on 3 June 1783 and arrived at Liverpool in August 1784.

Had you any knowledge of Doctor Trotter before that time, or how did you become acquainted with him?
He was recommended by one of his friends to one of the owners of the ship: I knew nothing of him before.

According to your judgment, in his capacity of surgeon, was he attentive to the slaves that were ill on board?
I thought him often very inattentive to his duty, and I thought likewise that he spent a great deal too much time in dress, and which I was often under the necessity of telling him of, or reproving him for.

Do you remember the number of slaves you purchased in that voyage?
Yes: 638.

Did you usually bring as many in any voyages before?
We brought more the voyage before that; we purchased 666, and buried twenty-six in the whole.

Do you believe any slaves could be kidnapped with impunity on the Gold Coast?
I really believe not.

Do you remember a man slave on board your ship attempting to destroy himself?
I do; and I really believe the man was perfectly mad, and I am sure so too.

Do you remember particularly flogging one of your seamen the voyage that Mr Trotter sailed with you?
I do; I flogged him for abusing the slaves, and being very insolent to myself – I believe it was the only time that any of the seamen were flogged that voyage.

Do you remember in any of your voyages having a number of parroquets on board, and how long since?
I do remember it – it was in 1784, rather sooner in the year than this month – I do not exactly remember the time.

Do you remember any accident happening to the parroquets in the voyage alluded to?
Yes – I remember they were all killed in one night – When I enquired the next morning how it happened, I found they had been killed by a black man belonging to the ship (he was not a slave); he had also told some of the people that he would do as much for me the next night. I asked him if he said so and he said, yes, with all the insolence in the world. I immediately ordered the people to confine him, and then held a consultation with my officers what we should do with him, and we all thought it was unsafe to keep him below; I therefore sent him to the mast head, where he was kept for about two days. At the end of the two days he sent word down by some people that he was very sorry for what had happened, and hoped that I would let him come down. I immediately ordered him to be brought down and let out of irons, and he came on the quarter deck to me, and begged pardon for what he had

down (*sic*) and hoped that would excuse him; I told him to go forward about his business; but all the remainder of the passage I took good care to keep the cabin door faſt during the night – he was a very troublesome turbulent man.

Was any particular treatment adopted for the recovery of the sick slaves on you arrival in the Weſt Indies?
We generally purchase all the vegetables we can on our firſt arrival, such as limes, oranges, and anything of that sort.

Did your slaves, soon after their arrival, recover their health?
They did mend very faſt, and do in general.

When slaves were offered to you for sale, did you make any enquiry to ascertain whether or not they were the property of the person who offered them to you for purchase?
I did not; they are not in general the property of those that bring them on board; those that sell them to us only act as brokers.

What enquiry did you use to make respecting the manner in which these brokers had come by them?
None; we do not doubt but they have a right to sell them.

Do the slaves in general appear much dejected when firſt brought on board?
Some of them do; but they in general soon mend of that, and are in general in very good spirits during the time they are on board the ships.

Had the slaves sufficient room, and were they tolerably well off as to comfort in other respects?
Yes, they had room enough to lay down, and were as comfortable as any body could expect on board a ship.

Could you walk about amongſt them without treading upon them?
Yes, certainly; it is done every night by the officers; I mean after they go to reſt.

Was the heat oppressive, and air very foul?
It was much hotter at some times than others; that depends chiefly on the weather; it is sure to be very warm when calm.

The enquiry is not concerning the heat of the climate, but whether the air was not very foul and offensive from the number of human bodies confined in a small place?
I never found any bad effects from the air.

Queſtion repeated.
It is sure that the air cannot be so good as upon deck.

Queſtion again repeated.
It is rather foul and offensive, but more so in calm weather than at other times.

Cannot you ſtate with any tolerable precision what number of men you carried in the men's room?

I cannot; I should suppose, from the number on board, that there must have been something short of 300 in the men's room.

What was the length and breadth of your men's room?
The breadth I think was about 26 foot, but the length I do not remember.

What space had each slave to lie in?
I do not know the space; I never measured it, or made any calculation of what room they had; they had always plenty of room to lay down in, and had they had three times as much room they would lay all jammed close up together; they always do that before the room is half full.

The accounts given to the committee by these two witnesses differed greatly both as to detail and the broad conclusions. Noble sought to discredit Trotter as someone given too much to strutting on deck in uniform, and neglectful of his duties. Trotter, in his turn, described Noble as abusive, interfering with treatment, capable of personal cruelty, and as being master of a ship where the living conditions of the male slaves constituted institutionalized barbarity. The resulting death rate was not in much dispute. Noble insisted that all the slaves he purchased had been sold to him legally, whereas Trotter suggested that 'prisoners of war' story was an invention.

Whose evidence was the committee likely to believe? If they were at the start to have tested the question of motivation, there was no obvious reason for Trotter to lie, while on the contrary there was good reason for the master of a slave ship to engage in some denial. And the committee would of course have interpreted these sessions within the context of evidence received from other witnesses. To describe Clement Noble as having been lying in his teeth, is probably not too extreme a judgement. It seems likely that the committee would have accepted Trotter's version of events as an informed and objective account of the wickedness of slavery, and he was speaking with the authority of a naval surgeon: Noble's answers when he was pressed by the committee as to the foulness of the air in the men's room give an acute sense of prevarication.

Noble may have been attempting to avoid the embarrassing truth, but his performance was modest compared with other pro-trade witnesses. One captain claimed that the holds of slave ships were 'redolent with frankincense'; another that the slaves could not have been treated with greater kindness if they had been in the 'nursery of any prominent family'. One Liverpool ship-owner even declared that the middle passage was among 'the happiest moments in a Negro's life'.[25]

The abolitionist cause had achieved enormous momentum by 1793, and the evidence given by Trotter and other witnesses showing the horrific details of the trade was so graphic and overwhelming as to make government intervention inevitable. Yet it was not until 1807 – fourteen years later – that the British Parliament banned the slave trade in its colonies and prohibited any participation by subjects of King George. The early successes of Clarkson and

---

[25] Thomas, *The Slave Trade*, 495, 416, 507

Wilberforce caused the opponents of abolition to rally. There was a barrage of petitions from ship-owners, manufacturers and the corporations of towns like Liverpool and Bristol, predicting that economic disaster would follow the abolition of the trade. The excesses of the French Revolution and the war that followed further strengthened the forces of conservatism. The outbreak of a bloody slave revolt on the French West Indian island of St Domingue, led by Toussaint l'Ouverture, was presented as an object lesson in the perils of tinkering with the status quo. The French doctrines of liberty, equality and fraternity made any kind of liberal enthusiasm in Britain seem subversive and unpatriotic. The government was reluctant to do anything that would split the nation and, led by Henry Dundas, minister of war and Pitt's special crony, continued to pay lip service to abolition while following delaying tactics. It was only in 1807, when the ideological ambiguities of the revolutionary war had been replaced by a more normal power struggle with Napoleon and national confidence restored by a series of decisive naval victories, that Wilberforce at last achieved his objective and saw the Slave Trade Act become law.

~ 5 ~

Northumbrian Interlude

I N 1784, Thomas Trotter was twenty-four years old with four years sea-going experience as a naval surgeon, spent in a variety of climates and conditions. He had learnt much about the practical elements of his profession, and had begun to develop clear and novel views on the genesis and treatment of that greatest of all eighteenth-century maritime scourges, scurvy. Applying observation in true Enlightenment fashion, he doubted the prevailing explanation that the cause of the disease lay in putrefaction. He had witnessed the effects of fresh vegetables and citrus fruits in the Channel, the West Indies and the North Sea while on *Berwick*, and had seen their benefits confirmed on the unhappy slaves of the *Brookes*. He had taken careful note of all the evidence and was anxious to present it to the medical professors in Edinburgh and develop his ideas more widely in a book on the subject.[1]

Trotter was also anxious to resume the academic study of medicine in order to master more deeply the current theories of disease, and to help him refine the raw material of his practical experience. The possession of a medical degree would also serve a practical purpose by raising the lowly status he enjoyed as a surgeon, and giving him the social prestige and academic credibility associated with being a physician. To achieve these ambitions, and be within easy reach of the great University of Edinburgh, Trotter left Liverpool and headed back to the north country. He did not, however, take up residence in his home town of Melrose, but established himself just over the border, as a surgeon and apothecary in the Northumbrian town of Wooler.

Wooler and the Borders

Built on a rise between the River Till and the Cheviots, Wooler was 46 miles north-west of Newcastle and 16 miles from Berwick, astride the ramshackle highroad that went from Morpeth to Coldstream, then across the border to Kelso, and ultimately to Edinburgh. The road was described by the traveller Arthur Young as being tolerable in part but execrable in most, but it was nevertheless important as the major route used by waggoners, whose huge wide-wheeled

---

[1] The first, 1786, edition of Trotter's *Observations on the Scurvy* received a luke-warm response. This seemed partly to be because it emphasized his practical experience rather than treated the subject on the usual theoretical level, and partly because reviewers were dismissive of a writer whose only claim to fame was service as a surgeon's mate in the navy with one voyage on a slaver. See *The Monthly Review* 74 (January–March 1786), 316–17

vehicles and teams of straining horses carried goods from England to Scotland.

Wooler was an important market town with a hinterland comprising the rolling green hills and broad valleys that had been formed by the Glen river to the north, and the Till and Breamish to the south and east. With poor soil, boggy uplands and valleys watered abundantly by a host of rushing streams, the area had long been given over to pastoral agriculture. Shepherds with flocks of scrawny sheep roamed the peaty uplands of the Cheviots and the lush pastures of the adjacent valleys. The development of more varied agriculture in the Borders had been delayed by the disruptive impact of the Anglo-Scottish wars of the late Middle Ages. The battlefield of Flodden lay just up the road and many of the great houses of the area had been designed for defence rather than for comfort. But things were changing. Led by the county's larger landowners, notably George Culley, who farmed in Glendale, George Hughes of Middleton Hall 2 miles south of Wooler, Sir John Delaval at Ford and the earl of Tankerville through his land agent, John Bailey, the agricultural revolution was in full vigour.[2] Estates and farms were being enclosed and ringed with hedges and stone walls to keep the semi-wild sheep of the hills at bay, and allow the introduction of new breeds from Derbyshire and Leicestershire. Pastureland was being improved, land was being drained, and fertility increased by the application of lime fertilizer. Isolated crops of oats, corn and greens were being produced, and the valleys of the Till and Breamish had proved to be ideal for the cultivation of turnips, drilled and grown on the new principles of Jethro Tull. At the same time attempts were being made to introduce new implements for ploughing and harrowing and more efficient threshing machines powered by horses circling in covered wheelhouses.

When Trotter arrived in Wooler, the region was dominated socially and economically by the nobility, gentry and large tenant farmers. Four miles to the east lay the castle and park of Chillingham, seat of the area's greatest magnate, the earl of Tankerville. As well as possessing a famous herd of primitive wild cattle, Tankerville owned huge swathes of the countryside and, indeed, the town of Wooler itself. North and south-west of him were the smaller estates of Sir Francis Blake and Edward Collingwood. Both were in the process of extending their homes, Fowbury and Lilburn Towers, into elegant modern mansions. Adjacent to Fowbury, across the Till stream, lay Westwood Hall, the home of John Orde, while beyond Lilburn lay the estates of Samuel Ilderton and the lands, village and hall that had belonged for generations to the Roddam family.[3] This was of particular interest to Trotter, as the current owner was Vice-Admiral Robert Roddam, who, as commander-in-chief at the Nore, had been responsible for the supply and repair of the North Sea squadron when Trotter had been serving on *Berwick*.

At the opposite extreme to the landowners and farmers was a mass of landless

---

[2]   John Bailey and George Culley submitted a report on these changes to the Board of Agriculture, which was published in various editions after 1794, entitled *A General View of the Agriculture of the County of Northumberland*

[3]   Little had changed when William Whellan compiled his *History, Topography and Directory of Northumberland* (London and Manchester, 1855)

labourers: there was little in between. In Northumberland, farm labourers, called hinds, were a highly mobile group, moving from area to area with their families as opportunities arose, and hiring themselves out for a year at a time. The standard of their temporary accommodation was primitive. Sharing the living space with their animals, the labourers were housed in hamlets of single-storey hovels or in long, low semi-barrack buildings, which often formed a courtyard with other farm structures.[4] The landscape featured none of the cheerful villages and well-tended thatched cottages that Oliver Goldsmith and foreign visitors so admired in the south of England. On the other hand, the diet of the Northumberland farm labourer was acknowledged to be among the best in the country, comprising a varied mix of mutton, pies, oats, beer, bread and cheese. Unlike the south of England, where more and more labourers were being given cash wages and expected to fend for themselves, in the north they received little in the way of money but were given board and lodging. Married labourers and their families were supplied with food as part of their contracts and often with a patch of land on which to keep an animal, while single farm servants lived adjacent to the farm house and ate together with their employers in the traditional fashion.[5]

Wooler was an important part of this rural economy. There were monthly markets for horses and cattle in January, February and March; markets for sheep, wool and the hiring of servants in July and October; and a market for corn every Thursday throughout the year. When Trotter took up residence in 1784, there were some 1200 inhabitants and 250 dwellings, shops and inns.[6] It was a working town with no pretensions to elegance, comprising a number of streets radiating from a central space where the markets were held. Many of its original crude thatched buildings, including the church of St Michael, had been destroyed by fire in 1722; the pace of repair and rebuilding in local pink sandstone with slate roofs had been slow: it had taken twenty years for even the church to be rebuilt. But it remained a town of artisans, shopkeepers and tradesmen, all working to supply the needs of the surrounding area. There were no retired army officers, no genteel ladies of limited means, and no lesser gentry. Wooler therefore offered none of the refinement found in the country towns described in the novels of Jane Austen. For the more privileged members of the community, the social life of the region was based in the homes of the local gentry rather than in Wooler itself. The standard of hospitality offered in the town's various inns was so poor that Sir Walter Scott, visiting a few years later, preferred to beg accommodation in a private home rather than patronize the *Black Bull*, the *Anchor* or the *Tankerville Arms*.[7] Likewise the London to Edinburgh mail coach service did not even stop in Wooler, preferring to change its horses and refresh its passengers in the *George Inn* at Haugh Head, a mile to the south.[8]

---

[4] Visiting the area sixty years later, Walter White found little improvement in these living conditions. See his *Northumberland and the Border* (London, 1856), 201–4
[5] J. Burnett, *Plenty and Want* (London, 1966), 21, 33
[6] Whellan, *History, Topography and Directory of Northumberland*
[7] Scott to William Clerk, 26 Aug 1791, printed in *The Memoirs of Sir Walter Scott Bart* (Edinburgh, 1837), 181–2
[8] Lt Colonel Paterson, *A New Description of All the Direct and Principal Cross Roads in England and Wales and Part of Scotland* (London, 1811)

Doctors and doctoring

It was not unusual for a medical practitioner like Trotter to establish himself in a small market town where he had connections, and where there seemed to be a need. Demand for the services of regular medical men had been increasing since the middle of the century, as growing agricultural and commercial prosperity had put more money into people's pockets, and standards of medical training and performance had risen. The *Medical Register* of 1779 stated that at least three thousand regular physicians, surgeons and apothecaries were operating in England, and that the number was steadily growing. Distribution, however, was not uniform. The university-trained physicians stayed in the cities and major towns, tending to the needs of the rich and fashionable. Indeed, the scales of their fees, their growing wealth and the way they ostentatiously dashed in their coaches from the bedside of one affluent patient to another had already attracted the attention of the Georgian period's many satirists. The medical needs of the bulk of the country were not catered for by physicians but by their humbler and more numerous brethren, the surgeons and apothecaries. In the smaller towns and rural areas, this group was becoming indispensable as the providers of medical services which were inexpensive and suited to what the population wanted.

Ill-health was ubiquitous in Georgian Britain. Disease and accident were respecters of neither rank nor age. A fifth of babies failed to survive infancy, and average life expectancy at birth was only forty years. And for every individual who died each year, there were a dozen whose lives were disrupted by illness. At first sight, therefore, Trotter's decision to establish himself as a surgeon-apothecary so as to support himself while he completed his medical studies and refined his conclusions on the nature and cure of scurvy was a sound one. According to the commentator Robert Campbell, 'An ingenious surgeon, let him be cast on any corner of the earth, with but a case of instruments in his pocket, he may live where most other professions starve'.[9] Apothecaries, many of whom were leaving their shop counters to visit patients in their homes, were also doing well and had become, according to Adam Smith, 'the physicians of the poor in all cases, and of the rich where the distress is not very great'.[10] Wooler must have seemed to be a place of opportunity for Trotter. If the Militia Ballot Lists of 1762 are anything to go, the area was poorly served in terms of regular medical services; although the town could boast five butchers and eight shoemakers, it had only one surgeon and no apothecaries.[11]

As a surgeon, Trotter had the advantage that in the treatment of some conditions there was no alternative to surgery. In broader medical areas, however, the fact that practitioners were available did not mean that their services would be used. Economics was an obvious factor. Specialist medical attention was within easy reach of the wealthy, but people of the 'middling sort', that is, shopkeepers, small farmers and artisans, were constrained by cost. Ironically, paupers and the mass of the industrious poor who lived on the breadline were often able to obtain medical attention at the expense of charities or the liberality of the

[9] R. Campbell, *The London Tradesman* (London, 1749), 57
[10] Adam Smith, *An Inquiry into the Nature and Causes of the Wealth of Nations* (London, 1776), I, 137
[11] Northumberland Militia Muster Roll, 1762, Morpeth Record Office, M46

pre-Victorian Poor Laws. There were factors other than cost in play. The sturdy individualism which marked British society had long inculcated a tradition of self-help and self-medication. In the eighteenth century, the maintenance of good health was not seen as the exclusive concern of professionals but as everybody's legitimate, almost daily, business. Like cooking, baking and home economics, 'kitchen physick' – that is the ability to treat the common diseases which afflicted family and servants through the administration of herbs, barks, purgatives and emetics – formed part of the skills expected of every competent housewife.

The tradition of self-medication was supported by a multitude of books offering medical and lifestyle guidance appropriate to the class of the reader. Although probably seldom seen in Northumberland outside the homes of the gentry, there was Tissot's 1766 *Essay on the Diseases of People of Fashion* and George Cheyne's 1724 *Essay on Health and Long Life*, both aimed at the affluent and the sedentary who could pay for medical care, and could afford to take to their sick beds. The pages of both the *Ladies' Magazine* and the *Gentlemen's Magazine* were likewise filled with health tips. For the 'middling sort' there was William Buchan's 1769 best-seller *Domestic Medicine*, while the needs of the poor were covered by John Wesley's popular 1747 *Primitive Physick*, which was practical and drew on folk remedies and easily found natural ingredients such as herbs, garlic and onions. Products needed to stock the family medical chest could be found in abundance, not only in druggist shops, but filling the shelves of chandlers, grocers and general dealers as well. At one extreme, there were natural remedies such as liverwort, cinnamon water, liquorice root, rhubarb, valerian, cream of tartar, camomile and gum arabic. At the other, proprietary medicines such as Dr James's Powders, Ward's Pills and Drops, Dr Steer's Oil for Convulsions, Cook's Rheumatic Powders, Mrs Norton's Mordant Drops and Dr Hooper's Female Pills were among the most popular. Many patent medicines contained opium to reduce pain, quell diarrhoea and induce sleep.

As Trotter got to grips with the challenges of his new vocation, he became increasing critical of the prevailing interest in self-medication. Based upon archaic medical theories and the staples of vomits, sweats and purges, it could also be dangerous. Skin diseases, for example, were often attributed by the ignorant to 'bad humours and foulness of the blood [which] must be carried off with a purge'. He wrote:

> purgative medicines differ extremely from one another . . . and it must often be dangerous to thrust them to common hands. I was once called to visit a farmer who had taken two ounces of saltpetre, instead of Glauber's salt. I found him in extreme pain about the stomach, with ghastly looks, an inter-mitting pulse, and cold sweats. A few minutes longer would have been too late to save him: by drinking plentifully of warm milk and water, with a brisk emetic, he was recovered. But I have known similar cases prove fatal.[12]

---

[12] T. Trotter, *A View of the Nervous Temperament being a Practical Enquiry into the Increasing Prevalence, Prevention and Treatment of those Diseases commonly called Nervous, Bilious, Stomach and Liver Complaints, Indigestion, Low Spirits, Gout etc.* (London, 1807), 109

The mania for purging frequently became habitual. Persons with nervous dispositions and sedentary occupations were particularly vulnerable as this 'produced a constipated state of body which the patients helped to relieve with laxatives and purges, often with catastrophic results'. The result of this desperate resort to medication was that

> some of the most drastic purgatives such as aloes and scammony, come at last to be in common use with them. The custom soon begets a habit; when the bowels are brought to that torpor and inactivity as never to be moved without the aid of a drug.[13]

Trotter was also fully aware that human nature and the ever-present threat of ill-health made people vulnerable to exploitation by what he called 'jugglers and mountebanks'. Medical science still lacked a scientific base so that resort to regular practitioners gave no guarantee of a cure and frequently brought little relief. There were plenty of alternative treatments available. The country was filled with wise women, bone-setters, herbalists, mesmerists, occultists and quacks offering cheap, mysterious and often magical remedies. Trotter could expect plenty of competition in his new career. He had no captive audience.

Establishing a practice

The task of setting up a practice was not easy for the new doctor. Some were lucky and inherited them from their fathers or other mentors. Others married the daughters of their masters or senior partners. Trotter had none of these advantages. He had to start from scratch. There were, however, some well-established principles to help him. Erasmus Darwin, advising a young relative in a similar position, stressed the need for 'visibility and cordiality', and making his face known in the community.[14] Trotter would undoubtedly have done this by being seen on market days, frequenting farmers' dinners and attending church. He would also have built a secure base for his practice by courting the Poor Law guardians to ensure that there was a queue of charity-supported patients at his door each morning. His fellow Edinburgh student, the distinguished American physician Benjamin Rush, certainly regarded this 'taking care of the poor' as an essential part of setting up a practice.[15]

In setting himself up, the support and patronage of old naval contacts was vital, and the most important of these was the distinguished vice-admiral who resided at nearby Roddam Hall. The contact he was able to establish with Roddam provided the connections with the local gentry he needed to establish the 'riding practice' that was the normal way of working for a surgeon apothecary in a rural area. The poor queued at his gate for treatment, but paying patients

[13] Trotter, *A View of the Nervous Temperament*, 110
[14] D. Kele-Hele (ed.), *The Letters of Erasmus Darwin* (London, 1963), 206–7, quoted in D. and R. Porter, *Patient's Progress: Doctors and Doctoring in Eighteenth Century England* (Stanford, 1989), 119
[15] L. H. Butterfield (ed.), *The Letters of Benjamin Rush* (Princeton 1951), I, 250–1, quoted in Porter, *Patient's Progress*, 121

expected house calls as of right. As a result, Trotter would have covered many miles a day across country on horseback in pursuit of his profession.

Successful face-to-face encounters with patients were vital to the establishment of a reputation. In dealing with the poor, a certain amount of 'authority and condescension' was judged to be appropriate by the experts.[16] Trotter was of the same mind and considered that direction rather than persuasion was needed, particularly when dealing with those whose problems lay in drink or the abuse of opiates and patent medicines. Dealing with paying patients was a different matter. One feature of the obsession with health and the tradition of self-medication was that patients frequently made up their minds as to what was wrong with them and called on a medical practitioner to confirm it and provide the predetermined treatment. It was difficult for medical men to exert 'authority' in this situation. Trotter had none of the instruments so familiar today to aid more objective diagnosis, and physical examinations were restricted to taking the pulse, observing skin tone, listening to coughs and wheezes and smelling any 'putrefaction'. Consultations were largely verbal. Patients would describe what was wrong with them and when it started. They would then go on to outline their lifestyles, sleeping patterns, eating habits and bowel movements. Trotter would have needed tact and skill in deducing the true nature of the ailment, reading between the lines and providing what he regarded as the correct remedy while at the same time satisfying his patients' whims. He later described these challenges in the following terms:

> The physician must often take a very circuitous route to put questions to his patients, that he may learn the real genius of the distemper. He must in many cases be guarded in his enquiries, lest he excite fears and suspicions in the irritable mind, which is observant of every trifle, jealous of a whisper, and once alarmed, however falsely, not easily quieted again.[17]

Edinburgh, scurvy and return to the navy

Whilst in Wooler, Trotter had more to do than establish his medical practice. In fulfilling his ambition to improve his professional knowledge and social status by acquiring an MD degree, there were lectures in Edinburgh to attend and connections to renew, especially with the distinguished and influential Dr William Cullen. As described in Chapter 1, Cullen's impact on Trotter's thinking was profound and beneficial. But in one area Trotter's hopes remained unrealized. This was his desire to challenge prevailing theory on the nature and cure of scurvy. The first serious challenge to the 'putrefaction' and 'fixed-air' theories propagated by Mc Bride had already been made in 1782, with the publication of *An Enquiry into the Source from whence the Symptom of the Scurvy and other Putrid Fevers arise*, by Dr Francis Milman. The critique contained in

---

[16] T. Perceval, *Medical Ethics; or a Code of Institutes and Precepts adopted in the Professional Conduct of Physicians and Surgeons* (Manchester, 1803), 272, quoted in Porter, *Patient's Progress*, 140
[17] Trotter, *A View of the Nervous Temperament*, 289–90

the book had begun to undermine the scientific credibility of fermentation, malt and wort,[18] but Trotter profoundly disagreed with Milman's alternative hypothesis that scurvy resulted from debility caused by poor diet. He was therefore anxious to produce his own book which would both challenge Milman and show that putrefaction and fermentation – notwithstanding their endorsement by Captain Cook – were false trails.

Trotter was not the only one. As he knew, opinion within the navy was turning away from malt and wort as a result of practical experience. The extensive use of these substances had done nothing to relieve the scurvy that had raged during the siege of Gibraltar in the 1780s. Likewise, his contemporary Gilbert Blane, when with Rodney's fleet in the West Indies, had established that malt and wort were ineffectual. However, the administration of vegetables and lemon juice in both Gibraltar and the West Indies had worked, and the fact had been registered by both practical naval doctors and up-and-coming naval commanders like Lord Hood and Captains Roger Curtis and Alan Gardner.[19] Nevertheless, the outside medical establishment was still wedded to putrefaction and fermentation and the official position of the lay administrators on the Sick and Hurt Board inevitably reflected that of the doctors. As late as 1786 it wrote, in answer to a proposal from an East India Company surgeon, that, although lemon juice had its merits, 'the method already pursued with the preparation of substances such as portable broth, wort, sauerkraut etc. are much more efficacious both for the prevention and cure of scurvy'.[20]

Trotter's first attempt to raise his ideas on scurvy with William Cullen at the University of Edinburgh was a disappointment. The great man acknowledged that he had received a written submission from Trotter during a lecture but, to the latter's dismay, never mentioned the subject again. Perhaps Cullen, who was now in his seventy-sixth year, was too old to reconsider the convictions of a life time. Nevertheless, Trotter pressed ahead with his book, and saw it published to luke-warm reviews in 1786 under the title *Observations on the Scurvy with a Review of Theories lately advanced on the Disease, and the Opinions of Dr Milman refuted from Practice*.

Wisely, Trotter did not choose scurvy or maritime diseases as the subject of the dissertation required to qualify for the prestigious degree of Doctor of Medicine. He decided to branch out and chose 'drunkenness and its effect on the human body' as his subject. In 1788, Trotter achieved his ambition and was awarded the MD degree of the University of Edinburgh. He was now ready and anxious to return to the Royal Navy, which was still his preferred profession. But it was not a good time to apply for readmission. In 1788, Britain was at peace and, with naval manpower fixed at less than a fifth of its wartime level, there were few vacancies for which Trotter could be considered. However, he

[18] See for example, *The Monthly Review* 47 (July 1782), 175–6, and 84 (January 1786), 316
[19] L. Gillespie, 'Observations on the putrid ulcer', *London Medical Journal* 9 (1785), 373–410; F. Thompson, *An Essay on the Scurvy showing Effectual and Practical Means for its Prevention at Sea*, 1790; Hood to Sandwich, 1781, in G. R. Barnes and J. H. Owen (eds), *The Private Papers of John, Earl of Sandwich*, Navy Records Society 78 (London and Colchester, 1938); Admiralty to Sick and Hurt Board (re Curtis), 10 September 1782, NMM, Adm E/43
[20] Sick and Hurt Board to the Admiralty, 28 Mar 1786, TNA, Adm 98/15

was in luck. In May 1789, Vice-Admiral Robert Roddam was appointed as commander-in-chief at Portsmouth. Knowing both Trotter's abilities and his ambitions, Roddam exerted influence on his behalf by asking the Navy Board to appoint him as surgeon to his flagship, the 98-gun *Barfleur*.[21]

Roddam's intervention on Trotter's behalf was perfectly normal. 'Interest' – that is, patronage and the exercise of personal influence in the appointment and promotion of friends and relations – was the oil that lubricated the machinery of Georgian administration, and Admiral Roddam was as much a part of the system as anyone else. His appointment as peacetime commander-in-chief at Portsmouth was based upon his reliability and experience at Sheerness during the American War; but he was sixty-five years old and was at the end of his career. As a patron, therefore, he was hardly an ideal choice. Nevertheless, when, to the thunder of salutes, he boarded *Barfleur* in Portsmouth Harbour on 3 May 1789, and hoisted the red ensign to her foremast to signify his assumption of command, he brought with him a retinue of twenty-one persons.[22] These comprised a personal staff which included a secretary, steward, cook and a coxswain, and a group described as 'servants', the pseudonym for 'followers'. Likewise, it is no surprise that a week later *Barfleur*'s captain was replaced by Roddam's brother-in-law, Robert Calder.[23]

Unfortunately for Thomas Trotter, the patronage system was not entirely applicable to the navy's technical officers like himself. All had warrants from the Navy Board, not the Admiralty. The boatswain, gunner and carpenter were 'standing officers' who were appointed to a ship as soon as she was launched and stayed with her for the rest of her career, while the others – the purser, master, chaplain and surgeon – were appointed following examinations or outside scrutiny of one kind or another. As a result, the selection of warrant officers tended to be immune to the patronage system. Roddam certainly had no luck when he tried to appoint his own nominees to *Barfleur* as master and chaplain,[24] and his request on Trotter's behalf was rejected on the grounds that the ship already possessed a perfectly competent surgeon. Nevertheless, now that Trotter had both the status of a physician and the known support of the local commander-in-chief, the Sick and Hurt Board had little difficulty in finding a vacancy for him. In October 1789, Trotter was delighted to learn that he had been appointed as surgeon to HMS *Edgar*, then acting as a guardship at Portsmouth.[25]

[21] Navy Board to Roddam, 18 March 1789, NMM, ROD 6/1

[22] Roddam, General Instructions, 8 March 1789, NMM, ROD 7/1

[23] *Barfleur* Muster Book, TNA, Adm 36/10794; Admiralty to Roddam, 12 May 1789, NMM, ROD 6/1

[24] Micah Martin and the Rev. George Cuthbertson were Roddam's nominees. Stephens to Roddam, 18 and 29 March 1789, NMM, ROD 6/1

[25] *Edgar* Muster Book, TNA, Adm 36/11017

— 6 —

Recalled to the Colours

T HE AMERICAN WAR had been an unparalleled disaster. With Britain outnumbered on land and sea by French, Spanish and Dutch forces, the American colonies had secured their independence, and attacks on British possessions in Gibraltar and India had only just been beaten off. A new government led by William Pitt took office in 1784, and applied itself to restoring Britain's power and prestige. Thin, sickly and austere, with no passions except for port wine, Pitt had nevertheless inherited his father's oratorical skills and ability to manage Parliament. Under his leadership the country's recovery was rapid. Government expenditure was slashed and the country's financial credit restored. The decline in transatlantic trade proved less than had been feared, but nevertheless stimulated a search for other markets in the East and the exploration of the Pacific, the Antipodes and the north-west coast of America by such men as James Cook, Matthew Flinders and George Vancouver.

The Royal Navy to which Thomas Trotter was dedicated and which he had now managed to rejoin had emerged from the American War in good state. The last-minute victory by Sir George Rodney over the French at the Battle of the Saints in April 1782 had restored morale, and his breaking of the enemy's line of battle, whether done accidentally or deliberately, had shown the solution to the tactical problem that had perplexed admirals throughout the eighteenth century. Since the time of Samuel Pepys, warships had been required to fight in long parallel lines. The doctrine was enshrined in the *Fighting Instructions* issued centrally by the Admiralty and reinforced by a set of signals that limited commanders to a prescribed range of manoeuvres. Alas, the instructions seldom matched the situations in which admirals found themselves, and to abandon the line of battle was an unforgivable sin. The consequence was that it became well-nigh impossible to achieve a decisive result. Creative commanders like Anson and Hawke found their own answer by pretending the enemy were in flight and signalling for a 'general chase' – the only excuse they had for breaking formation. But this was a high-risk strategy that broke all the rules. After Rodney's victory at the Saints things changed. The inadequacies of the old *Fighting Instructions* were obvious, and naval commanders-in-chief, led by Britain's senior and best-connected admiral, Lord Howe, began to issue *Additional Instructions* of their own that allowed them to take greater control. A more flexible signalling system was needed to back these changes and Lord Howe also applied himself to developing one.[1]

---

[1] B. Tunstall, *Naval Warfare in the Age of Sail: The Evolution of Fighting Tactics* (London, 1990),

The navy was also well equipped with stores, and the comptroller of the navy, Sir Charles Middleton, had continued to carry forward his improvements in the construction, coppering and arming of British warships. All these measures had received William Pitt's support. Although his priority was to cut government expenditure, Pitt spared the navy. He knew that in times of crisis the fleet had to be mobilized rapidly, and Middleton was able to take advantage of this good will and to exploit his relationship by marriage to the prime minister's confidant, Henry Dundas. Indeed, in the face of the taciturn and uncommunicative personality of Lord Howe, who was now First Lord of the Admiralty, Pitt came to rely more and more on Middleton's advice, often dealing with him behind Howe's back. The prime minister was thus persuaded of the need to maintain ships and stores in a high state of readiness, and even to invest in an expanded building programme.[2] By 1786, there were twenty vessels in commission as guardships, sixty ready to be mobilized at a moment's notice, eleven being built and twelve undergoing repairs. It was this unusual degree of peace-time readiness that gave Thomas Trotter the chance to realize his ambition to rejoin the navy.

HMS 'Edgar'

Trotter arrived at Portsmouth to take up his post on 16 October 1789. Built on the end of the flats of Portsea Island, Portsmouth was a walled town, fortified in the style of the early eighteenth century with an economy dominated by the Royal Navy and dockyard. It was a hectic, crowded, cosmopolitan place filled with sailors, soldiers, marines, dockyard workers, merchants, shop-keepers and street traders, and awash with inns, drink and women of easy virtue. Like other arrivals, Trotter would have made his way down the High Street, past St Thomas's church, the *Blue Posts* with its carousing midshipmen and the *George* inn, haunt of more sedate senior officers, before turning right at the Navy Board's slaughterhouse and meat store to go down Broad Street to the Point. Portsmouth Point, later immortalized in Rowlandson's cartoon, looked northwards over the huge flask-shaped harbour which formed the navy's principal base. On the right could be seen the cranes of the victualling wharf and the Navy Board's bakehouses and stores. Beyond that was the gun wharf, where ships loaded their artillery and powder and, further in the distance, the towering masts and smoke that marked the docks, building slips, smithies, ropeyards and timber stores of the royal dockyard. On the left, on the other side of the water, was the town of Gosport, where the Navy Board's brewhouses and cooperage were located and, facing Spithead, the famous Haslar Royal Naval Hospital. Immediately ahead, under the lee of the slopes and chalk quarries of Portsdown Hill, was the harbour itself, busy with wherries and boats, and thick with the masts and hulls of anchored warships. One of them was Trotter's destination, HMS *Edgar*.

117, 194
[2] P. Webb, 'The rebuilding and repair of the British Fleet 1783–93', *Bulletin of the Institute of Historical Research* 50 (1977), 194–209

Trotter's basic pay as a surgeon was £65 a year, but from this he was expected to provide his own instruments and the bulk of the medicines he used. There were, however, three 'perks': a monthly payment of twopence for every crew member; an annual bonus averaging, in time of peace, £32, from what was called 'Queen Ann's Gift'; and the right to charge seamen 15 shillings for each cure of venereal disease. He was also entitled to employ a 'servant' and thus enjoyed a modest piece of patronage which enabled him to introduce young men into the service. Thus, when Trotter joined his new ship, he took his nephew, Robert, who was there to find a place on the ladder which led to commissioned rank.[3]

HMS *Edgar* was a typical 74-gun ship of the time, similar to, but a sightly more modern version of, Trotter's first ship, *Berwick*. Built at Woolwich in 1779, she too was one of a class designed by Thomas Slade. All served with distinction during the Napoleonic Wars; they included Nelson's *Vanguard* and Collingwood's *Excellent*; *Goliath* and *Defence*, which fought at Trafalgar; and *Bellerephon*, which not only featured in the battle but brought the defeated Napoleon to Britain in 1815. *Edgar* had the same measurements as *Berwick* and had a complement of 590 officers, seamen and marines.

As *Edgar*'s surgeon, Trotter lived in more comfortable surroundings than had been his lot on *Berwick*. He had his own small cabin on the port side of the orlop deck towards the stern, next to the dispensary and adjacent to the cockpit, which in battle was converted into an operating theatre. But more significantly, he was welcomed as a full member of the wardroom, which gave him the advantage of being able to socialize with his equals and gave him access to an additional place to work illuminated by natural light.

Trotter's companions on *Edgar* were a mixture of the talent and eccentricity which was common in ships of war. The diary of an observant and sardonic midshipman called James Anthony Gardener tells us who they were.[4] *Edgar*'s captain, Charles Thompson, was a gruff, experienced though unimaginative officer who had held his rank since 1771, and had commanded the two-decker *Alcide* at the Battle of the Saints. He was gallant enough in action but was reluctant to depart from standard procedures.[5] He was punctilious in insisting that officers should wear full uniform when going ashore or on duty,[6] and in issuing bibles to his crews.[7] It was he who, as a vice-admiral in 1798, would be ejected from the Mediterranean Fleet by Lord St Vincent for denouncing as 'a profanation' his execution of four mutineers on a Sunday. The *Edgar*'s elderly first lieutenant, Robert Yetts, was likewise a product of the old Georgian navy

---

[3]   *Edgar* Muster Book, TNA, Adm 36/11017
[4]   J. A. Gardener, *Above and under Hatches* (London, 1955)
[5]   At the Battle of St Vincent on 14 February 1797, it was Thompson's failure to see or understand Sir John Jervis's signal to tack with the rear division he commanded that caused Nelson to wear *Captain* out of the line and attack the retreating Spanish, thus bringing about the pell-mell engagement which made his reputation. Thompson was nevertheless made a baronet after the battle. In his contemporary *Naval Biography*, Ralfe delicately summarizes the lack of distinction in Thompson's career in the diplomatic phrase 'he does not appear to have acquired the public notice which his merit and ability deserve'.
[6]   Gardener, *Above and under Hatches*, 48–9; Captain's Orders for *Elephant*, NMM, THO/1
[7]   Thompson to the Bible Society, 19 April 1787 and 20 October 1790, NMM, THO/1

and dressed as such. At the ship's commissioning, he is said to have worn an oversized uniform jacket with huge white lapels and skirts, a red waistcoat, nankeen breeches and black stockings. His professional obsession was the constant scrubbing of decks with water. The second lieutenant, a large, fiery Welshman called Nowell, was famous for his prowess in fencing and the long jump. The sixteen midshipmen on board were a mixed bunch and spent much of their time in pranks and amusements. None of this was Thomas Trotter's style; but happily there were individuals on *Edgar* with whom he could react at the intellectual level. The schoolmaster, Andrew MacBride, for example, was a brilliant mathematician, an admirer of Ossian and, like Trotter, a keen writer of both prose and verse. Unfortunately, he was unable to control his drinking. Another was the midshipman John Macredie, who, though notoriously absent-minded, was a Greek and Latin scholar who wrote both poetry and plays.

Gardener's comments on his colleagues are invariably acerbic. One, for example, is described as 'sickly, and as crabbed as the devil', another as 'an infamous tyrant' and a third as 'better acquainted with rope yarns and bilge water than Homer or Virgil'. Yet his brief description of Trotter shows nothing but respect and admiration: he was, he wrote, 'an excellent fellow with first-rate abilities, an able writer and poet'.[8]

During the time Trotter served on *Edgar*, she was manned and ready but remained comfortably anchored in Portsmouth Harbour. The watch-keeping system used at sea was not in operation and discipline was relaxed. Leave was seldom granted, to prevent desertion by the crew, but the men were entitled to receive visits by their 'wives'. The result was that hundreds of women, many of them prostitutes or good-time girls, flocked on board the already crowded men-of-war, enlivening the days with frolicking or fighting and staying the night to indulge in what one officer described as 'excess and debauchery that the grossest passions of human nature can lead them to'.[9] None of this could have helped the constant fight of Trotter and other surgeons against venereal disease.

Nevertheless, moored near the victualling yard and with a constant supply of fresh meat, bread and vegetables, the ship remained healthy. With two surgeon's mates, Alexander Crombie and George Walker, to help, Trotter's duties were light, and left him time to extensively revise and prepare the second edition of his *Observations on Scurvy*. At the same time he produced a pamphlet proposing a reform of the navy's medical department.[10] Here he pointed out the disadvantages of charging for venereal cures; of making surgeons pay for the medicines they dispensed; and of leaving admission examinations for naval surgeons in the hands of an outside body. And, although only thirty years of age and with limited naval experience, he also felt confident enough to question the wisdom of having the medical services run by civilian administrators. Like the army, he thought it should be headed by professionals under the leadership of a surgeon general, which would make it more effective and provide prestige and a career structure.

---

[8] Gardener, *Above and under Hatches*, 48–9
[9] Quoted in C. Lloyd, *The British Seaman* (London, 1968), 247
[10] T. Trotter, *A Review of the Medical Services of the British Navy with a Method of Reform Proposed* (London, 1790)

Trotter also had opportunities to further develop his theories on ship-borne diseases. One arose in December 1789 with the arrival of the *Deptford* with convicts sent back from Newfoundland. With her unfortunate inmates confined below in the wet and cold without adequate food, clothing or bedding, scurvy was raging. Trotter was sent aboard to give professional help. In just under three weeks he was able to restore the situation by issuing vegetables and lemon juice and by persuading the commander-in-chief to supply quantities of jackets, trousers, shirts, shoes, stockings and caps so that the vessel continued its voyage to Dublin.[11] His actions made such an impression that the Admiralty proposed to the Home Department that he should be given a guinea a day for his efforts.[12] Then in 1790, Trotter was ordered to look into a serious outbreak of typhus on the 44-gun *Gorgon*, recently arrived from Chatham, carrying troops of the New South Wales Rangers on their way to Australia.[13] He soon discovered that the disease had been brought on board by two deserters who had been lodged in the Savoy Prison, and had then rapidly spread through the crowded lower deck. Trotter immediately isolated and treated the sufferers in a hulk alongside, recruiting two female nurses. With extra meat and wine and a special diet of sago, currants and spices the disease was eradicated in a fortnight. Roddam and the authorities were so impressed that the Admiralty secretary, Philip Stephens, approached the War Office, proposing that Trotter be given a special bonus for his dedication in caring for the soldiers.[14]

Mobilization and disease

Trotter's time on *Edgar* lasted for six months. Then, an international crisis caused the fleet to be mobilized. The cause on this occasion was not the French. France was preoccupied with the early stages of its Revolution: the Bastille had been stormed, and the royal family had been forced to quit Versailles for Paris by the mob. This time it was Spain which activated the crisis by seizing British ships and fur-trading stations in Nootka Sound on what is now Vancouver Island, and claiming sovereignty over the north-west coast of America. Pitt responded immediately and, in the spring of 1790, initiated the Spanish Armament. Forty-three ships of the line were mobilized and orders were given for 55,000 men to be raised for service. There was a flurry of patriotic excitement that Trotter fully shared. He put aside his current interest in poetic themes drawn from nature and the Border country, and rattled off a stirring song called *The Cruize* full of naval daring. It was a great success in the theatre at Portsmouth, where it was included in Mr Yeo's current hit, *The Asiatic*.

The Spanish Armament had a profound effect on Admiral Roddam's command at Portsmouth. *Barfleur*, *Edgar* and the other guardships prepared for sea and, on 2 June, Roddam moved with his staff and followers to the *Royal*

[11]   Onslow to Thompson, 23 December 1789, Thompson to Purser Buchanan, December 1789, NMM, THO/1
[12]   Stephens to Roddam, 11 January 1790, NMM, ROD 6/1
[13]   Roddam to Trotter, 20 March 1790, NMM, ROD 7/1
[14]   Stephens to Roddam, 10, 12 and 13 March and 12 May 1790, NMM, ROD 6/1

William, originally carrying a hundred guns, now mounting eighty-four.[15] The vice-admiral was able to get Trotter appointed to the new flagship, describing him to the Admiralty as 'a regular bred physician, and one, whom their Lordships may remember, has given very successful proof of his professional skill on two or three similar occasions'.[16] Trotter took three weeks leave in London before leaving the *Edgar*. His purpose was not, however, the pursuit of pleasure, but the provision of damning evidence to the House of Commons Select Committee on the Slave Trade.

In addition to preparing the fleet for sea, Roddam was responsible for raising the men it needed from all over the south of England. A general press was activated on the nights of 4 May and 15 July, and *Royal William* was designated as the receiving ship for the impressment tenders that covered the area.[17] Like Lind and Blane before him, Trotter found the system disturbing from both the humanitarian and medical points of view, writing

> we must suppose that men of this description, at least those that are married and have children, leave a situation where they have enjoyments . . . consequently they must feel those pangs of separation at leaving a virtuous charge which are natural to human beings; but must now and then be aggravated by the most poignant distress, by resigning wives and children to beggary and want, and a thousand ills of which I can form no idea. Hence the dejection of spirits that makes them the first subjects for scurvy and the earliest victims of contagious diseases.[18]

The men – volunteers and victims of the press gang alike – were treated as prisoners, guarded by marines, crowded together in the hold of the tender with hatches battened down, and kept for weeks without bedding or changes of clothing. The first recruits were a mixture of merchant seamen seized from their ships and already predisposed to sickness following long homeward voyages, and vagrants picked up from the streets or the gaols. They were all, as Trotter graphically described

> mixed together in the same deck. Many of them bring from their hiding places the seeds of infection in their clothes, which are speedily extended to others. No method has yet been practised to clothe these people, and they often sleep for weeks on the boards without a bed; this, joined with the crowded state of the tender, never fails to render them sickly if the passage happens to be long and the weather bad.[19]

Trotter noted that of five thousand recruits who passed through the *Royal William*, no less than five hundred had to be sent immediately to Haslar Naval Hospital. He was now convinced that the navy's impressment system encouraged the

---

[15] *Royal William* Muster Book, TNA, Adm 36/10786
[16] Roddam to Stephens, 4 October 1790, NMM, ROD 6/1
[17] Stephens to Roddam, 3 May and 13 July 1790, NMM, ROD 12/2
[18] Trotter, *Medicina Nautica*, I, 45
[19] Ibid., 46

spread of typhus, and that changes in conditions were needed even before the men reached their ships and officially joined the navy. He would have liked to have gone further. Trotter argued that the new recruits should be sent to ships on home stations to learn their trade and gather their strength before being exposed to the rigours of sea-going men-of-war. And, like Lind, he believed that the mixture of infected rags and civilian oddments worn by pressed men should be replaced by a uniform which would promote good health and *esprit de corps*. In winter, this would consist of a blue jacket and trousers, a white waistcoat lined with flannel, and a round waterproof hat with a band carrying the name of the ship. An overcoat was optional. In summer, the outfit would be supplemented by a checked shirt with a black neckcloth and white trousers.

Both recommendations were in advance of their time and assumed a level of funding and administrative ethos that did not exist. The Admiralty nevertheless took the point and soon after ensured that clothing and bedding was issued to new recruits by the regulating officers who ran the Impress Service, rather than wait until the men were eventually posted to a particular ship.

The mobilization was fast and effective and Lord Howe was able to sail within four months with a Channel Fleet of thirty-five ships-of-the-line and still leave Roddam in Portsmouth with eight battleships and seventeen smaller vessels.[20] Stunned by the speed of the British response, Spain climbed down. The fleet was decommissioned and the tenders returned the newly recruited men to their home ports. As an act of generosity, the Admiralty awarded bonuses to all who had been swept up in the mobilization – one month's pay for seamen and two months' for officers.[21] The following April, a second successful mobilization followed the seizure by Russian forces of the fortress of Ochakov on the Black Sea.

With that alarm over, in August 1791 Roddam transferred his flag to the 98-gun *Duke*, taking his retinue and Thomas Trotter with him.[22] Robert Calder soon joined as the *Duke*'s captain, but Roddam's efforts to get rid of two lieutenants, both elderly and incapacitated by wounds or general lethargy, to make way for his protégées Lieutenants Grey and Daniel, proved difficult.[23] The Admiralty was now less willing to allow admirals to decide which officers were to be appointed to flagships. Fortunately, the problem was overcome. George Grey had ample interest, being a member of a prominent Northumbrian family, the son of the future Lord Howick and the brother of the Whig Member of Parliament Charles Grey, who, as Earl Grey, not only introduced the Reform Bill of 1832 and became prime minister, but gave his name to a well-known blend of tea.

Vice-Admiral Roddam's command lasted one more uneventful year. Trotter occupied himself with the problem of keeping water supplies fresh, and carried out experiments which showed that an improvement could be achieved by burning the casks until the interiors were charred. Then, on 15 June 1792, Roddam's

[20] List of ships, 6 August 1790, NMM, ROD 13/1

[21] Stephens to Roddam, 22 and 23 November 1790, NMM, ROD 6/2

[22] *Duke* Muster Book, TNA, Adm 36/11167

[23] Stephens to Roddam, 27 August, 19 September 1791, NMM, ROD/2; Roddam to Stephens, 5 September 1791, NMM, ROD/6/5

three-year appointment came to an end, and he was succeeded as commander-in-chief at Portsmouth by Admiral Lord Hood. With their patron in retirement, Roddam's men had to fend for themselves. Of the followers who remained, five found berths on other ships and eventually achieved commissioned rank,[24] while four seem to have transferred to the army.[25] Thomas Trotter was worried that he was still not high enough on the list of surgeons to qualify for half-pay. Roddam tried to find him a suitable berth. 'Sensible of how much import it is to have a man of science and ability in the character of a surgeon, especially on a foreign station' he wrote to his friend Rear Admiral Goodall, 'I beg leave to introduce Dr Trotter . . . His merits are not unknown to the physical and literary world and his recent publication has already received singular marks of approbation.'[26] Alas, it was still time of peace and there were few vacancies.

This phase of Trotter's career did not last long. At the end of 1792, war clouds appeared on the horizon as the Jacobins who now controlled France reacted to an inept invasion by the kings of Austria and Prussia by executing Louis XIV, unleashing a reign of terror at home, and sending ragged armies to spread their revolutionary ideals abroad. On 2 January 1793, the brig HMS *Childers* was fired at in the approaches to Brest and returned to England carrying pieces of a 42-pounder cannonball as evidence of French hostility. A month later, France declared war on Great Britain.

A major element of British strategy in its wars against France had always been the wealth and vulnerability of the West Indian islands. It is no surprise therefore that a military expedition to the Caribbean was prepared. But this time, there were political possibilities, for news had arrived that French royalists in Martinique were willing to hand the island over to Great Britain. A squadron of seven ships under Rear Admiral Alan Gardner was assigned to occupy the island. An eighth was chosen to bring the royalist leaders back to England. This was the 74-gun *Vengeance*, then a guardship at Chatham. In January, she was moved fully manned to Portsmouth to receive a new set of officers under the command of Captain Charles Thompson. Thompson needed a medical man for the voyage to the West Indies and already had first-hand experience of Thomas Trotter's abilities. On 7 February 1793, Trotter became surgeon of HMS *Vengence*.[27]

---

[24] James Yeo eventually became a knight and a commodore; George William Henry Knight and Hood Knight, post captains; and Thomas Parker a commander. George Grey secured rapid promotion, becoming a post captain the following year at the age of twenty-six, and was appointed as flag captain to Admiral Sir John Jervis during the expedition to the West Indies in 1793 in which his father, General Sir Charles Grey, commanded the troops. He proved himself indispensable to Jervis and went with him to command *Victory* at the Battle of St Vincent. He became commissioner of Portsmouth dockyard in 1804 and was made a baronet in 1814. Maintaining the family's political tradition, he married Mary, daughter of the Whig brewer and MP Samuel Whitbread

[25] Jonathan G. M. Nelham, Edward Osburn, John Tipper and Henry Bell

[26] Roddam to Goodall, 28 February 1792, NMM, ROD/6/5

[27] *Vengeance* Muster Book, TNA, Adm 36/11230

7

The Royal Hospital, Haslar

HMS 'Vengeance'

VENGEANCE arrived in Portsmouth after a wet and stormy trip from Chatham packed with men. In addition to her normal complement of six hundred, she carried another four hundred who were to be distributed to other ships in the squadron, and when Trotter joined her in February 1793, large numbers had been laid low with typhus. Sixty of the most serious cases were transferred to Haslar, while dozens remained sick on board. Trotter took stringent action to isolate the infected, fumigate the atmosphere, dry the decks with stoves and fires, pump out the hold, cleanse the ballast and ensure that the crew, their clothing, bedding and hammocks were clean and washed with soap. It took a month before the outbreak had been contained and the ship was ready for sea.[1]

On 10 March 1793, *Vengeance* sailed with orders to escort a convoy to Cork, then to join a squadron under Rear Admiral Alan Gardner off the Scilly Isles. The ship reached her rendezvous point on 24 March. Alas, she arrived too late: Gardner's force had passed the Scillies twenty-four hours earlier. Thompson waited for a week then returned to Portsmouth. *Vengeance* eventually left for the West Indies on 16 April as escort to an outward-bound convoy, and reached Barbados after an uneventful voyage on 11 June. Once again she was too late. Gardner's squadron was already off Martinique and the following day landed a mixed force of British and French royalist troops to attack the local republicans. It was a fiasco. The French royalist troops fired on each other and retreated in confusion, only a handful of loyalists rose in support of the invasion, and the recently reinforced republican forces resisted with vigour. After a week, Gardner abandoned the invasion. All the British were re-embarked together with most of the French royalists, though many supporters were left behind to face imprisonment and death at the hands of their republican compatriots. By October, Gardner's ships were back in England.

Trotter's time in *Vengeance* was unexciting. This, his third voyage to the West Indies, had brought no novelties, and the hoped-for occupation of Martinique had come to nothing. The only event of interest was when a swallow flew through the wardroom window when the ship was in the Atlantic, miles from

---

[1] Trotter, *Medicina Nautica*, I, 171

the nearest land. Trotter composed a poem to commemorate the event.[2] The medical conditions on *Vengeance* were unremarkable. Likewise, when the ship returned to England, the crew was in good health except for the usual cases of scurvy.[3]

What Trotter found interesting from the medical point of view was the condition of the ship when he joined her, ravaged as she was with typhus. His investigations revealed that half of the supernumeraries she had carried from Chatham had been transferred from the receiving ship, *Nemesis*, and that two of them had been afflicted with the disease when they came on board. The extended voyage to Portsmouth in bad weather with gunports sealed, hatches battened down, poor food, bad air, cold and damp, had provided ideal conditions for transmitting typhus, which had spread rapidly among the unseasoned, ragged landsmen who crowded her lower decks. The conditions on *Vengeance* – so like those he had encountered on *Gorgon* three years before – now made Trotter convinced that typhus was indeed contagious. Trotter was to have further opportunities of studying the disease in the months that followed, for on 27 December 1793 he was transferred from *Vengeance* to the naval hospital at Haslar. His reputation was now high enough to warrant a promotion to the newly created post of second physician at an increased salary of £200 a year.[4]

The Royal Naval Hospital, Haslar

Haslar Naval Hospital was one of the medical wonders of the age. Built on a low-lying peninsula adjacent to the town of Gosport on the opposite side of the harbour to Portsmouth and its dockyard, it was made up of a double block of buildings arranged around three sides of a quadrangle facing south-east over Spithead. The original design by the Navy Board's veteran surveyor, Sir Jacob Ackworth, had been for a huge square building with a central courtyard, but the supervising architect of the project, Theodore Jackobson, had eventually recommended that one side be left open to admit light and air. Built above huge vaulted cellars, the hospital was three storeys high, with a central span and two wings each measuring 560 feet. It was the biggest brick building in Britain, if not in Europe. As the original Admiralty instruction had specified, it was 'strong, durable and plain', and was built of red brick dressed with Portland stone. It had nothing in the way of embellishment, except a pediment over the main entrance carved by Thomas Pearce.[5]

The decision to build Haslar in 1744 represented a revolution in the care of seamen who were too ill to be treated on their own ships, and had to be sent ashore. Previously, it had been seen as a temporary problem, dealt with by the hiring of sick quarters from individual landladies, lodging house-keepers and

[2]   Trotter, 'The Swallow', in *Sea Weeds*
[3]   Trotter, *Medicina Nautica*, I, 188–92
[4]   Admiralty to Sick and Hurt Board, 27 December 1793, NMM, Adm E 44 (A)
[5]   H. Richardson (ed.), *English Hospitals 1660–1948: A Survey of their Architecture and Design*, Royal Commission on the Historic Monuments of England (Swindon, 1998); W. Tait, *History of Haslar Hospital* (Portsmouth, 1906), ch. 4

Fig. 6. Admiral Robert Roddam, mezzotint by H. Hudson
after Lemuel Francis Abbot. © National Maritime Museum, London

small private hospitals. The system had worked badly. Not only was it difficult
for naval surgeons to supervise the medical care of seamen scattered throughout the town, but the contractors had taken full advantage of the inevitable
opportunities for graft and fraud. There were stories of shared beds, poor food,
drunken nurses and lousy sheets. Men were encouraged to pawn their clothes
for alcohol, and desertion was rife. By 1740, it had become clear to the authorities that in time of war the existence of large numbers of sick and wounded
men was a permanent phenomenon which could not be adequately dealt with
by the contract system. Between the summers of 1739 and 1740, for example,
no fewer than 15,800 men had been invalided ashore. The Admiralty was also
encouraged by the success of the small hospitals which the navy had opened
in Lisbon, Jamaica and Minorca where alternatives were not available. After
years of debate, on 15 September 1744, the government agreed to a programme
of hospital building in England that would provide sick seamen with medical
care, appropriate drugs and suitable food, in purpose-built facilities far from
the temptations of drink and desertion. A prestige hospital was to be built at
Haslar with a capacity of 1500 patients, to be followed by smaller institutions at

Fig. 7. Admiral Earl Howe. Stipple engraving by E. Finden
after John Singelton Copley. © National Maritime Museum, London

Plymouth and in the Medway area.[6] As additional proof of Admiralty commitment, when Haslar opened its doors in 1758, Dr James Lind, the leading authority on naval medicine of the time, was appointed as its first physician in charge.

Haslar was an immediate success. By 1779, with the American War gathering momentum, the total of patients rose to 2100, making it four times the size of Guy's or St Thomas's Hospitals in London.[7] Patients were accommodated in the hospital's two wings, which between them provided eighty-four wards, each with its own water closet and washing area. Most were for general and surgical cases, although there were smaller rooms for those with measles, smallpox, fever and mental derangement. A recent addition had been a separate operating theatre introduced by senior surgeon Robert Dodds. Before that, operations had been carried out in the open wards to the distress of other

[6] N. A. M. Rodger, *The Command of the Ocean, 1649–1815* (London, 2004), 309
[7] Letter and Report from Dr J. Lind, Physician, Haslar, 1780, printed in Lloyd, *The Health of Seamen*, 202–3

patients. Haslar's central span was the location of the hospital's main entrance, offices, council chamber and dispensary, while additional facilities were located in the hospital's grounds, a so-called 'breathing area' of forty-six acres in which were located a cemetery, a mortuary, a short terrace of houses for senior staff and the church of St Luke. For the benefit of patients, the steward, Mr Trotman, had had the quadrangle between the three blocks tastefully grassed over and planted with flowers, though the area was surrounded with wooden posts and rails to prevent access.

No amount of grass and flowers could disguise the fact that Haslar was a military establishment, the first desire of whose inmates was to recover their health, the second to get access to drink, and the third to escape. To keep at bay the undesirables from Gosport who flocked to the hospital in the hope of selling alcohol and to prevent desertion from within, all outer doors were sealed, the lower widows were fitted with iron grills, the doors of the wards were locked at night, and the ends of the wings were linked by tall spiked railings. The whole area was surrounded by a wall 12 feet in height and, as an extra precaution, the grounds were patrolled at night by thirty soldiers under the command of a lieutenant and four non-commissioned officers.[8] But no security system is perfect and, of the 8949 men who passed though Haslar in 1794, 226 managed to desert.[9] In so doing the men showed both ingenuity and agility. They filled the locks on the ward doors with sand to immobilize them; lowered themselves from the upper windows with bed sheets; avoided the military guard; and then scaled the perimeter wall to escape.[10] It was, as a laconic report on one desertion suggested, a tribute to Haslar's skill in restoring the men to full fitness.

Organization and staff

Trotter's appointment as the hospital's second physician represented a considerable increase in its senior medical establishment. Up to then it had comprised only one physician, Dr John Lind, son of Dr James Lind, who had taken over from his father in 1783, two surgeons, Thomas Fitzmaurice and Charles Dodds, who had also effectively replaced his father in 1793, a dispenser, Nathaniel Taylor, who was seventy-three years old and in decline, and a part-time apothecary, Tristram Harper. They were supported by six assistant surgeons, eight assistant dispensers, a matron with ninety nurses, two dozen washerwomen, and teams of 'labourers', who acted as male orderlies and did much of the fetching, carrying and washing of wards and patients. On the administrative side, the hospital was run by an agent, helped by a small staff consisting of clerks, a ferryman, a porter, a barber, a plumber and a chaplain. Food and drink were the responsibility of the steward, supported by a butcher, a butler, a cook and various assistants.[11]

[8] *Remarks on an Examination of the Royal Hospital, Haslar, 29 March and 4 April 1794*, sent with Admiralty to Sick and Hurt Board, 9 Jun 1794, NMM, Adm E/45
[9] Blane, *Select Dissertations*, in Lloyd, *The Health of Seamen*, 198–201
[10] Crimmin, 'The Sick and Hurt Board and the health of seamen'
[11] *Remarks on an Examination of the Royal Hospital, Haslar*, and Tail, *History*, ch. 18

On arrival in December 1793, Trotter was given responsibility for the northern wing of the hospital, which included the isolation ward for smallpox. He quickly reviewed and reissued instructions on the routines that were to be observed. The day began at dawn, when the patients were woken and washed, beds were made, chamber pots emptied, windows flung wide, and the wards scrubbed and cleaned in true Royal Navy fashion. At 8 AM in summer and 9 AM in winter the assistant dispensers would then carry out an inspection to make sure the wards were clean and the patients out of bed, and to establish whether there had been any unusual medical occurrences during the night. The rest of the morning was taken up with the rounds of the physician, or where appropriate, the surgeon, accompanied by the dispenser and the apothecary to record progress and decide on treatment. Wards were visited in a set order, with the smallpox facilities last. To signify their importance, Trotter's prescriptions were written in red ink, and on no account were to be altered by the dispensers, whose job it was to make up and administer the medicines.[12]

Cleanliness was a major element in the hospital's regime, not only of wards, but of men. On arrival, patients were bathed in tubs with soap and warm water, shaved and had their hair cut. Shirts and underclothes were replaced by hospital shifts, and their own garments were fumigated and stored ready to be returned following discharge. Trotter's instructions specified that patients were to be washed daily, and their shirts and body linen changed twice weekly. Hair was to be worn short and the men were to be regularly shaved. Trotter was just as concerned with the patient's mental well-being. His instructions required nurses to show compassion, and never to treat patients 'unfeelingly or harshly'. He later wrote

> It is the lot of the sailor and soldier to languish under affliction and disease far from the cheering support and watchful attendance of his friends and relations; and hence a charge of another kind devolves on their physician, that nurses and others may be tender and assiduous in their respective duties.[13]

Trotter was, however, neither soft nor sentimental. Although he had a great admiration for the character and courage of sailors in meeting the hardships and dangers of their lives, he had no illusions about their foibles and weaknesses, or the propensity of a minority to malinger and fake illnesses. In the age of the press gang, the desire of a man to escape the service often resulted, he wrote,

> in a determination to watch for every opportunity for effecting his escape: it is also the source of numerous deceptions by making him assume diseases to be an object for invaliding. Hence he employs caustics to produce ulcers; inflates the urethra to give the scrotum the appearance of hernia; and drinks a decoction of tobacco to bring on emaciation, sickness at stomach, and quick pulse.[14]

[12] 'Directions for the visiting apothecaries and assistant dispensers in wards of the North Wing of the Royal Hospital, Haslar', printed in Trotter, *Medicina Nautica*, I, 27–8
[13] Trotter, *Medicina Nautica*, I, 27
[14] Ibid., 36–7

The detection of such tricks was the duty of the assistant dispensers. Indeed, they were the principal supervisors in the running of the hospital. As well as preparing and giving medication, they had responsibility for ensuring cleanliness, for keeping nurses up to standard and for the prevention of fighting among the inmates.

When Trotter arrived in December 1793, Haslar had 1300 patients in residence with an annual turnover of around 9000 a year. Only a fifth of these were surgical cases. The remaining four-fifths were made up of general medical conditions, 7 per cent being damp-related complaints such as rheumatism, coughs and bronchitis, and 17 per cent advanced cases of scurvy. Inevitably the sick list was dominated by typhus, of which 68 per cent of general patients were victims.[15] The winter of 1793–4 was mild, with no extremes of cold or wet. Nevertheless, ships discharged a steady stream of typhus cases into the hospital. In December, *Russell* and *Invincible*, returning from winter cruises, off-loaded a dozen men each, followed by *Colossus* and *Robust*, fresh from Toulon. In the first months of 1794, *Raisonable* was struck by an epidemic and sent in a hundred men. In March, fifty arrived from *Valiant* and more from *Caesar* and *Leviathan*. Unusually, soldiers also made their appearance, invalids from Lord Moira's invasion force, who were too numerous to be accommodated in special sick quarters organized by the army on the Isle of Wight. In the autumn of 1793 Moira's men had been packed into overcrowded transports for the short trip to the French coast but, finding their landing opposed, had then spent months at sea before returning home riddled with fever.[16]

Looking into the causes, Trotter confirmed his conviction that typhus thrived in damp, crowded conditions, with one man infecting another. In line with the thinking of the time, however, he concluded that it was spread through smells and bad air infected with the breath of the afflicted. He was later to write

> I am of the opinion with others, that the exhalations or excretions of the sick are the vehicles of contagion. It is these which impregnate the atmosphere with noxious matter; they affect in like manner, bed clothes or apparel, and every thing that can imbibe them, when in contact with the diseased body.[17]

Trotter noticed that the number of cases sharply increased following periods of bad weather, and put this down to the fact that the quality of the air deteriorated even further when the hatches of ships were battened down and their gunports sealed. The true reason, that typhus was transmitted by lice, was unknown at the time. In the case of Moira's force, he had been able to identify that the disease had begun with the arrival of a handful of infected individuals. The epidemics on *Raisonable* and *Valiant* had likewise been caused by the arrival of transfers

[15] Blane, *Select Dissertations*, statistics presented by Dr John Lind in Lloyd, *The Health of Seamen*, 202–5
[16] Trotter, *Medicina Nautica*, journal entries for 1793, I, 57–9
[17] Ibid., I, 53

of men from an infected *London*.[18] He had seen it all before in *Vengeance* and, three years previously, in *Gorgon*. Trotter was also struck by the poor condition of the men, many of whom had been weakened by the standard treatment of bleeding to reduce the fever, followed by the administration of arsenic. His answer, as before, was to supplement the basic rations of beef, bread and cheese with a strengthening diet of mutton, sago and a substantial quantity of wine. In so doing he attracted the criticism of colleagues, who regarded such treatment as bordering on the extravagant.[19]

By Georgian standards, Haslar was run with a satisfactory degree of efficiency and probity. True, there were instances when medicines and foodstuffs went missing, and when the clothes of the patients disappeared from the store. But this appears to have been due to the inefficiency, or the excessive work loads, of the clerks who were responsible. Captains too were found to be at fault by failing to list in detail the personal effects transferred with each man on the reverse of their sick tickets. From the medical point if view, Haslar seems to have been effective. Only 5 per cent of patients died, and investigators received no complaints from the men about their care, food or clothing.[20] Trotter, however, was neither complacent nor one to accept the status quo and work within the financial limits. The weaknesses in the hospital's administration quickly became clear to him and, as was his wont, he was soon drafting a memorandum on the subject. A more elaborate version was later published under the title *Remarks on the Establishment of Naval Hospitals and Sick Quarters*.

Improvement and reform

Haslar may have had an impressive health record, but it was clear to Trotter that the staff were overstretched and the operation was being run on a shoestring. The hospital had two fully equipped kitchens but only one cook, which made it impossible to serve meals simultaneously to all the inmates. Likewise, the assistant dispensers were so overloaded that they lacked the time to dispense the prescriptions themselves and had to leave it to the nurses, many of whom were illiterate. The numbers of senior medical and surgical staff were also too few to cope adequately with the number of patients. Trotter wrote:

> It muſt readily appear to every discerning person, that so few physicians and surgeons . . . for such an immense business, muſt be utterly unequal to the task . . . No man can suppose that one Physician is capable of doing juſtice to four or five hundred patients in one day . . . It is not merely the time spent at the sick bed . . . there muſt be hours left for ſtudy and reflection. Diseases will now and then appear where every thoughtful mind would wish to turn over Authors on the subject, and to canvas opinions, in order to give preference to a decided method or cure.[21]

[18]   Ibid., Journal entries for February and March 1794, I, 58–60
[19]   Ibid., entry for 1 April 1794, I, 60
[20]   *Remarks on an Examination of the Royal Hospital, Haslar*, and Tail, *History*, ch. 18
[21]   Trotter, *Remarks on the Establishment of Naval Hospitals and Sick Quarters with HINTS for their improvement* (London, 1795), 15

In Trotter's view, pay levels were also inadequate. Physicians received £200 a year, surgeons and their assistants, £150 and £90 respectively, the assistant dispensers £50 and the nurses only £12.[22] For senior men, these emoluments were poor in relation to the rewards that were possible in civilian life, and compared badly with what was paid at all levels in the medical services of the army. Almost in recognition of this, those employed in Haslar and Stonehouse were allowed to engage in private practice, thus reducing further the time available for sick seamen. Accommodation for staff was also insufficient.[23]

Trotter was particularly critical of Haslar's administrative framework. The hospital was governed by a council consisting of the seven most senior staff, led by the first physician. The medical and administrative challenges of accommodating, feeding, visiting, treating and monitoring the medical progress of such a large body of patients were formidable enough. To have to deal additionally with the disciplinary problems created by over a thousand reluctant and potentially unruly inmates, many eager for drink or escape, was an additional burden that deflected attention from the hospital's main purpose. In Trotter's view, Haslar should be made a regular naval establishment, with a captain in overall charge, supported by lieutenants to keep order and give leadership to the men.

The bulk of Trotter's proposed improvements were eminently practical. It was only when he elaborated them for publication that he became almost lyrical. He felt, for example, that the washing of the men in tubs was demeaning and proposed the construction of bathhouses so they could 'bathe like gentlemen'. These would include rooms of different temperatures and would, if built properly, 'become as famous as those of Baiae in the days of ancient Rome'. Likewise, the grounds should be turned into a farm with dairy cattle, poultry and an orchard to provide milk, eggs and fruit for the sick. 'How grateful is a dish of salad after a long cruise', he wrote, 'How delicious an apple, a pear or a plum after a long sickness on board?' Trotter was also a visionary. To him Haslar should be developed into a teaching and research centre for naval medicine. Its staff would be financially compensated for these additional duties, and would be supported by a medical library available only to naval surgeons, who would have 5 shillings docked from their pay to meet the cost of the books.[24]

Trotter did not allow these proposals to be pigeon-holed. He raised his more practical suggestions with Sir Roger Curtis, chief of staff to the commander-in-chief, Lord Howe, with whom he had struck up a mutually supportive relationship. Both Curtis and Howe were well known for their concern for the health of seamen and reacted quickly. Rear Admirals Caldwell and Gardner, supported by Captains Donnett and Nicholls, were ordered to carry out an inspection of the hospital. The visit lasted two full days, both Fridays, 28 March and 4 April 1794, and their findings were issued in early June.[25] Although they avoided the knotty question of pay, many of their proposals showed signs of Trotter's influence, most notably in recommending increases in the number of

---

[22] Tail, *History*, ch. 18

[23] *Remarks on an Examination of the Royal Hospital, Haslar*

[24] Trotter, *Remarks on the Establishment of Naval Hospitals* and *Medicina Nautica*, I, 15–27

[25] *Remarks on an Examination of the Royal Hospital, Haslar*

medical assistants, clerks and cooks, the provision of more accommodation for staff on the site, and the introduction of greens and mutton to make the diet more suitable for the sick. The total cost of these improvements was estimated to be £13,604.[26] Most significant of all was the recommendation that Haslar and Plymouth Hospitals should become regular naval establishments, subject to the Articles of War and under the command of a governor and a team of assistants who were sea officers. Thus, on 14 August 1794, Captain William Yeo was appointed the first naval governor of Haslar, supported by three naval lieutenants.[27] Thomas Trotter was not, however, present at the hospital to witness the implementation of the reforms he had so effectively advocated. On 5 April 1794, he had been promoted to be physician to the Channel Fleet under Lord Howe.[28]

[26] Sick and Hurt Board to Admiralty, 28 February 1795, NMM, Adm F/25
[27] Admiralty to Sick and Hurt Board, 14 August 1794, NMM, Adm E/45
[28] Admiralty to Sick and Hurt Board, 9 April 1794 NMM, Adm E/45

8

Physician to the Channel Fleet

W HEN WAR WAS DECLARED, Britain had taken immediate advantage of the disarray in revolutionary France. A sea-borne expedition seized her major West Indian islands; anti-republican risings in Brittany and the Vendée were supported; and Lord Hood's fleet occupied the great Mediterranean base of Toulon, destroying ships, stores and timber before it was ejected by an artillery major called Bonaparte. But there were opportunities for the French as well. Festering political discontent in Ireland and the existence of huge convoys in the western approaches carrying the wealth of the world to the city of London offered irresistible targets. Sadly for French ambitions, the revolutionary turmoil had had a disastrous effect on the organization and leadership of their navy. Yet it was still formidable, with eighty-two ships of the line, and even if traditional discipline had been weakened, a new and aggressive fighting spirit seemed to have replaced it.

Lord Howe and the 'loose' blockade

The British government did not see the immediate threat from France as lying in great fleet actions, but in attacks on merchant convoys by naval squadrons or privateers. In the front line of the battle to defend this economic lifeline lay the Channel Fleet, commanded by Britain's most experienced sea officer, Admiral Lord Howe. An earl in his own right, Howe was a member of the Whig aristocracy with distant links to the royal family. His grandfather had been Scrope Howe, Member of Parliament for Nottingham, who had voted to place William of Orange on the English throne, and had been ennobled as a result. His mother was Maria-Sophia Kielmansegge, said to be the illegitimate daughter of George I. Howe was one of the most prestigious figures in the Georgian navy. A captain since 1746, he had rapidly acquired a reputation as an outstanding organizer and combat officer. He had fired the first shot in the Seven Years' War, and had unflinchingly led the line when Hawke had chased the French fleet to its doom amid the gales of Quiberon Bay in the 'Glorious Year' of 1759. He had fought against superior forces in the American Revolutionary War and had commanded the fleet that had finally frustrated the Spanish siege of Gibraltar in 1782. Howe had also been a leading figure in moves to give fleet commanders greater tactical control over their captains in battle and in developing a signalling system that would enable them to communicate their intentions. In 1790, this was ready, in the form of his *Signal Book for Ships of War*. It consisted of sixteen flags that enabled 160 separate numerical orders to be sent. Number 1, for example, meant 'Enemy in sight', while number 16 signified 'Engage the enemy more closely'.[1]

Howe's innovations and tactical vision gave him an unrivalled prestige in the service. Nelson described him as 'the great, the immortal Earl Howe . . . the first and greatest Sea-officer the world has ever produced',[2] and Admiral Lord St Vincent is said to have worn blue trousers with his uniform in imitation. Thomas Trotter, from the humbler vantage point of a surgeon, extolled his virtues of loyalty, integrity, independence, humanity, modesty and piety and regarded him as 'a model for the conversion of the modern Great'.[3]

Howe's taciturn manner and saturnine colouring had earned him the nickname 'Black Dick'; but his concern for his men also caused him to be known as 'the sailor's friend'. Conscious that every manoeuvre and action depended on muscle power and morale, he had, as a captain, put method into shipboard organization by writing elaborate instructions on how his ship was to be run. He had also pioneered a system in which seamen were divided into divisions, each under the immediate command of a lieutenant and a group of midshipmen, who were responsible for their cleanliness and well-being.

Lord Howe was the government's obvious choice as commander-in-chief of the Channel Fleet. Unfortunately, he was sixty-seven years old, tired, of delicate health and smitten with gout. Knowing his limitations, Howe had only agreed to take on the responsibility after the personal intervention of King George III. In the circumstances, he inevitably came to rely heavily on his chief of staff, captain of the fleet, Sir Roger Curtis. In many ways, Curtis was a good choice. A friend and confidant of the admiral, Curtis was not only an experienced captain, but an accomplished diplomat who did much to protect and support Howe during his period of command. He was also cautious. Caution is an invaluable quality in a chief of staff whose commander is active and aggressive; but Howe was no longer the man he had been. However powerful his vision and scientific approach, his instincts had been forged in the 'old' Hanoverian navy and they now returned to blunt his edge. He worried about the seaworthiness of his ships; he was alarmed by the dangers of maintaining a tight blockade of the French coast; and he was pessimistic about the abilities and zeal of his captains.

In July 1793, the Channel Fleet sailed to impose a blockade on the French naval base of Brest. But it was neither continuous nor close. Howe believed that the best way to conserve his resources was to conduct a 'loose' or 'open' blockade – that is, to leave frigates on watch outside the port, and withdraw the main fleet to the sheltered waters of Torbay to await news of French movements. The fleet left its anchorage occasionally to ensure the safety of the West Indian and Mediterranean convoys, but Howe's attempts to find and engage the enemy came to nothing and merely confirmed his doubts about the capabilities of his

[1] R. Knight, 'Richard, Lord Howe', in Peter Le Fevre and Richard Harding (eds), *Precursors of Nelson, British Admirals of the Eighteenth Century* (London, Chatham, 2000), 289–90, at 289; D. Syrett, *Admiral Lord Howe* (Stroud, 2006), 115

[2] Nelson to Howe, 7 January 1799, N. H. Nicholas, *The Despatches and Letters of Vice-Admiral Lord Viscount Nelson* (London, 1846), III, 219

[3] Trotter, *Medicina Nautica*, III, 62

ships and the competence of his captains. As a result, the first year of the war produced little in terms of action except for dramatic engagements between frigates. The first of these, when *Nymphe* captured *La Cléopâtre* in fifty minutes flat, was greeted with such rejoicing by a public hungry for victory that the triumphant British captain, Edward Pellew, was knighted. The popularity of Howe on the other hand sank, with cynics referring to him dismissively as 'Lord Torbay' after the fleet's principal haven. Black Dick remained typically unmoved and uncommunicative.

The combination of Howe and Curtis at the head of the Channel Fleet was, in one respect, wholly beneficial. Like his chief, Curtis was concerned with the health and welfare of the men. He was one of those captains who was convinced of the benefits of lemon juice as a cure for scurvy and in 1782 had written a report to the Admiralty extolling its use.[4] Likewise when his ship, *Brunswick*, had been afflicted by a 'putrid and highly infectious fever' at Spithead in 1791 he had instituted a comprehensive regime to cleanse the ship and the crew. He later published a pamphlet on the subject, half of which was devoted to the methods he had used to eradicate the disease, and the other half to giving advice to his fellow captains on the maintenance of health and hygiene.[5] What Curtis said and the way he said it so closely accorded with Thomas Trotter's own ideas that Trotter quoted it in its entirety in his *Medicina Nautica*.

Trotter promoted

At the beginning of the campaigning season of 1794, Howe decided to appoint a physician of the fleet. The appointment was partly a consequence of Howe's concern for the health and welfare of his crews, but it reflected a heightening in the aggressive instincts of commanders. Fighting a national war of ideologies seemed to produce a fierce determination to win and a realization that healthy crews were as important as seaworthy ships. The presence of a senior medical figure on their staffs to give advice was therefore important. For the first time, physicians could be found serving with all major fleets. In May 1793, Lord Hood appointed Dr John Harness to the Mediterranean Fleet. On 5 April 1794, Lord Howe did the same in the Channel, selecting Thomas Trotter for the task. In 1795, Primrose Blair was made physician to the proposed Leeward Islands Squadron under Rear Admiral Christian; and, in the years that followed, Lord St Vincent and Lord Nelson made similar arrangements, using Andrew Baird, John Snipe and Leonard Gillespie.

Why was Thomas Trotter chosen for this important, and comparatively new, assignment? He was not particularly senior, being only half-way up the list of surgeons. He had never been a member of Howe's retinue or part of his patronage network. Likewise there is no evidence that the ailing Howe, with all the burdens of fleet administration, supply and tactics on his shoulders, was

---

[4] Admiralty to Sick and Hurt Board, 10 September 1782, NMM, Adm/E/42
[5] R. Curtis, *The Means used to Eradicate a Malignant Fever which Raged aboard HMS Brunswick at Spithead in the Spring of the Year 1791, with some Observations on the Most Probable Means of Preserving the Health of a Ship's company* (1791)

familiar with current literature on naval medicine or with Trotter's previous record. However, his captain of the fleet, Sir Roger Curtis, certainly was. The similarities of view between Curtis and Trotter on the prevention and cure of maritime diseases and the need for vegetables and lemon juice in combating scurvy, are striking. Indeed, Trotter became a welcome visitor at Curtis's home at Gatcombe House and composed an elegy to commemorate the death of Curtis's daughter's pet dog. In later years, they maintained a lifelong correspondence, and Trotter's second son carried the Christian name 'Curtis'. It is therefore likely that Sir Roger Curtis played an influential part in securing his appointment, and that it was he who drew Howe's attention to the merits and work of Thomas Trotter.

As physician to the Channel Fleet, Trotter's job was to ensure the effective treatment of ill-health among the ships of the fleet, supervise the work of the surgeons, and prevent the onset of disease by encouraging hygienic practices and good diet. He relished the opportunity. Dedicated to his profession, inexhaustible in his reading, convinced that the good health of seamen was vital to the effectiveness of the navy, and with a fund of ideas on the causes of diseases like scurvy that had crippled fleets in the past, Trotter was keen to put his theories into action. With the steady support of the commander-in-chief, he was not disappointed. Howe's confidence was such that he allowed Trotter to issue orders in his name without previous approval, and invariably backed any recommendation he made to the Admiralty. With the assistance of his subordinate surgeons, who were required to submit regular reports, Trotter was able to extend his influence and to develop his ideas further. Openly following the example of Gilbert Blane, he began to record information and data on the health of the fleet and to draw conclusions from what he found.

When Thomas Trotter was appointed physician to the Channel Fleet in April 1794, he did not join the *Queen Charlotte* as a member of Lord Howe's staff. Unlike Gilbert Blane with Admiral Rodney and Leonard Gillespie with Lord Nelson, he never became part of the social life of the flagship, nor did he enjoy the chit-chat at his admiral's dining table. Instead, Trotter established his base on a hospital ship called *Charon*. Commanded by George Countess, she was intended to act as a floating hospital and supply ship for medicines and anti-scorbutics to the Channel Fleet. With two decks and originally of forty-four guns and a crew of three hundred, *Charon* had been built at a time when powerful cruising ships were popular, but by 1793 her design was obsolete.[6] She was too small to stand in the line of battle and too slow to act as a commerce raider, but with one of her decks disarmed, she was ideal for her new purpose. And to this end, in addition to her surgeon and two mates, she carried a hospital staff of sixteen – a matron, Martha Simons, five nurses, three male assistants, six washerwomen and a baker, James Chamberlain.[7] *Charon* was not, however, unarmed and marked by red crosses in the manner of modern

---

[6] *Charon* was built in 1778 after a design by Sir Thomas Slade. She measured 140 feet on the gundeck and 16 feet 4 inches in the hold, and was of 879 tons. For details and plan, see P. Goodwin, *Nelson's Ships* (Conway, 2002), 88

[7] Muster Roll of *Charon*, TNA, Adm 36/11831

hospital ships. One deck still carried artillery, and her crew of 120 included gunners and fifteen marines.

Trotter joined *Charon* at the beginning of April 1794. She had arrived at Spithead a month before, fully manned and provisioned.[8] In addition to normal supplies of beef, beer and medicines, *Charon* carried 14,000 gallons of lemon juice and 116,000 pounds of sugar. This was intended for a squadron being prepared to attack the French Indian Ocean base of Mauritius. Its commander, Rear Admiral Alan Gardner, had asked for the lemon juice in order to counteract the scurvy that would be inevitable on such a long voyage, and the Admiralty had agreed.[9]

The Battle of the 'Glorious First of June'[10]

Across the Channel in France, 1793 was the high point of the terror and disruption caused by the Revolution. Prisons were overcrowded, the guillotine took its daily toll, discipline and the rule of law disintegrated. Then the harvest failed, threatening national catastrophe. To save the situation, French diplomatic agents in the United States were ordered to buy a huge quantity of grain and other foodstuffs, and to hire as many ships as were needed to send it home. On 2 April 1794, a convoy of 117 merchant vessels, heavily laden with grain and West Indian produce, sailed from the Chesapeake for France, escorted by Rear Admiral Vanstable and a small naval squadron.

In England, rumours of French activities arrived in the first months of 1794. Then in April, it was learnt that a fleet was preparing at Brest with the objective of meeting the grain convoy in mid-Atlantic, seeing it safely home and sweeping the seas of British commerce as it did so. In command was Rear Admiral Louis Thomas Villaret-Joyeuse. Villaret-Joyeuse was an active and intelligent officer. He had learnt his trade in Indian waters with Suffren, one of the French Royal Navy's most aggressive and original admirals, and was in no way overawed by the British. A member of the minor nobility who had been a lieutenant at the outbreak of the Revolution, he had established his republican credentials, thrown in his lot with the regime and been rewarded with rapid promotion. Robespierre may have had confidence in Villaret-Joyeuse's loyalty, backed by the ever-present threat of the guillotine, but to make sure, he had appointed a Jacobin activist called Jean-Bon Saint-André to the fleet as a kind of joint commander and political commissar. Saint-André's job was to instill revolutionary enthusiasm and self-sacrifice among the men and to keep an eye on the officers.

Lord Howe, who had spent much of the winter resting at his house in Grafton Square or taking the cure at Bath, returned to Portsmouth in March. The fleet was by this time in reasonably good condition. So were the men.

---

[8] Captain's Log of *Charon*, TNA, Adm 51/189
[9] Admiralty to Sick and Hurt Board, 17 and 24 December 1793, and 4 January 1794. NMM, Adm E/44b and 45
[10] For the most up-to-date account of the battle and its consequences, see M. Duffy and R. Morris, *The Glorious 1st of June: A Naval Battle and its Aftermath* (Exeter, 2001)

Trotter reported that, out of a total complement of some 22,000 men on the line-of-battle ships, only 725 were sick. In April, Howe received his orders from the Admiralty. They were to escort the East and West India convoys clear of the western approaches, then to intercept the French grain convoy, dealing with any warships he encountered as was appropriate.

On 2 May, Howe set sail from Spithead with thirty-two ships-of-the-line and thirteen smaller vessels, including *Charon* with Trotter on board, and the accompanying convoys. As they passed down the Channel, they were joined by more merchantmen from the western ports. Two days later, they were off the Lizard. To observers on the shore, the convoy and its escort were an impressive sight and a demonstration of British maritime power. The sea was filled with white sails as far as the eye could see. From the decks of *Charon*, Trotter and his companions could count no less than 228. That afternoon, the convoys parted company and turned south, escorted by a squadron commanded by Rear Admiral George Montagu to see them safely as far as Cape Finisterre. Howe, with the remaining vessels, headed for France.

A reconnaissance of Brest showed that twenty-two big ships and a large number of smaller vessels were still in the anchorage. Villaret-Joyeuse had not yet sailed. But the following day, the wind swung round to the north-west. To avoid being blown onto the rocks of the Brittany coast, Howe stood out to sea. When he returned to Brest a fortnight later on 19 May, the French had gone. Fearful for the safety of Montagu's squadron, Howe turned south-west, but that night met one of his frigates bearing dispatches. From these, Howe learnt that a small French squadron under Rear Admiral Nielly had not only sailed from Rochfort, but had encountered the British Newfoundland convoy at sea, capturing many of its merchant ships and its single naval escort. But there was more. From a loquacious French corvette, Montagu had learn the rendezvous point at which Villaret-Joyeuse was to meet the grain convoy. It was between 45° and 48°N and at 16°W – that is, some 430 miles due west of Brest.

Howe headed into the Atlantic, retaking the captured ships of the Newfoundland convoy as he went. A week later, having reached 16°W, he turned and sailed north as far as 48°N, looking for the French. There he retraced his steps, though, with the wind from the south, the closest he could get was south-east. The Channel Fleet was now in two columns, with a flying squadron consisting of four fast 74-gun ships to windward. Then, on the morning of 28 May, a large body of ships was sighted ahead some 10 miles to the south, in the eye of the wind. A reconnaissance soon established that it was indeed the French fleet. For Howe, the good news was that he had found Villaret-Joyeuse's ships in the vastness of the Atlantic. The bad was that they had what was called the weather gauge. In other words the French were to windward of their opponents and could therefore decide the time of any attack or, indeed, escape over the horizon whenever they chose. The need to occupy the weather gauge, and so dictate the course of any engagement, had long been an article of faith among British admirals, and for the next few days it became Howe's principal objective.

The French showed no alarm at sighting the British fleet. Indeed, Villaret-Joyeuse's ships could be seen adjusting their line and trimming their sails before heading south-east in a loose line of battle. The French admiral was content to take his time and distract the British from the grain convoy, somewhere to the west. By the afternoon, it was blowing a moderate gale with squalls of rain. Rear Admiral Pasley's flying squadron was in close pursuit, and as dusk approached began a fierce exchange of cannon fire with the huge 100-gun *Révolutionnaire* in the French rear. A few more of Howe's ships were able to join in, but when night fell, he called off the action.

Dawn next day found the two fleets sailing on broadly parallel courses, heading south-east with a light breeze and a heavy swell, the French still to windward. At mid-morning, Howe put his plan to seize the weather gauge into action. At a flutter of signals from the flagship, the line of British warships tacked and headed close-hauled in order of sailing diagonally south-west. Howe's intention was to punch his way through the enemy's rear. As the British approached and began to fire on the three French vessels that blocked their path, Villaret-Joyeuse reversed course to succour his beleaguered ships. In this he succeeded, but at the cost of allowing Howe to pass through his rear, gain the windward position, and put two French battleships out of action.

Next day, 30 May, the mist which had hung white over the water all night was replaced by fog, so dense and impenetrable that any kind of action was impossible. It did not fully clear until noon on the following day. Howe was anxious to get a decisive result, but feared that he lacked the time to do so. In an act of moral strength and true leadership, he decided to postpone his attack until the morrow.

Sunday 1 June found the two fleets sailing westwards on parallel courses over a calm sea, the British line now to the south and to windward. Tucked behind the line further southwards were Howe's smaller vessels – the frigates ready to tow away any damaged ships, the others – including *Charon* – out of harm's way. For the British, however, daylight brought a shock, for during the night Villaret-Joyeuse had been joined by three of the Rochfort ships-of-the-line. The French now outnumbered their opponents, though in terms of firepower, the two sides were broadly equal. Howe waited until his crews had fortified themselves with breakfast then, at 7.30 AM, initiated the battle by hoisting signal no. 34 – 'having with the wind of the enemy, the admiral means to pass between the ships in the line for engaging them to leeward'. His intention was that each ship should turn, head at right angles for the French, fire a broadside into the stern of their opposite numbers as they passed through their line, then turn and finish them off from the leeward side. To try to ensure that there was no misunderstanding, he then hoisted signal no. 36 – 'each ship independently to steer for and engage her opposite in the enemy's line'. Unfortunately, Howe's second signal failed to achieve its purpose. Some captains were now unsure as to the side on which they should engage the enemy. In the event, when they reached the enemy line, only *Queen Charlotte*, *Marlborough*, *Defence*, *Royal George*, *Queen* and *Brunswick* broke through it: the others engaged from the windward.

From the decks of the *Charon*, Thomas Trotter had a grandstand view as the British ships slowly turned in response to Lord Howe's signals and headed in line abreast towards the French line. At about 10 AM, they reached point-blank range and unleashed their first broadsides. The battle area was soon obscured by smoke and the engagement became a series of bloody encounters between individual ships. To the rear of the flagship, Trotter watched in awe as Howe took the *Queen Charlotte* through the French line, guns blazing on both sides as she simultaneously took on Villaret-Joyeuse's 100-gun *Montagne* and the smaller *Jacobin*. Her broadside smashed a hole the size of a coach in the vulnerable stern of the French flagship and caused hundreds of casualties as cannonballs sliced through the whole length of the gun deck. It was only the loss of the *Queen Charlotte*'s topmasts that enabled her opponent to escape. Trotter later recaptured Howe's tactic and the resulting scene in a heroic poem:

> Meanwhile revolving in his manly soul
> Fate's ftern decrees, that human might control,
> Britannia's Hero bade the signal fly,
> And the loud cannon shakes the vaulted sky;
> Quick thro' the trembling hoft he darts his course,
> And swift as lightning deals the thunder's force.
> Huge piles of smoke in curling volumes rise,
> Obscures the seas, and darkens all the skies;
> Save when the flash illumines the sev'ring cloud,
> Gleams round the maft, or quivers thro' the shroud,
> Wide o'er th'embattled Line the fight extends,
> The ocean bellows, and the welkin rends;
> Till, far and near, the echoing concave bounds,
> With hoarser clangors and remoter sounds.
> Now thro' the smoke some ftately vessel rears,
> Now half-disclose'd her painted form appears;
> There crash the ftayless mafts, and ftrew the deck,
> And leave the shatter'd hull a helpless wreck.[11]

The French fought with ferocity during the battle. But superior British experience and discipline eventually triumphed. By noon, twelve French ships had lost all or two masts, and six – *Sans Pareil, Juste, Northumberland, América and Impetueux* and *Achille* – had been captured, while one, *Vengeur*, had sunk after a bloody duel with the *Brunswick*. French casualties were approaching seven thousand. On the British side, *Defence* and *Marlborough* had been dismasted, three ships had lost one mast each, and five had lost their topmasts. Trotter estimated casualties at 288 killed and 810 wounded. Nor had the French shot made any allowance for rank. Among the seriously wounded were thirty-seven junior officers, one captain and three rear admirals, two of whom, Pasley and Bowyer, had lost a leg, while seventeen officers and three captains had been killed or fatally wounded.

By midday, exhaustion was beginning to set in, and the fighting petered out. At about 1 PM, Villaret-Joyeuse pulled out of the battle and formed his manageable ships into a line behind which his more seriously damaged consorts could find refuge. By this time, Lord Howe was physically and emotionally

---

[11] 'Suspiria Oceani: a Monody on the Death of Richard, Earl Howe K.G.', in Trotter, *Sea Weeds*

exhausted. He had been on the quarterdeck continually for four days, wrapped in his overcoat, occasionally dozing in an armchair. He had been impressed by the stubbornness of the French defence and feared that Villaret-Joyeuse's movement posed a threat to his own battered ships. Supported by the cautious Curtis, he decided to go on the defensive. Strings of signals ordered the fleet to rally round the flagship and secure the prizes. The battle was over.

Victory and rewards

Villaret-Joyeuse gathered what was left of his shattered fleet and limped back to Brest, apprehensive about his reception. He need not have worried. In the approaches he met Vanstable and the grain convoy that had escaped detection by the British. The Revolution, and Villaret-Joyeuse's head, were saved. In the hastily repaired great cabin of the flagship, Saint-André wrote his report. Individuals who had shown a lack of civic duty – and had, he hinted, thereby prevented a victory – were identified, but the story he told was one of the triumph of republican virtue. The heroic deeds of individual sailors were held up for emulation and his description of the loss of the *Vengeur*, its men fighting to the last and crying 'Vive la République' as they struggled in the water, became the stuff of legend. Thomas Trotter, who had spoken to the officers commanding the boats which had plucked the freezing men from the sea, flatly contradicted this story, but made no impact.

In years to come, when the sailing navy reached maximum effectiveness and British admirals spoke in terms of annihilation, Lord Howe's failure to pursue the shattered French provoked criticism. Nelson himself later expressed a determination to avoid 'a Lord Howe victory', by which he meant one that was incomplete and not fully exploited. But in terms of the standards and expectations of the eighteenth century, Howe's achievement had been unprecedented. For four days, he had manoeuvred his fleet by signal alone; he had seized the windward position with astonishing tactical skill; and had then deliberately broken the enemy's line, and secured both victory and a bag of captured ships. Cuthbert Collingwood reflected the mood of the moment when he wrote in a letter to a friend:

> We who are seamen were well acquainted with the great professional abilities of Lord Howe; but he has outdone all opinion that could be formed. The proceedings of the 1st June were like magic, and could only be effected by skill like his. I scarce know how to give you an account of it.[12]

The British participants in the battle seemed to sense that they were witnessing something remarkable. Many wrote memoires and diaries recording their experiences on what was to be called 'the Glorious First of June'. The battle also generated its own collection of supporting anecdotes. There was, for example, the encounter between Captains Edward Pakenham of *Invincible* and James

---

[12] Collingwood to Sir Edward Blackett, 15 June 1794, E. Hughes (ed.), *Correspondence of Lord Collingwood*, Navy Records Society 98 (London and Colchester, 1957), 46

Gambier of *Defence*. Gambier was a devout evangelical Christian who spent much time on prayer meetings, the distribution of improving texts and the suppression of swearing. Sweeping past *Defence* as she rolled mastless in the swell, Pakenham yelled through his speaking trumpet 'No time for Prayers today Jemmy. But don't worry – whom the Lord loveth He also chastizeth.' Gambier called back politely to ask how many of the *Invincible*'s hard-drinking Irish crew had been killed. In reply, Pakenham shouted 'Damn me if I know. They won't tell me for fear I stop their grog.'

Another anecdote told by Barrow reflects perfectly Howe's temperament and relationship with his crews. He wrote that, after the battle,

> A deputation of petty officers and seamen requested Bowen [the Sailing Master] to ask Lord Howe if they might have the gratification of congratulating him on the victory he had gained, and of thanking him for having led them so gloriously . . .
>
> On receiving them on the quarterdeck, Lord Howe was so affected that he could only say, with a faltering voice, and his eyes glistening with tears, 'No, no, I thank *you* – it is you my brave lads – it is you, not I, who have conquered'.[13]

Sea officers, topmen and gun crews were not the only individuals who performed well that day. Deep in the gloom of the cockpit, the surgeons and their mates had also done their duty. Even when the battle was over, their work went on well into the night. Robert Forrest of the *Brunswick* had 112 seriously wounded men to deal with; Thomas Romney of *Marlborough* 90; Richard Shepherd of the *Royal George* 72; and Alexander Browne of the *Queen*, 69.[14] *Defence*, with 49 casualties, presented a different picture. There, her surgeon Dr James Malcolm, though a good physician, was incapable of performing amputations, so the whole responsibility fell on his mate, a cheerful Irishman called Youhall, who worked for twenty hours out of twenty-four, almost without a break.[15]

In the aftermath of the battle, with the contribution of the surgeons still fresh in everyone's mind, Trotter seized the opportunity to raise the problem of the status of naval surgeons with Lord Howe and Sir Roger Curtis. Receiving an encouraging response, Trotter organized a general meeting of the surgeons of the fleet. There had long been resentment among naval surgeons over their modest pay and low status, particularly when they compared themselves to colleagues in the land forces. In the army, regimental surgeons held commissions and wore a uniform. Naval surgeons had neither. Likewise, army surgeons received on average £198 a year and were entitled to half-pay of 5 shillings a day. In the wartime navy, the basic pay plus Queen Ann's Bounty averaged only £108 plus the cost of a servant, valued at £12, and the payment of 15 shillings for each venereal cure. Likewise, out of 473 surgeons on the list,[16] only 125 were

---

[13]   John Barrow, *Life of Richard Earl Howe* (London, 1838), 268–9
[14]   Journal entry for 1 June 1794, Trotter, *Medicina Nautica*, I, 54
[15]   William Dillon, *A Narrative of My Professional Adventures*, ed. M. Lewis, Navy Records Society 93 (London and Colchester, 1953)
[16]   *Steel's Navy List* for 1795

entitled to half-pay, the most senior receiving only 2 shillings and 6 pence a day. It was small wonder that recruitment was difficult and that there were large numbers of vacancies in the medical branch, particularly at the lower level of surgeon's mate.

The result of the meeting of the surgeons convened by Trotter was a petition to the Admiralty, sent through Lord Howe. In a surprisingly short period of time, the initiative brought results. On 8 August 1795, the Admiralty introduced wholesale changes in the conditions of naval surgeons and made substantial increases in their emoluments. Basic pay remained the same, but a flat sum was added to replace the notorious charge for venereal cures, while the twopence per capita payment was continued to reflect the size of the ship in which a surgeon was employed. The result was that average emoluments went up to £210 a year.[17] Pay for surgeon's mates was likewise increased by £1 a month, giving senior men on 74-gun ships who owned their own instruments £5. There was equally good news on half-pay. The number of those eligible was increased to 320 – effectively including anyone with five years' experience – and the top rate was doubled to 5 shillings a day. Taking into account the financial pressures on the government and the leisurely pace of Georgian bureaucracy, these changes represented an enormous achievement for Trotter.

On 2 June, the British fleet remained hove to among the floating debris of the battle, disposing of the dead, repairing damage to ships and rigging, and securing their prizes. Thomas Trotter was ordered to board each of the captured French ships and report on the men's medical condition. Trotter and the prize crews that were now in control were shocked by the filthy conditions and overcrowding aboard the French ships. All were infected with typhus, *Northumberland* and *Sans Pareil* so badly that many members of the British prize crew caught it and eventually died. The French prisoners brought the disease with them to the British ships and Trotter had to take rapid measures to contain the disease. The sick were isolated, the holds fumigated, the decks cleansed and dried with smoke and fires, and clothes and bedding washed and aired. Even so, when the fleet returned to Portsmouth, five hundred men had to be transferred to Haslar Hospital. Typhus continued to rage among the French prisoners of war even after they had been brought ashore. It did not disappear until the end of September.[18]

In England, news of the British victory was received with enthusiasm. Church bells rang throughout London, ships in the river were covered in flags, the Opera House interrupted its performances to sing 'Rule Britannia', and

---

[17] The new rates gave the surgeon of a third-rate 74-gun ship the following:

	£	s	d
Pay	65	3	6
Compensation for a servant	12	7	8
2d for every man	62		
£5 per 100 men in lieu of venereals	30		
Queen Anne's Bounty (war rate)	43	8	1
Total	212	19	3

Nepean to Stewart and reply, November 1798, NMM, Adm E/47

[18] Journal entries for end of June 1794, Trotter, *Medicina Nautica*, I, 55–6

the windows of every house and public building were illuminated at night in celebration. Lord Howe returned to Spithead on 13 June, to the thunder of gun salutes, the strains of the red-coated band of the Gloucestershire militia playing 'See, the conquering hero comes', and the cheers of the crowd which packed the ramparts to gaze in awe at the battle-scarred ships and their prizes. A fortnight later, King George himself arrived at Portsmouth to salute the victors. He was accompanied by members of the royal family, government ministers and the Board of Admiralty. The following day was sunny with blue skies – ideal for the ceremonial. In the morning, the king went to the dockyard, boarded Lord Howe's own barge and was towed round to inspect the ships at anchor. As he passed, each vessel fired a royal salute and manned the yards with cheering sailors. He then boarded the *Queen Charlotte* to greet an emotional Lord Howe and present him with a sword studded with diamonds. There were rewards for others as well. Vice-Admirals Thomas Graves and Sir Alexander Hood were made barons, the latter choosing to be known as Lord Bridport; three rear admirals and Roger Curtis were made baronets; the captains received gold chains and medals; and there were promotions all round.

But a cloud hung over the ceremony. Dissatisfied with the performance of some of his captains, Lord Howe had avoided giving names in his victory despatch to the Admiralty and limited himself to a bald outline of the action, only mentioning Sir Roger Curtis, Sir Andrew Douglas (the captain of his flagship) and the senior officers who had been wounded or died in the engagement. But four days later, on 6 June, he had written a second despatch that not only gave a more detailed account of the battle but also listed the names of those officers whose conduct he regarded as particularly meritorious. Unfortunately Howe – or to be more precise, Sir Roger Curtis who was widely believed to have written the document – had been careless and omitted the names of a number of people who had performed well. The most notable of these were Rear Admiral Caldwell and Captain Cuthbert Collingwood of *Barfleur*, the flagship of Rear Admiral Bowyer who *had* been mentioned. This had serious consequences, as the contents of the despatch were printed in the *London Gazette*, and the granting of both honours and the victory medal was restricted to those on the list. Lord Howe had tried to cover himself by explaining that he had only named the officers whose actions he had actually seen, and that there were no doubt others whose conduct had been equally admirable. But Collingwood and the other officers whose names had been omitted regarded their exclusion as a slur on their honour and retained a lifelong feeling of resentment.

Lord Bridport takes command

In Britain, the Glorious First of June brought the euphoria of victory, but in France, there was no sense of defeat. The convoy with its vital supplies of grain had arrived safely, and their fleet had fought with revolutionary fervour. The loss of a few ships was a minor consideration. Likewise, Britain was as commercially and politically vulnerable after the battle as before it. In spite of continuing revolutionary disruption, the French navy remained dangerous and aggressive. Within months, its first commerce-raiding squadron was at sea.

With the victory celebrations concluded, the Channel Fleet, first under Howe then under his successor, Lord Bridport, returned to its normal routines. One change was the deployment of a squadron off Ushant, a small wind-swept Atlantic island some 30 miles to the west of the Brittany coast, to support the frigates watching Brest and provide time for the Channel Fleet to arrive if the French tried to break out. But with bad weather and an active enemy, the weakness of the policy of open blockade became daily more obvious. In the first month of 1795, for example, Villaret-Joyeuse managed to sneak out of Brest and captured over a hundred homeward-bound merchant vessels off the Scillies. By the time the Channel Fleet knew what was happening Villaret-Joyeuse was back in port.

Storms continued intermittently for months and, early in February 1795, produced a crisis. Torbay, the principal haven for the Channel Fleet was ideally suited to give protection from the prevailing westerlies, but on the 13th, the wind veered and began to blow with increasing violence from the south-east – right into the bay. At anchor were 34 British line-of-battle ships and 16 frigates. The gale steadily increased in intensity, decks were lashed with sleet, and a heavy swell set in from the seaward. Careering madly with such violence that they threatened to tear their anchors from the ocean bed, the ships faced disaster. Fortunately, anchors and cables held and when the wind eventually moderated, the fleet was safe. But for Lord Howe it was the last straw. Already physically ailing and under strain, the great storm broke his nerve and he begged to resign. The government had just been reshuffled, and the new First Lord of the Admiralty, Lord Spencer, wanted continuity. He therefore refused Howe's request. However, as a compromise, he agreed that the admiral could take leave and command the fleet from Bath or London while his second-in-command, the tetchy Lord Bridport, did all the work at sea. It was not a happy solution. Relations between the two men became tense, Bridport frequently ignored his letters and the clumsy triangular route along which all communications and orders had to pass between the Admiralty, Howe and the fleet caused delays and failures of coordination.

Four months later, in June, came a new threat. Learning that the British were transporting a royalist army to Quiberon Bay to foment rebellion, Villaret-Joyeuse put to sea to intercept the convoy. This he failed to do, but he did find the squadron off Ushant under Vice-Admiral William Cornwallis. Heavily outnumbered, Cornwallis turned and conducted a fighting retreat up the Channel. When news reached Lord Bridport, the Channel Fleet, attended by Trotter in the Hospital Ship *Charon*, put to sea and on 22 June found Villaret-Joyeuse off the Isle de Groix near Quiberon Bay. In a brisk action, Bridport captured three French line-of-battle ships before the enemy fleet withdrew. Anxious to avoid the perils of that wild stretch of coast, Bridport did not follow and contented himself with seeing the invasion force safely landed. From that time on, another small squadron was deployed off Quiberon Bay in support of the rebellion.

If further proof of the inadequacies of open blockade were needed, it came in December 1796, when a French force carrying 15,000 troops under Rear Admiral Morard de Galles took advantage of thick weather to slip out of Brest.

Preparations had been going on for months and the British were well aware of them. What they did not know was its destination. As a result, Bridport had sent two detached squadrons to watch the likely exit routes – one under Sir John Colpoys, the other under Sir Roger Curtis, now a rear admiral. In fact, the expedition's destination was Ireland. In military command was the ruthless revolutionary general Lazare Hoche, accompanied by the impatient Irish patriot Wolfe Tone. Amid appalling weather and winds that scattered their ships, the French arrived in Bantry Bay in a blizzard on 22 December. Eight ships were missing, one of them the frigate on which Morard de Gales and Hoche were travelling. A landing was impossible, so, after a week of gales and snow and still without their commanders, the French limped back to Brest. The expedition achieved nothing; but this was solely due to the weather. Neither Colpoys nor Bridport knew what the French were up to until it was all over.

The Bantry Bay fiasco was the final act of a depressing year. Victorious French armies had swept all before them in the Rhineland and Italy, shattering Britain's ally, Austria, while the newly revolutionized Dutch and the Bourbon Spanish had both joined the French. Britain was exhausted and the government dispirited. Then, to add to its discomfort, in February 1797, a group of French frigates escaped yet again and landed 1500 troops in Fishgard, Wales. Most were former convicts under the leadership of an American adventurer. They were quickly rounded up, but the government was dismayed. Fortunately news arrived soon after of the decisive defeat of a superior Spanish force off Cape St Vincent by the fleet under Sir John Jervis on St Valentine's day. There were stories of derring-do in the battle by up-and-coming Commodore Horatio Nelson. This provided a much-needed tonic to public confidence in the navy, even if it did nothing for the reputation of the Channel Fleet. The only exciting news from home waters was provided by the adventures of separate frigate squadrons operating out of Falmouth.

In April 1797, Howe's resignation as commander-in-chief of the Channel Fleet was accepted at last. Spencer at the Admiralty was disenchanted with Bridport's performance, but had no alternative but to appoint him as his successor. Trotter, to whom Lord Howe was a hero who had supported him in a way that had not been forthcoming from Bridport, was dismayed.

$$\text{---}\ 9\ \text{---}$$

The Conquest of Scurvy

WHILE HOWE AND BRIDPORT played cat and mouse with the French in the Channel, the greatest potential threat to health at sea continued to be scurvy. For decades the navy's operations had been undermined by the disease, which would appear after only six weeks and steadily turn the crew into enfeebled invalids. Even on the outbreak of the Revolutionary War, memories of its devastating impact during the Siege of Gibraltar and Rodney's campaigns in the West Indies were fresh. Yet within a decade, scurvy had been all but overcome and consequent improvement in the navy's health was an important factor in its victories in the Napoleonic Wars. How this came about, and what role Thomas Trotter played in the transformation, will be the subject of this chapter.

'Observations on the Scurvy'

When the Revolutionary War began, Trotter was one of the leading public voices discussing the problem of scurvy. His views had recently been published to favourable reviews in the second, 1792, edition of what he now called *Observations on the Scurvy with a review of the opinions lately advanced on that disease and a new theory defended.* The book ranged over a number of naval diseases, but scurvy remained Trotter's special interest. The revision of the book had given him the opportunity to present his current thinking on the disease.

The causes, he argued, fell into two classes. First, there were the 'predisposing' conditions which did not themselves cause scurvy but made the men vulnerable to it; and second, there were 'occasional' causes, which actually led to its appearance. Trotter had no disagreement with medical men like Lind and Blane, or with naval officers like Curtis, that the 'predisposing' causes comprised a damp and cold atmosphere, foul air, fatigue and an inadequate diet. Like them, experience had also led him to believe that the most vulnerable members of the crew were those with melancholy temperaments and 'lazy, inactive and slovenly people called skulkers'.[1]

It was obvious to Trotter that much of this was inevitable in crowded warships at sea for long periods. When on watch, the men were exposed to rain and spray and frequently came below soaked to the skin. The ships were damp and, in winter, cold. At sea, water was not only taken on board as they

---

[1] Trotter, *Observations*, 41

shouldered their way through the waves, but leaked through the working of their timbers and imperfectly caulked, or sealed, decks. And the dampness of the atmosphere was made worse by the obsession of some officers with swabbing the decks with water. Foul air was just as inevitable when hundreds of men were packed into the poorly ventilated accommodation decks. Another source lay in the tons of sand and shingle ballast that were spread in the lowest part of the hold to maintain stability. Not only did all the dirt washed out of the vessel ooze down to this level, but the ballast itself, especially that taken from the River Thames, was frequently filled with rotting 'animalculae'. There were well-recorded cases of men being suffocated when working in the bowels of the ship. Trotter, who was a keen follower of the new science of chemistry, referred to this gas as 'fixed air', or 'choke-damp', the same term he used for the noxious gases found in coal mines. He was later to make a special study of the subject.

Trotter was not, however, pessimistic. As a true son of the Enlightenment, he was a firm believer that understanding led to 'improvement', and was impressed by the beneficial changes already taking place in the navy. He listed the most significant as the use of wind sails, air pumps and fumigation to remove foul air; the avoidance of excessive deck swabbing and use of portable stoves to dry the atmosphere; and the introduction of the divisional system to keep the men clean, dry and occupied. With typical optimism, he concluded:

> The complete mode of discipline carried out in HM ships at this time throughout the navy is, on the whole, so happily conducted for answering the purpose of the service and securing the health of the ship's company, that it almost anticipates any remark that I have made . . . It is not just health that is the fortunate result of these judicial forms of discipline: the morality of seamen is undergoing a revolution for the better. Nastiness, drunkenness and theft are almost banished from a man of war; the rough sailor is daily losing his ferocity of manners while the true courage which distinguishes the British tar is increased and blends itself with more polished notions of principle and honour.[2]

Trotter may have been in harmony with other medical authorities on the background conditions which encouraged scurvy, but he disagreed with current views on the circumstances that triggered the disease. Experience had made him doubt that scurvy was a disease of putrefaction and sceptical as to the effectiveness of the three 'cures' then in vogue, namely sauerkraut, elixir of vitriol and infusions of malt or wort. In his book, Trotter examined and rejected each in turn. The value of sauerkraut was curtly dismissed. Not only were its effects as an anti-scorbutic 'trifling', but it was far more expensive than the fresh vegetables available in home ports.[3] Its introduction had nevertheless been founded on the practical experience of the Dutch navy. The other

---

[2] Ibid., 171–3
[3] Ibid., 180–1

supposed cures had no such pedigree and were based on abstract theorizing. Elixir of vitriol was given short shrift as a 'mere placebo' which passed through the body with no observable effect.[4] Likewise, the use of malt and wort to stimulate internal fermentation in accordance with the 'fixed air' theories of Dr McBride were dismissed. 'After long analysis', he said, 'I have not seen it attended with any good effect.'[5]

Trotter was also dissatisfied with the writings of Lind and Blane on the subject. While acknowledging their contributions to naval medicine and recommending that their works should have a place in the libraries of the captain of every man of war, he found their views on scurvy inadequate. Trotter applauded the accumulation of data, observations and evidence in favour of the beneficial effects of lemon juice and acid fruits which Blane had produced, but was worried that his work suffered from a lack of enquiry into the reasons. Lind, although Trotter hailed him as 'the father of Nautical Medicine' and repeated many of his recommendations in his own books, came in for greater criticism in relation to scurvy. He had reached accurate conclusions on the benefits of lemon juice whilst on *Salisbury*, even if the effect had been undermined by a problem with the process of producing the concentrated 'rob' which destroyed its benefits. Unfortunately, Lind had become sidetracked by a conviction that the cause of scurvy was the consumption of indigestible salt meat and mouldy water in a damp atmosphere which blocked perspiration, and had decided that the answer to scurvy lay in changing the whole environment rather than making a simple addition to the diet.[6]

Trotter had few complaints as to the quality of the foodstuffs which made up the seaman's rations. Salt meat, he wrote, was now prepared to 'the greatest possible perfection'.[7] Butter and cheese were adequate but constituted a small proportion of what was consumed. The vegetable elements consisted of flour, biscuit, raisons, dried pease, the universally unpopular oatmeal, which was made into burgoo porridge for breakfast, and the no less unpopular sauerkraut. The latter could be easily replaced with a more attractive alternative of pickles and greens; and burgoo could be made attractive and beneficial by adding molasses. A further possibility was the substitution of oatmeal by cocoa and sugar, as had proved popular in the West Indies.

The apparent anti-scorbutic element in beer also attracted Trotter's attention. The use of beer as food as well as medicine had a long pedigree. When at Haslar, Trotter thought that the stronger version of porter was effective and, like his contemporaries, had been struck by the fact that, at sea, scurvy frequently appeared after the beer had run out. The problem was that of volume. A seaman's entitlement was one gallon of beer a day and storage space was limited on warships. Trotter's solution was ingenious – to double the strength and half the allowance.[8]

---

[4] Ibid., 182–5
[5] Ibid., 190
[6] Ibid., 76
[7] Ibid., 204–6
[8] Trotter to Howe, 15 May 1795, NMM, Adm/E/45

Trotter did not, however, see the key to the prevention of scurvy as tinkering with beer. He was now convinced that the immediate causes of scurvy lay in a lack of vegetable matter in the seaman's diet. 'Where it abounds', he added, 'the disease in unknown.'[9] Prevention therefore lay in the ample supply of fresh vegetables, notably greens, onions and leeks, which could be added to beef or pork to form a stew. Other items, like lettuces, radishes and spring onions could be eaten raw as salad; and the salinity of the meat could be corrected by the use of onions, pickles, red cabbage and cucumbers. As regards a cure for scurvy once it had been acquired, he went on:

> From what we ourselves have seen of this disease, or learnt from the writings of authors, we believe that fresh vegetables of all kinds will cure it, and that those fruits abounding with an acid, such as the citrus classes, are more effective than others . . . [Indeed] the superior efficacy of the acid fruit in the cure of scurvy is so well ascertained, that it might seem superfluous to add any fresh remarks to what is so fully admitted.[10]

Why vegetables and citrus acted so powerfully against scurvy was still a mystery. However, Trotter was impressed by the discovery of oxygen by Priestley and had begun to move towards the view that it was the existence of oxygen in acid fruits that purified the system. But in 1792, he was still unsure, later writing

> Whatever, therefore, may be the theory of sea scurvy, we contend that vegetable matter imparts a *something* to the body, fortifies it against the disease: and that in proportion to the quantity of this *something* imparted, making allowance at the same time for external causes which counteract its effect on the constitution, the symptoms will sooner or later disappear.[11]

A modern physician would endorse Trotter's position on vegetables and fruit, notably citrus. By the middle of the twentieth century it had been scientifically established that scurvy was a disease resulting from a deficiency of the vitamin C needed to synthesize collagen in humans. Even if Trotter did not know the reason why, the remedies he was proposing to combat the disease were correct in theory. Unfortunately, there were severe problems when applying them in practice. In particular, green vegetables were seasonal, laborious to obtain, bulky to transport and only storable for a limited time. Likewise, the method he proposed of cooking them in a broth would have reduced the potency of the vitamin C. It was no wonder that, in the event, naval commanders preferred to rely on more easily stored and longer-lasting supplies of lemon juice.

Trotter was not, in fact, an unconditional enthusiast for citrus juice. He called it 'cold and fat-consuming' and believed that it had the side effect of debilitating the system. He was therefore adamant that lemon and other juices should only be used as *cures* for scurvy, and should not be distributed in order to prevent it. Prevention lay in providing ample supplies of fresh vegetables. It

---

[9] Trotter, *Observations*, 40
[10] Ibid., 215, 151
[11] Trotter, *Medicina Nautica*, I, 420–6

was, he wrote twenty-seven years later, all very simple.[12] Indeed, even in 1792, he expressed astonishment that 'scurvy, a disease whose cause and cure are so well ascertained, is still the scourge of long voyages and a sea life'.[13]

The assault on scurvy

Trotter was not the only one to think this way. Based on its practical experiences in Gibraltar and the West Indies, the navy as a whole was coming to the same conclusion and was increasingly impatient with the unwillingness of the medical establishment ashore to recognize the effectiveness of lemon juice. The first step in the path that was to lead to the conquest of scurvy in the Royal Navy was not, therefore, taken by a member of the medical profession, or by Gilbert Blane or any other of Lind's 'disciples'. It was taken by Alan Gardner, now a rear admiral. In December 1793, he asked for a supply of anti-scorbutics for the squadron he was to command in the attack on Mauritius. Like others, Gardner had seen the effects of lemon juice in the West Indies and was uninterested in wort, malt, elixir of vitriol and the other substances that had been foisted on Captain Cook and, indeed, were still being issued to all ships going on distant voyages.[14] Reflecting the growing current of naval opinion, Gardner had written to the Sick and Hurt Board, saying that

> as lemons are, I believe, deservedly acknowledged to be the best anti-scorbutics and being usefully packed will contain their good qualities for several months . . . I must further beg leave to suggest to you whether a few chests of lemons may not be productive of great benefits to the crews of the respective ships.[15]

Significantly, the composition of the board had recently undergone an important change. Earlier in 1793, for the first time, two naval surgeons, Dr Robert Blair and Dr James Johnston, had been appointed to join Sir William Gibbons and Robert Lulman as commissioners. There was an immediate change in style. Previously, commissioners had all been laymen and they had been obliged to seek outside medical advice. The arrival of Blair and Johnston on the board gave it the confidence to make quick decisions without outside reference. It also attuned it more closely to the growing recognition within the navy that the cure for scurvy lay in citrus fruits. Thus, without further ado, the board sent Gardner's proposals to the Admiralty with its support, recommending a supply which would give each man a daily ration of ¾ of an ounce of lemon juice and two ounces of sugar to be taken with ½ pint of rum and one pint of water.[16] The Admiralty agreed and the supplies were made ready. But at the last minute there was a change of plan. In the face of preparations in the French

[12] T. Trotter, *A Practicable Plan for Manning the Royal Navy* (London, 1819), 45

[13] Trotter, *Observations*, 151

[14] For example, *Discovery* was so supplied on 11 February 1791, *Assistance* on 14 June 1791 and *Providence* on 10 January 1794. NMM, Adm E/44a and 45

[15] Gardner to Sick and Hurt Board, 4 December 1793, NMM, Adm FP/36

[16] Sick and Hurt Board to Admiralty, 13 December 1793, TNA, Adm 98/118; and NMM, Adm FP/36

Channel ports, the expedition against Mauritius was cancelled. Only *Suffolk* and the sloops *Argo* and *Swift* under the command of Commodore Peter Rainier remained destined for India. *Charon* accordingly supplied Rainier's ships with the lemon juice and sugar they needed, then began to off-load the rest at Haslar Hospital.[17] Lord Howe then intervened to ask that the remaining supplies be reserved for his ships. As a result they were loaded back onto *Charon*, under the control of the recently appointed physician to the Channel Fleet, Dr Thomas Trotter.[18]

In his new post, Trotter was keen to put his ideas on the prevention and cure of scurvy into action. In his first year, his task was made easier by the way the fleet was deployed, since Howe's policy of open blockade meant that ships spent much of their time in Spithead, Plymouth or Torbay, where supplies of vegetables and fresh meat were available. In the second, Trotter's efforts were frustrated by strategy and the weather. The strategic factor was the pattern of cruising followed by Lord Bridport. As we have seen, instead of spending much of its time in its home anchorages, the Channel Fleet was now deployed in squadrons off the French coast for periods of up to four months, well beyond the time at which scurvy normally appeared. The second factor was the weather. The winter of 1794–5 was the worst ever recorded. From December to March there were severe frosts, bitter cold and deep snow. The Thames and the Medway froze over. In Norfolk, Parson Woodford noted in his journal that the birds fell dead from the trees, that ice on ponds had to be broken to allow livestock to drink, and that his chamber pot was frozen solid. On land, sheep and cattle perished, and not a scrap of greenery or vegetables could be found for miles around the major ports. For months, supplies of fresh meat and vegetable became impossible to procure.

In these conditions, scurvy was inevitable and lemon juice the only answer, imposing enormous strains on the stocks of the Sick and Hurt Board. At the beginning of March 1795, Trotter wrote to the Lord Howe, asking urgently for 100 gallons of lemon juice. A month later he repeated the request and proposed a series of ameliorating measures such as limiting the use of salt beef.[19] The Sick and Hurt Board did its best and sent thirty chests of lemons and oranges, but it was not until the end of May that the juice arrived. Meanwhile, Trotter was forced to rely on the supplies still on *Charon*. When Vice-Admiral Colpoys sailed for a month's cruise in March, he was only able to supply one third of what was needed. Inevitably, scurvy re-appeared. A month later, in April, a squadron left under the command of Rear Admiral Waldegrave. With *Charon*'s stocks of juice now almost exhausted, Trotter bought a dozen chests of lemons in the local markets. Fortunately, Waldegrave was one of those officers who were convinced of the value of citrus fruits and, encountering a Swedish vessel at sea, promptly bought another sixteen chests.[20] When he returned to port two months later, there was not a single case of scurvy in the squadron.

[17]   Admiralty to Sick and Hurt Board, 13 March 1794, NMM, Adm E/45
[18]   Admiralty to Sick and Hurt Board, 23 April 1794, NMM, Adm E/45
[19]   Trotter to Parker, 20 April 1795, NMM, Adm E/45
[20]   Admiralty to Sick and Hurt Board, 12 June 1795, NMM, Adm E/25

Meanwhile, Trotter turned his attention to supplying the fleet with fresh vegetables. Fortunately, the weather had sufficiently improved for supplies to be available. Calculating that 50 pounds of greens and 10 of onions would be needed for each hundred men, he demanded 50 hundredweight of greenstuffs a day for the fleet. Dr James Johnston, the Sick and Hurt Board's commissioner at Haslar, was expected to find them, and was alarmed. He regarded his duty as providing extra items for the sick, not supplying vegetables for the fleet in general. He asked the Sick and Hurt Board for guidance, and undertook to find only 20 hundredweight of greens.[21]

Trotter began to scour the area around Portsmouth for citrus fruit and fresh vegetables himself. He later wrote:

> I took care to inform their Lordships that I had attended the vegetable stalls on market days as well as the gardens in the neighbourhood and there found an abundance for our consumption. . . . The reader may smile at the idea of the Physician of the Fleet attending the stalls at a vegetable market, or perambulating the country to acquire the produce; but it never appeared to me below the dignity of the profession; nor did I consider it a mean task to serve the salad with my own hands from the *Charon*'s quarter deck. The good effects of these refreshments were astonishing; we had only to regret that they were not sent sooner.[22]

Trotter's actions in denuding Portsmouth of supplies of fruit and vegetables did not make him popular with local citizens. As he reported

> A lady of rank, who was in the custom of giving large dinners to small parties, complained that she could no longer procure oranges and lemons for her company. She said 'it is a shame that the nation's money should be expended in this way, Captain P tells me that these things are not good for sailors, and what is worse, this Physician can persuade Lord Howe of anything!'[23]

Supplies of lemon juice arrived from the Sick and Hurt Board just in time to supply each of Bridport's ships with 30 gallons before they sailed in mid-June 1795 to fight the French off the Isle de Groix. Unfortunately, the quantity was inadequate and, in their haste to leave, they had failed to load all the vegetables available. After two months, scurvy broke out again. By mid-September, Bridport's eight largest line-of-battle ships had 1008 cases.[24] At the same time, many of the ships stationed off Quiberon Bay were so weakened by the disease they had to be sent home.

Trotter and *Charon* went with Bridport's fleet when it sailed in June, but the demands on Commissioner Johnston did not stop. He came under pressure from Admirals Colpoys and Waldegrave to supply the fresh vegetables and

[21] Correspondence between Johnston and the Sick and Hurt Board (with annexes), 2–4 June 1795, NMM, Adm F/26, printed in R. Morris, *The Channel Fleet and the Blockade of Brest 1793–1801*, Navy Records Society 141 (Aldershot, 2001), 69–72

[22] Trotter, *Medicina Nautica*, I, 129

[23] Ibid., III, 324

[24] Ibid., I, 125 and 138, Journal entries for 17 August and 20 September 1795

was harangued by individual captains who sent their ships' boats to Haslar, demanding supplies. Johnston had no choice but to find 40 hundredweight of vegetables a day to meet the demand.[25]

That scurvy did not become worse was due to Trotter and *Charon*. The hospital ship was present throughout as part of Bridport's fleet, acting as an isolation ward for those with contagious diseases and ferrying seriously ill or wounded men to hospital ashore. Trotter had ensured that she was supplied with special ingredients for the sick – cocoa, porter, pickles and sauerkraut to make salted provisions more palatable, and milk and eggs for puddings. Increasingly, *Charon* and her successor, *Medusa*, began to shuttle between Portsmouth and the fleet, distributing lemon juice and quantities of fresh vegetables.[26] It was on one of these trips that Trotter suffered an accident that was to incapacitate him, and eventually bring his naval career to an end. The circumstances of the battle off the Isle de Groix have been described in the last chapter. After the engagement, in order to provide the surgeons with what additional assistance he could, Trotter visited the ships, including *Irresistible*, whose captain, James Grindall, had been severely wounded. Clamouring up the steep sides of the line-of-battle ship from a small boat, a sudden lurch threw him off balance, and threatened to pitch him into the sea. In the scramble to hang on, he ruptured himself. It was a devastating development for Thomas Trotter. It almost immediately began to restrict his mobility and activities as physician of the fleet, and left him in pain and discomfort for the rest of this life.

The Sick and Hurt Board found it increasingly difficult to meet the growing demand for lemon juice. By June, its supplies were almost exhausted. In mid-September, when Bridport's scurvy-ridden fleet returned home, Trotter repeated his excursions to the local markets in search of fresh vegetables. Also, in place of lemons he produced 100 bushels of green apples – an addition that he found to be widely popular. These measures were effective and at the end of the year, Trotter was able to report that the scurvy had been contained and that the health of Bridport's fleet was satisfactory. He had proved his point, and was able to write:

> However vague and uncertain the records of naval transactions left this point on former occasions, the late occurrences in the Channel Fleet have sufficiently established the fact that Scurvy can always be prevented by fresh vegetables, and cured effectually by the lemon, or the preserved juice of that fruit.[27]

The point was also taken by the admirals, the captains of the fleet and by the Admiralty. All this was to Trotter's credit. The Sick and Hurt Board, however, was uneasy, taking the view that its responsibilities were restricted to providing food for the sick and procuring citrus juice: it was the job of the Victualling

---

[25] Sick and Hurt Board to Admiralty (with enclosures from Johnston), 15 June 1795, NMM, Adm F/26
[26] Trotter, *Medicina Nautica*, I, 126–7 and 139–40, Journal entries for 17 August and 20 September 1795
[27] Ibid., I, 423

Board to supply vegetables as a routine part of the naval diet. The Admiralty agreed and, when at the end of August orders were sent to re-supply the squadron off Quiberon Bay, it was made clear that the Victualling Board was responsible for the vegetables.[28] Unfortunately for Trotter, when in December he began ordering vegetables for the relief squadron, he was rapped over the knuckles for doing it himself and not 'using the usual channels'.[29]

The triumph of lemon juice

Trotter's argument that fresh vegetables were the best way of preventing scurvy seemed to have won the day. But events now took the issue down another path. In March 1795, news arrived from Commodore Rainier that *Suffolk* and her convoy had successfully arrived in the East. More significantly, *Suffolk* had fewer men on the sick list than when he had left Spithead, and none had scurvy after a voyage of over four months. He attributed this to the daily distribution of lemon juice and sugar. A minor outbreak had been easily dealt with by increasing the ration.[30]

The significance of what had happened was clear and the effect was immediate. In March, Vice-Admiral Sir George Keith Elphinstone was ordered to attack the Dutch colony at the Cape of Good Hope. One of his first acts was to write to the Sick and Hurt Board, asking that a supply of lemon juice be provided to all the ships under his command. The letter is remarkable in that it is identical in wording to that written by Gardner in December 1793. Elphinstone added only five words to Gardner's original letter so that the key paragraph now read

> I must further beg leave to suggest to you whether a few chests of lemons *or a quantity of juice* may not be productive of great benefits to the crews of the respective ships.[31]

The Admiralty agreed. Unfortunately, the citrus juice did not arrive in time, but with Trotter's help, Elphinstone was able to buy fifty chests of lemons before he sailed. This was enough to get the expedition to the Cape, but did not prevent scurvy thereafter. The Admiralty too responded quickly to Rainier's experience. On 21 April, it ordered that *Hector* and *Sheerness*, both 'being prepared for distant service', should be supplied with lemon juice and sugar.[32] From then on, all ships bound for distant stations were so supplied: supplies of malt and wort were dropped.

Trotter's activities had done much to establish lemon juice as the major weapon in the battle against scurvy, but he began to suspect that impatient naval officers wished to issue it as a preventative rather than hold it back as a

[28] Admiralty to Sick and Hurt Board, 27 August 1795, NMM, Adm E/45
[29] Sick and Hurt Board to Admiralty, 9 December 1795, NMM, Adm F/26 and Admiralty to Sick and Hurt Board, 10 December 1795, NMM, Adm E/45
[30] Rainier to Sick and Hurt Board, 29 September 1794, NMM, RAI/4
[31] Elphinstone to Sick and Hurt Board, 19 March 1795, NMM, Adm F/25
[32] Admiralty to Sick and Hurt Board, 21 April 1795, NMM, Adm E/45

cure. In May, he wrote to Lord Howe expressing his concern and suggesting that scurvy would be better prevented by doubling the strength of beer and increasing supplies of fresh meat. The Admiralty sent the correspondence to the Sick and Hurt Board and asked for a definitive opinion.[33]

The board's reply, sent on 27 May 1795, was unequivocal. It was sceptical of Trotter's claims regarding the value of fresh meat and beer as anti-scorbutics, but had no doubts about citrus fruits. Rainier's experience, it wrote, had confirmed that the juices of lemons and limes were 'the most powerful anti-scorbutics in nature', and that 'when taken daily, there had never been an incidence of failure'. It therefore recommended that lemon or lime juice should be supplied daily as 'the best substitute for fresh fruit and vegetables with a salt diet'. True, these items were expensive, but much of the cost could be defrayed by dropping malt and halving the ration of oatmeal.[34]

In June, the Admiralty began to distribute citrus juice and sugar on an *ad hoc* basis. Meanwhile, demand from individual commanders for lemon juice continued to rise. In June 1795, Admiral Duncan of the North Sea Fleet demanded that his ships should be supplied with lemon juice in the same way as Lord Howe's.[35] The Sick and Hurt Board was non-plussed: existing supplies were just not adequate. It temporized, pointing out that citrus juice was supposed to be used when beer and vegetables ran out, and that the North Sea Fleet's proximity to its home ports ought to make this unlikely. But scurvy on Duncan's ships forced the board's hand, and it agreed to supply lemon juice and sugar, though to conserve its dwindling supplies insisted that it be used only for the sick.[36] Then, in August, the Cabinet decided to send 30,000 troops and a naval squadron under Rear Admiral Hugh Christian to attack the French West Indies. It was the largest and best-equipped expedition ever to leave British shores and, on Spencer's instructions, carried ample quantities of lemon juice.[37] In the event, Christian's force was scattered and forced to turn back in November by some of the worst gales the Channel had ever seen; but orders were given that the smaller replacement expedition under Cornwallis should likewise be generously supplied.[38]

In 1796, Spencer's Admiralty was now ready to implement the new policy formally. On 26 January, it wrote to the Sick and Hurt Board saying that 'in view of the proven beneficial effects of lemon juice and sugar . . . it is their Lordships' intention to supply a competent portion of these articles for general use with the fleet when fresh provisions cannot be provided'. The board was ordered to begin procuring them, to give an estimate of costs and indicate

[33] Admiralty to Sick and Hurt Board (with attachments), 19 May 1795, NMM, Adm E/45

[34] Sick and Hurt Board to Admiralty, 27 May 1795, NMM, Adm F/25, printed in Morris, *The Channel Fleet*, 65–8

[35] Admiralty to Sick and Hurt Board, 15 June, NMM, Adm E/45

[36] Sick and Hurt Board to Admiralty, 19 and 24 June 1795, NMM, Adm F/26

[37] Memorandum by Spencer, 25 August 1795, *Barham Papers*, Navy Records Society 32 (London and Colchester, 1910), 4; Trotter and Johnston to Christian, 25 September 1795, J. S. Corbett (ed.), *The Spencer Papers*, Navy Records Society 48 (London and Colchester, 1913), 150–2

[38] Sick and Hurt Board to Admiralty, 1 January 1796, NMM, Adm F/26; Admiralty to Sick and Hurt Board, 25 February 1796, NMM, Adm E/45

which items of diet could now be dropped or changed.[39] The reply came ten days later in a paper significantly entitled *Remarks on the intended supply of lemon juice to the fleet as an article of diet for the prevention of scurvy*. Noting that it was now 'a fact . . . that the daily consumption of lemon juice can prevent scurvy', the board went on to answer the Admiralty's questions. Assuming that 60,000 men would have to be supplied centrally, it estimated that 171,093 gallons of juice and 24,442 hundredweight of sugar would be needed annually. The total cost of these two items would be £112,429, but if the recommended changes in diet were made, the extra cost would fall to £27,997.[40]

The decision to introduce lemon juice and sugar as part of the naval diet was working its way smoothly through the system. By the end of 1796, the details of distribution had been settled. The lemon juice was to be supplied in partitioned boxes similar to those used to transport gin, each containing eighteen round glass bottles with a total capacity of 9 gallons, and the Victualling Board was given responsibility for its distribution. The squeezing and bottling of the juice was, however, judged to be so complex that the Sick and Hurt Board was to remain in charge of supplying it. Finally, instructions to pursers and surgeons were prepared and circulated.[41] At this point, however, the administrative machine lost momentum. This was not due to any lack of enthusiasm for lemon juice in the Sick and Hurt Board. Indeed, in August 1795, Robert Lulman had been succeeded by Gilbert Blane, then head of St Thomas's Hospital in London. Blane had had no part in the board's original recommendation to issue lemon juice and sugar as a regular item of diet, but like Trotter, was an advocate of citrus as a cure for scurvy.[42] Nor did the board lose any of its vigour. In addition to normal duties, it took over responsibility for the appointment of all medical staff, devised new instructions for surgeons, and continued to test the medical profession's latest bright ideas. These included Dr Smyth's system of eliminating contagion by filling ships with gas, Dr Wilkinson's stomach belt, which, it was claimed, would prevent yellow fever, and Dr Patterson's proposals that scurvy could more easily be eradicated by administering an oxygen-producing mixture of nitre and vinegar than by using perishable citrus fruits.[43]

---

[39] Admiralty to Sick and Hurt Board, 26 January 1796, NMM, Adm E/45

[40] Blair to Nepean, 4 February 1796, NMM, Adm F/26, printed in Morris, *The Channel Fleet*, 142–5. The exact costings were based on the supply of 1 ounce of lemon juice and 2 ounces of sugar daily to 60,000 men, giving a total of 171,093 gallons of the first and 24,441 hundredweight of the second. Lemon juice was currently available at 4 shillings a gallon, and sugar at 64 shillings a hundredweight – giving total costs of £34,218 and £78,211

[41] Sick and Hurt Board to Admiralty, 16 February 1796, NMM, Adm F/20; Admiralty to Sick and Hurt Board, 14 March 1796, NMM, Adm E/45; Victualling Board to Admiralty, 27 May 1796, NMM, Adm D/40; Sick and Hurt Board to Admiralty, 9 and 18 November 1796 NMM, Adm F/27

[42] In the standard works, it is curious that historians give credit to Gilbert Blane for this change even though he was not appointed a commissioner until the end of August 1795 – well after the recommendation had not only been made, but was being implemented. Strangely, Blane is likewise given credit for introducing Jenner's smallpox vaccination in the navy as well (see T. Fulford and D. Lee, 'The Jenneration of disease: vaccination, romanticism and revolution', in M. O'Neill and M. Sanders (eds), *Romanticism* (Abingdon, 2006), 322–43) – another assertion for which there appears to be no documentary evidence

[43] Admiralty to Sick and Hurt Board, correspondence between October 1795 and December 1796, NMM, Adm E/45

The problem was that the market in Britain was incapable of supplying such huge quantities of citrus fruit. The Sick and Hurt Board had previously had difficulty in meeting even the amounts needed for curative purposes. Distributions made before July 1795, for example, had left stocks exhausted. The following March, there were only 24,000 gallons in store.[44] If the market had problems in supplying the board with this modest quantity of juice, then a demand of 171,000 was clearly beyond its capacity. Tenders issued in 1796 and 1797 only produced bids to provide 10,000 and 30,000 gallons respectively at prices far in excess of those estimated.[45] The amount available in Britain was quite inadequate. The board realized this, and began to seek new sources in the West Indies and Portugal.

The Admiralty had no choice but to suspend the policy. For the immediate future, general distributions of lemon juice would only be made to ships going on foreign service.[46] As before, fleets in home waters would receive it for curative purposes only. Trotter, who had been opposed to a general distribution from the beginning, welcomed the news. He returned to the fray, stressing the superior properties of fresh vegetables for the prevention of scurvy and recommending that they be issued with double strength beer and molasses.[47]

For the Channel Fleet therefore nothing changed, and regular outbreaks of scurvy continued to occur in spite of Trotter's attempts to supply fresh vegetables. This situation continued for the next four years while the Sick and Hurt Board quietly increased its stocks of citrus fruit. The admirals became uneasy. In July 1799, Rear Admiral Berkeley complained about the poor condition of the Channel Fleet and the illogicality of current policy on the supply of lemon juice. As he pointed out, ships on blockade duty were often at sea without access to a port for far longer that ships on foreign stations.[48] His protest was accepted, and with stocks now healthier, the Sick and Hurt Board recommended that ships on home stations could now receive supplies of lemon juice and sugar, though at only half the rate given to ships on foreign service. The final breakthrough came in 1800. As will be described in the next chapter, Lord St Vincent, who had become an enthusiast for lemon juice, took command in the Channel, and demanded that his fleet should receive the full amount.[49] The Admiralty concurred and decreed that lemon juice should henceforward be issued generally, not just as a cure but as a preventative against the scourge of scurvy. This was not what Thomas Trotter had advocated. 'From the whole of my reports from the surgeons of the ships of the line', he glumly recorded, 'I

---

[44] Sick and Hurt Board to Admiralty, 25 May 1796, NMM Adm F/26 and of 21 November 1796, NMM Adm F/27 printed in Morris, *The Channel Fleet*, 151–2, 158

[45] Sick and Hurt Board to Admiralty, 21 November 1796, NMM Adm F/27 printed in Morris, *The Channel Fleet*, 158; and Sick and Hurt Board to Admiralty, 27 January 1797, NMM Adm F/27

[46] Victualling Board to Admiralty, 8 November 1796, NMM Adm D/40, printed in Morris, *The Channel Fleet*, 157–8

[47] Trotter to Nepean, 5 January 1797, NMM, Adm F/27

[48] Berkeley to Sick and Hurt Board, 1 July and response 19 July 1799, NMM, Adm F/30 printed in Morris, *The Channel Fleet*, 395–6

[49] St Vincent to Admiralty, 10 June 1800, and reply of 21 June 1800, TNA, Adm 1/116 and Adm 2/948 printed in Morris, *The Channel Fleet*, 486, 514

do not find a single fact that can justify the general use of lemon juice as lately administered.'[50]

The effect of lemons on the health of the Royal Navy after 1795 was so dramatic and the subsequent conquest of scurvy so rapid that many have asked why it took the authorities so long to issue citrus juice as a regular item of diet. The original explanation, propagated first by the Victorian sociologist, Herbert Spencer, and re-presented in Lloyd and Coulter's 1961 classic, *Medicine and the Navy*, was that the Sick and Hurt Board, the Admiralty and its admirals negligently ignored the medical evidence presented by Lind, and only eventually introduced lemon juice because his 'disciples', like Trotter and Blane, fortuitously reached senior positions in the service, and were able to persuade them to see sense.[51] In the 1980s, however, writers began to realize that this explanation was too simple, and that a great deal of responsibility lay with the medical establishment for failing to take the evidence for citrus juice seriously and for stubbornly sticking to putrefaction theories. They still argued, however, that admiralty officials and admirals needed persuasion to convince them of the need to issue lemon juice.[52] Nevertheless, whatever version of events was in favour, one element remained consistent – namely the supposed role of Gilbert Blane. On the one hand he was seen as a 'disciple' who kept pushing Lind's findings on the establishment; on the other, he was a gentleman, which meant that the powers that be were prepared to listen to him, whereas they ignored the views of ordinary naval surgeons. Indeed, it is also claimed that Blane was responsible for the Sick and Hurt Board recommendation to the Admiralty to issue lemon juice generally in the navy. Lloyd and Coulter say that it was Blane, 'now a Commissioner' who persuaded 'the Admiralty in 1795 . . . to sanction an issue of juice and fruit on a far more generous scale than ever before'. Carpenter, in his definitive *History of Scurvy and Vitamin C*, refers to 'the recommendation made by the Board, soon after Blane had joined it, that lemon juice be authorized as a regular issue in the Royal Navy'. Even as late as 2003, Stephen Bown in *Scurvy: How a Surgeon, a Mariner and a Gentleman Solved the Greatest Medical Mystery of the Age of Sail*, wrote: 'In 1795 Blane was appointed a commissioner to the Sick and Hurt Board. Using the results of the trial aboard the *Suffolk* and drawing on his own reputation, social standing and intimate acquaintance with many of the lords of the Admiralty, he persuaded the Admiralty to issue lemon juice as a daily ration aboard all Royal Navy ships.'[53]

The role of Blane in this matter is an important element in the 'Lind disciple' theory. Yet there is no truth in it. As has been shown, the Sick and Hurt Board's endorsement of lemon juice, and its recommendation that the Admiralty

---

[50] Trotter, *Medicina Nautica*, III, 390

[51] H. Spencer, *The Study of Sociology* (New York, 1879)

[52] S. F. Dudley, 'The Lind tradition in the Royal Navy Medical service', in C. P. Stewart and D. Guthrie (eds), *Lind's Treatise on Scurvy* (Edinburgh, 1853), 378–9; S. R. Bown, *Scurvy: How a Surgeon, a Mariner and a Gentleman Solved the Greatest Medical Mystery of the Age of Sail* (New York, 2003), 181; D. J. Harvie, *Limeys: The Conquest of Scurvy* (Stroud, 2005), 196

[53] Lloyd and Coulter, *Medicine and the Navy*, III, 321: K. Carpenter, *The History of Scurvy and Vitamin C* (Cambridge, 1986); Bown, *Scurvy: How a Surgeon, a Mariner and a Gentleman*, 181

distribute it generally, was made on 27 May 1795. Blane joined the board three months later in August 1795, by which time the lemon-juice case had been made and won.[54] James Johnson and Robert Blair are the people who deserve credit for this spectacular change of naval policy, not Gilbert Blane. Yet so insidious is the 'Lind disciple' theory that Alan Gardner's decision to demand lemons in December 1793 is also said to have been made due to the influence of, and on 'the advice of his friend Blane', just as Elphinstone's similar request was made 'on the advice' of Trotter.[55] There is no evidence to support either of these assertions.

Likewise, the documents relating to the conquest of scurvy provide no support for the standard story of bureaucratic inertia and eventual enlightenment through the agency of 'Lind's disciples'. On the contrary, the picture which emerges is a quite different one. It shows that the laymen who ran the Admiralty and the Sick and Hurt Board until 1793 were in fact anxious to solve the problem of scurvy, but were totally dependent on specialist advice for a cure. Alas, since the idea of nutritional deficiency was unknown at the time, the physicians who ran the outside medical establishment had difficulty in offering a single solution and, when they did, backed theories of putrefaction that proved to be false trails. Meanwhile, within the navy, officers and surgeons were increasingly becoming frustrated by the lack of progress and by the fact that practical experience had demonstrated to them the effectiveness of citrus juice. As a result, on the outbreak of war in 1793, the admirals took matters into their own hands, insisted, with the backing of the Sick and Hurt Board, whose members now included former naval surgeons, on being supplied with lemon juice, and saw that like-minded men, like Trotter, were appointed as their medical advisers. They needed no persuasion from 'disciples' or anyone else on the subject. Indeed, their conviction of the benefits of lemon juice was the reason for the selection of these medical men, and was not the consequence of it. A radical adjustment of the traditional version of events is called for.

---

[54] The Admiralty informed the Sick and Hurt Board of Blane's appointment on 19 August 1795, NMM Adm E/45
[55] Lloyd and Coulter, *Medicine and the Navy*, III, 320, 322

Shore-Based in Plymouth

The Spithead mutiny

COMING AFTER THE SET-BACKS OF 1796, the victory off Cape St Vincent revived the national spirit and restored confidence in the navy. But the mood did not last. Two months later came news of the worst possible kind – the Channel Fleet had mutinied. On Easter Sunday, 16 April 1797, the seamen refused to sail and announced that the fleet would remain at its anchorage at Spithead until their grievances had been satisfied. The principal demand was for higher pay, but there were calls for improvements in victuals, and in the treatment of the sick and wounded. Rates of pay were a matter of real concern to the men. Army salaries had recently been increased, whereas naval pay had not risen since 1652, and had failed to keep up with rapid rises in the cost of living over the previous two years. There was also an unspoken grumble over the operation of the recent Quota Acts, which required every county to furnish a set number of men for the service. In their anxiety to comply, local authorities had offered anyone who came forward bounties amounting to £40, £50 and, in one instance, £64. Since the normal bounty for a volunteer able seaman was £5, there was a wave of resentment at a system which heaped riches on untrained landsmen while denying it to those with real skills.

The mutiny was in modern terms a strike and a collective decision to down tools. It was well organized and co-ordinated by a group of delegates, two elected by each ship. It was also moderate in its aims and comparatively non-violent. Discipline was maintained and normal routines carried out – even to the extent of firing salutes to mark the king's birthday and visits by foreign royalty. Complaints over conditions had been stirring for months. Indeed, Lord Howe had received a number of anonymous petitions from individual ships as early as February, but they fell victim to the three-legged correspondence between Howe in Bath, the Admiralty in London and Bridport in Portsmouth.

Bridport advised a conciliatory approach and, in private, ministers were said to be sympathetic to the seamen's demands. Within a week, the government agreed to increase naval pay, and began to prepare a royal pardon for all involved in the incident. However, the legal process took too long and, on 7 May, the mutiny broke out again. This time there was bloodshed when the mutineers were fired upon. The seamen were angry and over a hundred officers were ejected from their ships. Fortunately, the necessary legislation was now in place, and, wishing to avoid further confrontation, the Admiralty played its trump card – Lord Howe. In spite of his age and his gout, the old admiral travelled down to Portsmouth and was rowed from ship to ship, listening to the men's demands and trying to convince them of the government's good faith. On 15 May he succeeded, and the mutiny ended with a celebratory procession and banquet. Two days later the Channel Fleet was back at sea.

Thomas Trotter was a witness to all these events, but avoided mentioning them in the journal he later published in his *Medicina Nautica*. Indeed, the only reference he made to the mutiny at the time was to register annoyance that the men had complained of the lack of fresh vegetables in the diet and the inadequacy of care for the sick. He was upset and confronted the mutineers, later writing:

> From my firſt appointment to the laſt hours in which I served in the fleet, my utmoſt exertions were employed to give the sick all the comforts which a sea life is capable of. The hospital ship of the fleet was even ſtored with delicacies and a bill of fare such as no hospital in Europe at this moment can equal. Even the supply of vegetables was more than anticipated by my own advice two years before. In the new medical arrangements of the ships and hospitals, the Admiralty had aĉted with unbounded benevolence . . .
>
> When I remonſtrated with the delegates, as the leaders of the mutiny ſtyled them selves, for this part of their conduĉt, they seemed abashed: and when they saw the comforts which were provided for them in the Medusa hospital ship they were aſtonished. These complaints concerning the sick were therefore never more heard in the service.[1]

Some elements within the government were convinced that the mutiny was concerned with more than a desire to improve pay and conditions and had a subversive political dimension. They saw the machinations of French sympathizers and United Irishmen behind the disturbances. While it is true that the mutiny which subsequently broke out at the Nore had a more political tone, no convincing evidence has ever been produced to show that these fears were justified. Indeed, Aaron Graham, the London magistrate sent to Portsmouth to carry out secret investigations into connections between the Spithead mutineers and republican agitators and propagandists, found nothing of any substance. Thomas Trotter, who was present from the beginning to the end of the whole business, was of the same view. As he later explained:

> It has been thought that seamen are a body of men not capable of much refleĉtion; and seldom found to aĉt with consiſtency and decision. This opinion, however, in the present business was proved to be erroneous. The founders of the mutiny were all men about middle age, married and had children. Their families were daily claiming relief from them: provisions for the two preceding years, 1795 and 1796, had been enormously high, and they found themselves ſtarving . . . By this account it will appear that the original cause of the mutiny was a seaman's grievance, and not to be charged to the levelling doĉtrines of the times.[2]

---

[1]   Trotter, *A Practicable Plan*, 26–7
[2]   Ibid., 22–3 and 27

Fortunately for the British, the Directory that then ruled France was too pre-occupied with its own troubles to take advantage of the disarray at Spithead and then the Nore. It was the navy of their ally, the Dutch, who posed the real threat. In October, it put to sea, and was defeated by the North Sea Fleet under Admiral Duncan in a bloody engagement off Camperdown. Like the Battle of St Vincent, it gave the nation a much-needed tonic. The fleet which only months before had been in a state of mutiny had not only returned to its duty, but had achieved a hard-fought victory. More were to follow. But by now the spotlight had turned southwards. Moulded into a formidable fighting machine by the discipline and iron will of Sir John Jervis, now ennobled as Lord St Vincent, the Mediterranean Fleet attacked Tenerife, then blockaded Cadiz. In 1798, it returned to the Mediterranean to look into reports of a huge French force mobilizing in Toulon. This was, of course, the expedition aimed at occupying Egypt and ultimately threatening British interests in India led by the Directory's leading general, Napoleon Bonaparte. Arriving too late to pre-vent the army's embarkation in May, a division of St Vincent's fleet under Rear Admiral Horatio Nelson scoured the Mediterranean looking for it. It reached Egypt too late to prevent a French landing but, finding their fleet at anchor in Aboukir Bay, attacked immediately and achieved a victory of unprecedented proportions. Britain exploded in relief and joy, and Nelson became a national icon.

The Bridport years: into the shadows

In contrast to their colleagues in the Mediterranean, the operations of the Channel Fleet generated neither glory nor excitement. Bridport was now in his seventies and was becoming increasingly pessimistic and prickly. Short of frigates and battered by gales, he continued the policy of loose blockade that proved unable to prevent supply ships entering the French ports or war-ships from leaving them. In August and September 1798, there were two more attempts to land in Ireland, the first led by General Humbert, the second by Commodore Bompart. In April 1799, a fleet under Admiral Bruix evaded Brid-port and sailed south for Spain. In August he returned with a joint Franco-Spanish fleet of forty line-of-battle ships. Worried by Bridport's health and his ability to deal with such a threat, Lord Spencer at the Admiralty decided that Bridport had to go. In April 1800, Lord St Vincent succeeded him in command of the Channel Fleet.

The relegation of the Channel Fleet to the sidelines was paralleled by Tho-mas Trotter's own situation. Up to 1797, Trotter had been highly effective, both in terms of the health policy of the fleet and of influencing wider issues. His recommendations on the organization of hospitals, his proposals for improv-ing the pay and conditions in the naval medical branch, and his advocacy of vegetables and lemon juice as a two-handed answer to scurvy, had been acted on with surprising speed. Indeed, the appointment of naval surgeons to the Sick and Hurt Board in 1793 echoed the proposals to professionalize the naval medical service made in his 1790 leaflet *A Review of the Medical Services of the British Navy with a Method of Reform Proposed*. Trotter's success was rooted in his knowledge of naval affairs and the practicality of his proposals, but the key to his effectiveness was the fact that he had acquired the support and backing of a powerful patron. With Lord Howe behind him, Trotter had been able to punch well above his weight.

After 1797, all this changed. Trotter's first problem was the hernia he had suffered boarding *Irresistible* at the Isle de Groix. Now, he was unable to perform his duties at sea. Instead of accompanying the fleet and being in close contact with the commander-in-chief, Trotter was left behind in Portsmouth or Plymouth. With Howe this might not have been a problem, but Lord Bridport was a more formal kind of commander. If Trotter had been at the admiral's side, he would have been able to make him aware of the medical imperatives. But he was not, and they went by default. In March 1798, for example, Bridport decided, without consulting Trotter, that he no longer needed a hospital ship.[3] *Medusa* was converted into a troop transport. From then on, Trotter's name was included in the crew list of the three-decker *Atlas*, though the muster book shows that he was only on board when the ship was at anchor in Plymouth or Cawsand Bay.[4] Five months later, Bridport wrote to the Admiralty suggesting that Trotter could be usefully employed ashore checking the quality of foodstuffs, sitting on medical boards and supervising the treatment of the fleet's sick in the naval hospitals. Spencer balked at passing these suggestions on to Trotter, sensing that such duties were insultingly routine for a physician.[5] Ironically, lacking guidance as to his duties, Trotter made himself useful by doing much of what Bridport had suggested.

St Vincent and the Mediterranean discipline

The arrival of Lord St Vincent as new commander-in-chief in April 1800 provided Trotter with an opportunity. Sixty-five years old, grim and smitten with gout, St Vincent was then the most formidable and demanding of commanders with a reputation as a savage disciplinarian. Although capable of personal acts of kindness and humour, the face he presented to the world was that of a stickler for detail who drove himself hard, who suffered fools not at all, and who ruled officers and men alike through fear. Of modest social origins himself, he had little respect for those whose main qualification for promotion was connections with the aristocracy; and, having been hard-up for most of his career, he was dismayed that when riches fell his way following the capture of French West Indian Islands in 1794–5, he and his co-commander, General Sir George Grey, had been censured by the House of Commons for their financial activities. As commander-in-chief, he had drilled the Mediterranean Fleet into a fighting machine that had triumphed over the Spanish in the battle he had adopted as his title. Now, to the dismay of many captains, St Vincent began to impose the same discipline in the Channel, introducing a fierce management style and a system of close blockade that tested the fabric of his ships and the

[3]   Bridport to Trotter, 16 March 1798, NMM, MS 62/111
[4]   Muster Roll of *Atlas*, TNA, Adm 36/12163 and 36/12164
[5]   Bridport to Spencer, 27 August 1798 and reply, British Library, Althorpe MSS

Fig. 8. Admiral Lord Bridport. Stipple engraving by S. Freeman
after Lemuel Francis Abbot. © National Maritime Museum, London

nerves of his officers. He was also determined to keep the men healthy. In the
Mediterranean, St Vincent had inherited both Hood's practice of supplying
vegetables, onions and lemon juice, and his fleet physician, Dr John Harness.
By the time St Vincent took command in the Channel, he had become an
enthusiast for citrus juice and, in June 1800, ensured that it should be issued
generally to the Channel Fleet instead of being restricted to the sick.[6]

The new commander-in-chief must therefore have been delighted with his
first letter from the Channel Fleet's physician. In it, Trotter warned of the dangers of malingering and desertion and the need to avoid hospitalization which
often resulted in men being returned to their ships with infected clothing and

[6] St Vincent to Admiralty, 10 June 1800, and reply of 21 June 1800, TNA, Adm 1/116 and Adm
2/948, printed in Morris, *The Channel Fleet*, 486, 514

Fig. 9. Admiral Lord St Vincent. Engraving by H. Robinson
after John Hoppner

bedding. He proposed that in future no man should be invalided without his personal authority; that surgeons should be required to report regularly to him as in the past; and that a careful watch should be kept on infected material brought from hospitals. The admiral promptly accepted his proposals.[7] St Vincent was also appreciative of Trotter's efforts in supplying vegetables to unhealthy ships on their arrival at Plymouth, but stressed that they should never remain longer than their orders allowed. Alas, the harmony was not to last. In July, there was confusion over the provision of fresh supplies to *Superb* and *Temeraire*, and their departures were delayed. Assuming that Trotter was responsible, St Vincent fired the following broadside:

[7] Trotter to St Vincent, 10 May 1800, St Vincent to Admiralty, 14 May 1800, TNA, Adm 1/116

I very much disapprove your officious interference to prevent His Majesty's
ships under my command from putting to sea the moment their beer, water
and provisions are complete, which is ordered to be done with the utmost
possible dispatch, and I desire you will discontinue this practice.[8]

For St Vincent, the wording of the letter was unremarkable and no different
from the normal language he used when addressing erring subordinates. Trotter, however, was deeply upset. He refused to reply, withdrew cooperation and
avoided any further communication with the commander-in-chief. St Vincent
seems to have been surprised by Trotter's reaction. In a letter recommending
him to his successor, the Hon. William Cornwallis, he later explained in a
slightly puzzled tone that Trotter had taken 'offence at my presuming to differ
from him in opinion touching the length it was necessary to retain ships in
port to refresh their crews'.[9]

The confrontation did not stop there. In October 1800, St Vincent issued a
'General Memorandum' encouraging ships' captains to ensure that sailors wore
flannel next to the skin as a preventative measure against catarrhs, coughs and
colds. The wording was unfortunate in that it contained a diatribe directed
against the medical service:

He most seriously exhorts the captains of the ship composing the fleet under
his command, to inculcate this doctrine in the minds of their surgeons; who
from caprice and perverse opposition to every wholesome regulation grossly
neglect this important duty.

Trotter interpreted St Vincent's reproach as an insult to his reputation and to
that of his colleagues. He commented:

They are a respectable body of professional men; faithful and humane in the
discharge of their office; and earning the humble pittance that they receive
from their country with as much integrity as any class of men whatever. Men
that had received a share of polite, as well as medical education, could not but
be deeply wounded by the language of this order.[10]

Trotter's time as St Vincent's physician of the fleet had lasted only two
months. To fill the vacancy afloat, the commander-in-chief moved the surgeon of the *Ville de Paris*, Dr Andrew Baird, to the flagship *Royal George*.
Baird was a well-known advocate of citrus juice, and his views coincided
with St Vincent's. The admiral's concern with good health paid dividends,
and when the fleet returned in September after a cruise of 121 days, only
sixteen men had to be sent ashore on health grounds. The sick quarters
which had been prepared in the expectation of legions of invalids remained
empty. This success had been built on improvements made by Trotter, and
it was unfortunate that the admiral's secretary Benjamin Tucker, who had

[8] St Vincent to Trotter, 13 July 1800, COR/11, printed in Morris, *The Channel Fleet*, 533
[9] St Vincent to Cornwallis in 1803, quoted in Lloyd and Coulter, *Medicine and the Navy*, 166
[10] Trotter, *Medicina Nautica*, III, 93–6

no knowledge of his work, attributed it entirely to the efforts and skill of Andrew Baird.[11]

Trotter's inability to go to sea and his estrangement from Bridport and St Vincent removed his power base. His proposals to the Admiralty were now little different from those that were regularly received from other medical luminaries and had to be evaluated like everyone else's. The fact that the Sick and Hurt Board no longer consisted of laymen but comprised three medically qualified commissioners hindered rather then helped the acceptance of Trotter's proposals. Indeed, a disadvantage in the new system which soon became apparent was that members began to disagree strongly over professional issues. Relations between Dr Robert Blair and Dr Gilbert Blane were particularly acrimonious. During the preparation of the new *Instructions to Surgeons* that were eventually issued in July 1800, Blair even walked out, refused to cooperate and wrote a long letter to the Admiralty denouncing many of the changes. The reply of his colleagues was no less caustic.[12] Blair then resigned in a huff. With opinion within the board divided, it was unlikely that suggestions from Trotter would be automatically approved. His proposals that shortages of lemon juice could be compensated for by doubling the strength of small beer were twice dismissed;[13] his proposal that apples should be supplied in the absence of citrus fruit got nowhere;[14] and his recommendation that a separate building should be built at Haslar for smallpox cases was rejected. The board preferred the cheaper alternative of sealing off part of the existing building by bricking up some of the doors and entrances.[15]

Trotter was, however, becoming increasingly aware that the campaign against scurvy was being threatened by a shortage of citrus fruits, and by their comparatively brief shelf life. In the spring of 1800, he learnt that a chemist working in Temple Bar, called Coxwell, had produced a crystallized form of lemon juice. Trotter obtained a sample, satisfied himself as to the chemistry and recommended it to the Admiralty. At the request of the Sick and Hurt Board, Trotter provided technical details and, during the summer, tested the substance on *Superb*, *Ajax* and *Renown*.[16] Meanwhile, the board asked Sir Roger Curtis at the Cape of Good Hope and Lord Hugh Seymour in the West Indies to conduct trials.[17] Unfortunately, distance and administrative problems intervened. Curtis failed to take action, and nothing was heard from the West Indies, where Seymour had died. Only when his papers were examined in January 1802 was a report discovered on a trial held on *Cambridge* six months previously. It was, alas, unfavourable.[18] This, plus the proximity of peace, put

---

[11] Tucker II, 33, 207, *Naval Miscellany*, Navy Records Society 92 (London and Colchester, 1952), 478
[12] Blair to Nepean, 20 December 1798; Sick and Hurt Board to Nepean, 4 January 1799, both NMM, Adm F/29
[13] Sick and Hurt Board to Admiralty, 27 May 1795 and 5 January 1797, NMM, F/26–7
[14] Sick and Hurt Board to Admiralty, 3 October 1801, NMM, F/32
[15] Sick and Hurt Board to Admiralty, 29 September 1797, NMM, E/46
[16] Trotter to Admiralty, 10 July, 19 July, 28 September 1800, NMM, E/47
[17] Sick and Hurt Board to Admiralty, 14 July 1800, NMM, F/31
[18] Sick and Hurt Board to Admiralty, 27 January 1802, NMM, F/32

paid to the idea. Alas, whether this was a lost opportunity will never be known, as the claims made for the crystals have never been confirmed.[19]

Hospitals and fumigation: tilting at windmills

Shore-based, and with time on his hands, Trotter began to get involved in areas that were only loosely connected with his responsibilities. Following his time at Haslar and the publication of his *Remarks on the Establishment of Hospitals and Sick Quarters*, he saw himself as an expert on the subject and there was much in the naval hospital at Plymouth with which he disagreed. At first he was circumspect, but in early 1799 there were outbreaks of typhus on *Saturn*, *Captain* and *St Uranie*. As physician of the fleet, he was entitled to check on the progress of seamen who had been hospitalized. Now, he became a regular and increasingly unwelcome visitor, complaining that men were being sent back to their ships with infected clothes and bedding; that patients complained about nauseous wine and poor food; that there were delays in treatment. He also clashed with his colleagues over diagnoses. On 23 October, the hospital's physician, Dr Walker, formally complained about Trotter's interference, and Captain Creyke, the naval commander of the hospital, sought him out and challenged his right to be there.[20] The Admiralty supported Creyke, and Trotter was banned from visiting without the permission of the physician.[21]

Another windmill at which Trotter tilted was Dr Carmichael Smyth's proposal to eliminate contagion on warships by using fumigation. It was commonly agreed that diseases like typhus, typhoid and malaria were spread by foul air. Smyth was convinced that the rapidly advancing science of chemistry could provide an answer. His proposal was that the holds of infected ships should be impregnated with nitrous gas, which would result in the double benefit of neutralizing the offensive vapours in the atmosphere while at the same time reacting with them to produce oxygen. The Sick and Hurt Board, faced with increasing typhus in the fleet as forced recruitment brought in the sweeping of the slums and the prisons, was keen to try out his idea. The system was used on the hospital ship *Union* in November 1795, and was ordered for ships of a typhus-riddled Russian squadron operating with the North Sea Fleet the following February.[22]

In June 1797, nitrous fumigation was used on the frigate *Niger* in Plymouth. Trotter got wind of it and was horrified. In a long letter to the Admiralty, he argued that the answer to contagion lay in cleansing ships, men and clothing, expelling the infected atmosphere, and replacing it with fresh air. In his view, Smyth's system was impractical, the production of breathable oxygen was uncertain, and the chemical agent he favoured was 'the very substance

[19] Carpenter, *History of Scurvy*, 91, 234, 251

[20] Sick and Hurt Board to Admiralty, 23 November 1799; Trotter to Admiralty, 24 October 1799; Walker to Creyke, 23 October 1799, NMM, F/30

[21] Admiralty to Sick and Hurt Board, 1 November 1799, NMM, E/47

[22] Admiralty to Sick and Hurt Board, 19 November 1795 and 16 February 1796, NMM, E/45. Smyth published *An Account of the Experiment made at the Desire of the Lord of the Admiralty on Board the Hospital Ship Union* (London, 1796) to celebrate the success of the test

that every intelligent officer is hourly employed to drive from the decks of HM ships'.[23] Experiments nevertheless continued. After trials on *Maidstone* in September, the Admiralty ordered that it should now be used on all ships sailing for foreign stations.

Trotter was too preoccupied in 1797 to do more than denounce fumigation in his *Medicina Nautica*, but a visit in November to the frigate *Nymphe*, which was being treated with Dr Smyth's method, stimulated another letter to the Admiralty. This time he pulled no punches. Fumigation was, he wrote 'useless and ineffective'; and he recommended that trials should be discontinued as 'this branch of Medical Practice entirely rests on speculative ideas on the nature of contagion'.[24] Trotter's views had no effect and, in the Sick and Hurt Board's new *Instructions to Surgeons*, Smyth's system was endorsed. Smyth was later awarded a prize of £5000 for his work. Trotter switched his attack to the pages of the *Medical and Physical Journal*, becoming involved in a debate with one of Smyth's supporters, a Dr Yeats.[25] What becomes clear from these exchanges was that the science of chemistry was insufficiently advanced to provide conclusive evidence one way or the other. Carmichael Smyth's fumigation method enjoyed a brief period of popularity, but by the 1830s it was widely recognized that although effective as a disinfectant, the vapour was so acrid and abrasive that it could only be used in empty spaces.[26] It was eventually replaced by less harmful procedures such as the carbolic acid spray.

The argument over fumigation provides an insight into Thomas Trotter's attitude at this stage in his career. He was not yet forty years old but, as physician to the Channel Fleet under Lord Howe, he had carried responsibility for the health of the crews at a crucial time, and had been instrumental in converting an array of theories about scurvy into a programme of action that established vegetables and citrus juices as routine parts of the naval diet. Unfortunately, as Trotter's hernia became more incapacitating and his declining influence more apparent, he became increasingly cantankerous. His exchanges with Dr Yeats over the best way to cleanse the foetid atmosphere of crowded warships were examples of this trait, concluding with the assertion that Smyth would rather leave to

> a court physician the indelicate task of purifying foul utensils which a cleanly nurse at Haslar Hospital or a decent London chamber maid would effectively correct with soap and water and throwing up the sashes, . . . to the entire discredit of this new-fangled prophylactic, and the utter confusion of all medical necromancy.[27]

This growing feature of Trotter's style was not lost on the critics. Discussing volume three of *Medicina Nautica*, the *Monthly Review* commented:

[23] Trotter to Admiralty, 2 July 1796, NMM, E/45
[24] Trotter to Admiralty, 4 November 1797, NMM, E/46. The definitive account of Smyth's system was published in 1799 under the title *Effects of Nitrous Vapours in destroying contagion*
[25] Trotter to the Editors of the *Medical and Physical Journal* 3 (January–June 1800), 1 February 1800
[26] Society for the Diffusion of Useful Knowledge, *Penny Cyclopaedia* 15 (London, 1839)
[27] Trotter to the Editors of the *Medical and Physical Journal* 3 (1800), 245–7, 429–33 (4 May 1800)

The author takes much pains to endorse, whenever he can, the attention to proper ventilation as the best means of preventing and removing fevers; . . . but he can never do this without at the same time throwing out very harsh observations against the use of mineral acids as destroyers of infection. This seems to be a favourite and lasting ground of invective with Dr Trotter; who, on the subject of contagion, seems to have acquired an extraordinary degree of irritability.[28]

It was not an unreasonable comment.

———•———

[28] *Monthly Review and Literary Journal* 44 (1804), 194

Honours and Half-Pay

Trotter's estrangement from Bridport and St Vincent removed him from any involvement in the day-to-day health problems of the Channel Fleet, but it gave him the time he needed to make a longer-term impact through his writings. In 1796, he had produced *Medical and Chemical Essays*. It was a short work containing discussions of scurvy among convicts in New South Wales, a case of heart disease at Haslar, and methods of keeping water 'sweet' at sea. Following its publication, Trotter began work on what was to become his major contribution to naval medicine. It was entitled *Medicina Nautica: an Essay on the Diseases of Seamen* and was clearly seen by its author as an important work. The operations of the Channel Fleet, he explained in the preface, provided an unparalleled field of investigation from which valuable conclusions could be drawn about a range of maritime diseases, including scurvy. The book would be of value both to specialists and to medical readers in general and would be based upon practical experience rather than theory.[1]

Trotter followed some of Blane's statistical methods in his work, but prided himself on producing a more profound examination of the subject. Volume one, which was published in 1797, comprised a chronological journal or 'General Abstract' detailing the operations and health of the Channel Fleet from 1794 to 1796; two 'Discourses', one of which dealt with the organization of naval hospitals, the pay and conditions of the naval surgeons, the character of seamen, uniforms, diet, recruitment and impressment; the other with maritime diseases, notably ague, typhus, yellow fever, rheumatism, dysentery and scurvy. With that completed, Trotter turned his attention to compiling volume two. Following the same format, he continued the story with a general abstract of the Channel Fleet's health and activities up to 1799; followed it with a section which dealt with contagion, ventilation and fumigation; and concluded with case histories of pioneering surgical operations. Trotter's hope that *Medicina Nautica* would become an important contribution to thinking on naval medicine seems to have been realized. A second edition was soon published and was immediately translated into German.

Meanwhile, having returned to duty as physician of the fleet, Trotter continued to make a positive contribution to the health of the fleet in two areas, the eradication of smallpox, and the closing of large numbers of gin shops in Plymouth.

---

[1] Trotter, *Medicina Nautica*, I, Introduction

The taming of smallpox

Smallpox regularly occurred in the navy. The disease was less widespread than typhus or scurvy, but its effect was more deadly and it could spread rapidly on a crowded warship. Trotter believed its occasional appearance was inevitable as the disease was endemic on land, and ships could never be isolated from the shore. In port, there were constant comings and goings by wives, bumboat women, boat crews and workmen. Trotter estimated that 10 per cent of seamen had never had smallpox or its milder variant, cowpox, and were therefore vulnerable.

It was known that protection from the disease could be acquired by some form of vaccination – that is, by deliberately introducing matter infected with smallpox into an individual so as to promote a mild reaction and subsequent immunity. Aristocratic travellers like Lady Worsley Montague had brought the technique back with them from Turkey early in the century, but its use had been limited to members of the royal family and the upper classes. Announcements advertising the service appeared in London and provincial newspapers, but demand was variable as many feared the procedure or objected to it on religious grounds. Forward-looking surgeons occasionally experimented with it on ordinary folk. It was tried out in Newgate Gaol, and in both the army and the navy. However, once detected, the standard response to smallpox was to do nothing more than segregate the patient and allow the disease to run its course.

With smallpox regularly appearing in ships of war, it is no surprise that Trotter had tried out this form of vaccination on *Charon* and *Orion* as early as 1794. The disease appeared over a hundred times during his time as physician to the Channel Fleet, and in the first volume of *Medicina Nautica* he urged that vaccination should be introduced into the navy, supported by an educational campaign aimed at winning over the seamen.[2] At that stage the idea was in advance of its time, and introducing even small quantities of smallpox into the body was risky – but things were about to change. Working in Gloucestershire, Dr Edward Jenner observed that agricultural workers who had had the milder disease of cowpox were immune to smallpox. During the 1790s, he had carried out a number of experiments in which patients were infected with cowpox then, after the symptoms had subsided, with smallpox. As a result, he was able to establish on a scientific basis that inoculation with cowpox did indeed give immunity against smallpox, that the reaction was mild, and that the disease was not transmitted through bad air. His results were published in his *Inquiry into the Causes and Effects of the Variolae Vaccinae* in 1798, and were confirmed in an analysis by a Dr Pearson which appeared later the same year.

Jenner's work was controversial but its importance to the navy was quickly appreciated. Trotter added a section reporting developments in the second volume of *Medicina Nautica* and he and a growing number of naval surgeons began to apply pressure in favour of introducing the new-style vaccination. When Trotter reported the appearance of smallpox on *Cumberland*, *Gibraltar*

---

[2] Ibid., 386–9

and then *Ville de Paris*, he used the opportunity to recommend it.[3] Others added their weight. Surgeon Veich of *Magnificent*, who had recently returned from the West Indies and had looked into the new development on arrival, wrote advocating its adoption.[4] Surgeon Weeks of *Argonaut* complained of the high incidence of the disease among newly joined marines and proposed that all recruits should be vaccinated.[5] Surgeon Moffatt of *Endymion* introduced the system himself, was successful, and wrote recommending that it be introduced generally in the fleet.[6] In July, the Sick and Hurt Board authorized trials on *Triumph*, but so strong had the pressure become that on 15 September 1800 it endorsed the proposal, and the Admiralty accordingly ordered that vaccination should be made available to any seaman in the fleet who wanted it.[7]

Naval surgeons quickly took advantage of the ruling. It was used on individual ships and Gibraltar was the location of the first mass vaccination. Although it was voluntary, persuasion no doubt helped to secure a wide coverage. The results were good, and Trotter organized a subscription among the surgeons of the fleet in order to present a suitable token of appreciation to Dr Jenner. A gold medal was selected and the following February it was sent with a congratulatory letter to Jenner, asking him to accept it in the name of the surgeons of the navy, which began:

> I am confident that no token of respect bestowed on a benefactor of the human race was ever conferred from more honourable or disinterested motives. It will not be less acceptable to Dr Jenner that it comes from a body of officers connected, by the exercise of their profession, with the most brilliant period of our naval history.[8]

The solid support given to his vaccination theory by the navy and the award of the gold medal, which was the first public acknowledgement of its importance, must have been greatly appreciated by Jenner, who had begun to encounter the hostility of a number of sceptics. To make sure that neither these criticisms nor the recent change of government should cause any alteration in naval policy, at the end of February 1801 Trotter wrote via Sir Thomas Troubridge at Plymouth to the Admiralty, now headed by Lord St Vincent, rehearsing the threat posed by smallpox, and reiterating that vaccination, which had now been 'approved by the best physicians of the age', should continue in use.[9] Fortunately, the benefits of vaccination were so clear that there was no going back, and the navy continued to apply the technique, though only on a voluntary basis, for the next fifty years.

[3] Trotter to Admiralty, 14 and 23 August 1800, NMM, F/31
[4] Sick and Hurt Board to Admiralty, 7 August 1800, NMM, F/31
[5] Sick and Hurt Board to Admiralty, 2 September 1800, NMM, F/31
[6] Sick and Hurt Board to Admiralty, 13 Sept 1800, NMM, F/31
[7] Sick and Hurt Board to Admiralty, 15 Sept 1800, NMM, F/31 and endorsement, printed in Morris, *The Channel Fleet*, 559
[8] Trotter to Jenner, 20 February 1801, printed in Dr Alexander Cockburn's address to the Harveian Society, 12 April 1845, giving a 'Biographical sketch of the late Dr Thomas Trotter, Physician to the British Fleet', *Edinburgh Medical Journal* 64 (1845), 430–41
[9] Admiralty to Sick and Hurt Board with Trotter's letter, 28 February 1801, NMM, E/48

Dissipation and gin shops

During his last months with the Channel Fleet, St Vincent continued to drive forward his measures for improving the health of the fleet. Bedding was aired and decks dry-scrubbed to keep down the damp; soap was issued to the men to enable them to wash; and the pig sties were moved from the forecastle so that it could be used as a dispensary. One of St Vincent's captains, John Markham, introduced a further improvement by moving the sick bay from the orlop deck into the forecastle so that the sick could benefit from air, light and the proximity of the galley stove. In June 1800, the debilitating effects of rum on the health of the men became St Vincent's target. The Sick and Hurt Board sympathized, and increased the supply of malt liquor and wine so as to replace spirits in the fleet.[10] A month later St Vincent turned his attention to the opportunities for debauchery when the crews went ashore, writing 'their only gratification [is] in getting beastly drunk with ardent spirits in the lowest brothels, from whence they return to their ships with their blood in a state to receive every disorder arising out of such practices'.[11]

Trotter had every opportunity to see what happened when the fleet was in. Every ship or squadron that arrived in Plymouth disgorged hordes of sailors, jaded after months of blockade duty and eager for booze and women. Hundreds of public houses opened to meet the demand until the streets of the town were filled with them. Trotter had long been a critic of the issue of ardent spirits and had regularly advocated the benefits of beer and wine. Now he saw at first hand the impact of the drunkenness and vice which the gin shops promoted. In February 1801, he wrote to Sir Thomas Troubridge, commander in the port, drawing his attention to the situation and denouncing the irresponsibility of the local magistrates in issuing liquor licences to all comers. St Vincent had sight of the letter, of which, like the first he had seen from Trotter a year before, he fully approved. He sent it straight to the Admiralty, demanding that action be taken.[12] The matter was referred to the home secretary, the duke of Portland, who promptly reined in the Plymouth magistrates. As Trotter reported with satisfaction in *Medicina Nautica*, two-thirds of three hundred pubs in Plymouth were closed as a result. As in the days of Lord Howe, the support of a powerful backer had ensured that Trotter's recommendations were acted on. St Vincent ceased to command the Channel Fleet on 17 February 1801, but there was no change of policy since his new post was no less than that of First Lord of the Admiralty itself.

Pay and conditions

As described in Chapter 8, the pay increases that had been granted following the memorial Trotter had presented on behalf of naval surgeons in 1794 in the

---

[10] Sick and Hurt Board to Admiralty, 28 June 1800, NMM, F/31 with St Vincent's letter of 24 June, printed in Morris, *The Channel Fleet*, 518–20
[11] St Vincent to Admiralty, 8 July 1800, TNA, Adm 1/116, printed in R. Morris, *The Channel Fleet*, 531–2
[12] St Vincent to Admiralty, 10 Feb 1801, TNA, Adm 1/118, enclosing Trotter's letter of 9 February 1801, printed in Morris, *The Channel Fleet*, 619–20

aftermath of the Glorious First of June had done much to create parity with pay in the medical branch of the army. A calculation done in 1798, for example, showed that annual pay for surgeons in the cavalry and infantry stood at £226 and £190, while that of naval surgeons varied from £269 on 100-gun ships to £116 on small sloops.[13] Half-pay, however, was a continuing source of complaint. In Georgian times, its receipt was vital to the survival of officers who were unemployed or had retired. Half-pay was not a 'pension' in the modern sense: it was technically a retainer to ensure an immediate return to service in time of crisis – yet it served the same purpose. All army surgeons received it, yet no more than half of those in the navy did so. And of these, only twenty were eligible for the 5 shillings a day paid to army surgeons. Of the rest, a hundred got 3 shillings a day and the remaining two hundred received 2 shillings and 6 pence.

In December 1797, a group of surgeons meeting at the Navy Tavern, Portsea, petitioned the Admiralty to ask that the situation be remedied. Their claims were moderate. They did not ask for the number of potential recipients to be increased, but merely proposed that the number in the senior group be increased to eighty, and the second to a hundred and twenty with a small rise of sixpence a day. The Admiralty did its sums, but in view of the favourable rates of pay, did nothing. Trotter added his weight, seeing half-pay as central to raising the prestige and standards of naval medicine. St Vincent's transfer to the Admiralty in 1801 gave him the opportunity of writing a letter to the new First Lord. It began in heroic style:

> While the naval prowess of this country has confessedly, in the present day, transcended its former greatness, it is nothing more than sound policy to preserve by every means our exalted superiority . . . Our greatness is solely due to the *unrivalled excellence in practical seamanship of our officers and seamen*. It is therefore, the *vital part* of the machine that is our glory. No people on earth can wrest from us this prerogative; but disease may rob us of health; a medical establishment, duly administered, can alone prescribe those means of prevention from sickness, which has often, and may again unnerve the naval arm. Let not then, my Lord, the precious hours of your administration be wasted in viewing the models of visionary or plodding projectors, or in surveying the new mud-ponds in our dockyards; the *living powers* that put ships in motion are more worthy of the attention of Earl St Vincent![14]

Trotter's proposals were also modest. He accepted the adequacy of current levels of pay, and merely suggested that the method by which it was calculated should be simplified. In place of an accumulation of personal pay, Queen Anne's Bounty, compensation for a servant, a lump sum for venereal cures and twopence for every crew member, he proposed a single payment based on a daily rate. Half-pay was another matter. Here Trotter recommended that it should become the entitlement of all surgeons, the most

---

[13] Sick and Hurt Board to Admiralty, 6 February 1798, NMM, Ad F/28
[14] Trotter to St Vincent, printed in *Medicina Nautica*, III, 35–8

senior two hundred receiving 5 shillings a day, the next two hundred 4 shillings, and the rest 3 shillings. He also proposed that physicians should be paid between £2 and £1 a day according to the size of the fleet they served. At that time, the rank was still a novelty with only two holders, Trotter and Andrew Baird, who was now with the fleet of Sir Hyde Parker and Lord Nelson, confronting Copenhagen. There was no official regulation covering the pay of physicians, but the Admiralty was paying each £1 a day. A third physician, John Harness, had retired the year before, and was receiving half-pay of 10 shillings a day.

Trotter's other proposals were of a more general nature and harked back to his 1790 leaflet. First, all medicines should to be supplied free by the navy. Second, the Admiralty should lay down a programme of study for all aspirant naval surgeons, comprising a two-year programme of lectures in anatomy, surgery, medicine and chemistry, followed by six months practical experience in a hospital.[15] It was a forward-looking programme in which only the changes in half-pay needed extra funding. Unfortunately, in this instance Trotter's eloquence was ineffectual. Peace was in the offing, the Admiralty was thinking about demobilization, and Lord St Vincent, though devoted to the navy, was a Whig who saw it as his duty to cut government expenditure rather than increase it. Trotter's proposal had come at the wrong time. It was not until after the outbreak of the war with Napoleon that these issues were settled.

When Admiral William Cornwallis arrived as St Vincent's replacement in February 1801, Trotter felt able to resume his full duties as physician to the Channel Fleet. But his disagreement with the staff of Plymouth Hospital rumbled on, and one of Trotter's first acts was to write to the new commander-in-chief, repeating his previous complaints.[16] The result was that the Hospital's physician and surgeons produced a long, detailed and convincing 'rebuttal of the scandalous calumnies propagated by Dr Trotter'.[17]

On the more positive side, his campaigns against the multiplicity of pubs in Plymouth and in favour of Jenner's system of vaccination of the fleet continued. He also met Lord Nelson, who had arrived in Plymouth to raise his flag on the *San Josef*, before joining the campaign that was to culminate in the Battle of Copenhagen later in the year. Nelson was having trouble with his good eye, had an ophthalmic complaint and was worried by a membrane which was growing over the pupil. Trotter prescribed 'a dark room – and bathing the eye every hour with spring water, which in 24 hours had a surprising effect, and in two days the inflammation was entirely gone',[18] Nelson's eye complaint was thus cured in time to enable him to famously fail to see Parker's signal to withdraw at the climax of the battle.

---

[15] Trotter to St Vincent, printed in *Medicina Nautica*, III, 42–6
[16] Trotter to Troubridge, 30 January 1801, Trotter to Cornwallis, 2 March 1801, NMM, E/48
[17] Sick and Hurt Board to Admiralty, 28 April 1801; Creyke to Sick and Hurt Board, 9 April 1801, NMM, E/48
[18] Trotter, *Medicina Nautica*, III, 107

Tributes, peace and marriage

Trotter's period of service as physician to the Channel Fleet saw a vast improvement in the navy's health. In the last years of his service, Trotter may have had little involvement with the day-to-day problems of the Channel Fleet, but the long-term improvements in health he had introduced under Lord Howe, the scope and utility of his writings, and his seniority gave him enormous prestige within the naval medical service. Even St Vincent had to 'confess that he is thought of very highly by his brother officers'.[19] As early as July 1797, Trotter's efforts were acknowledged by the fourteen surgeons of the Cape of Good Hope Squadron, who presented him with a gold snuff box in appreciation of his 'professional abilities successfully directed to the Welfare of the British Navy and in gratitude for long and unwearied exertions on behalf of the surgeons'.[20] The funds raised on this occasion must have exceeded the cost of the snuff box, for they also sent him a pair of silver coffee pots that can be seen in the National Maritime Museum today. To crown it all Lord Howe, writing to acknowledge receipt of a copy of *Medicina Nautica*, added his tribute:

> It will always be a matter of grateful reflection to me that I was the means of nominating you to your present station. And I may justly congratulate yourself and the country on the important changes which have taken place in ships and hospitals by your advice and exertions: and the zeal and activity which have been spread through out the service by your example.[21]

Trotter's return to duty after St Vincent's replacement did not last long. In October 1801, preliminaries of peace were signed with the French Republic, and negotiations for a final settlement began. Hostilities ceased, the Royal Navy's blockading squadrons were withdrawn and the Channel Fleet returned to Torbay in what Trotter described in his journal as 'the most perfect health'.

Trotter's last months of service were not arduous. But he was not idle. This time, Trotter found himself a wife. His choice was Elizabeth Juliana Everitt, who had been born twenty-eight years before in Botley, Hampshire, where her family lived. Her father, Michael John Everitt, came from nearby Fareham. He had been a naval officer who, months after his marriage in December 1773, had gone to the West Indies as a lieutenant under the patronage of a neighbour, Rear Admiral Clark Gayton. There he had been replaced as a side effect of one of Admiral Rodney's ploys to get a son prematurely promoted, and had unexpectedly been sent back to England in time for his daughter's birth in December 1774. When Everitt returned to the West Indies, Gayton's patronage began to pay dividends. In 1779, he was promoted commander of a small sloop called *Badger*. Eighteen months later, he was promoted again to be acting captain of the 64-gun ship *Ruby*, handing over command of *Badger* to another

[19] St Vincent to Cornwallis in 1803, quoted in Lloyd and Coulter, *Medicine and the Navy*, 166
[20] Dr McCallam to Trotter, NMM, MS 62/111
[21] Howe, printed in preface to T. Trotter, *A Proposal for Destroying Fire and Choak-Damps of Coal Mines; and their Production Explained in the Principles of Modern Chemistry: Addressed to the Owners and Agents of Coal-Works etc* (Newcastle, 1805)

up-and-coming officer, Horatio Nelson. But then tragedy struck. In June 1779, *Ruby* and two consorts were in pursuit of the enemy frigate *Prudente* off Haiti. Before surrendering, the Frenchman loosed off a desultory broadside at long range, which did little damage but killed two of *Ruby*'s crew. One was Captain Michael Everitt. His loss was deeply felt, and a tablet to his memory can still be seen in the church of Ss Peter and Paul in Fareham. Little Elizabeth, at the age of four and a half, became an orphan without powerful friends. For her to be courted at the age of twenty-eight by the physician of the fleet must have been a triumph and a relief for Elizabeth's family. The indications are that Trotter was equally delighted.

In April 1802, peace negotiations with France were sufficiently advanced for the navy to be demobilized, and for the majority of officers to be retired from the service. Thomas Trotter was one of them. Yet even now, as he was about to leave the navy for civilian life, his colleagues were moved to pay him another tribute. This time it took the form of a handsome set of silver tea plate engraved with a Latin inscription giving his qualifications and praising his achievements. Trotter then relinquished his post and, after sixteen years and nine months in the Royal Navy as mate, surgeon and physician to the Channel Fleet, finally retired on half-pay of 10 shillings a day.

Trotter headed north for London, where he was married to Elizabeth Everitt in the church of Marylebone in July 1802. The newly-weds then boarded the coach for the four-day journey to Newcastle, where Trotter had decided to settle and set himself up in private practice.

THE NEWCASTLE YEARS

12

Married Life and Civilian Practice

City and society

NEWCASTLE was an ancient town built on the steep sides of the north bank of the River Tyne, 10 miles from its mouth. Originally a border stronghold, at the beginning of the nineteenth century the city was a seat of local government, a market town and a major port, its waterfront crowded with warehouses and quays and its river filled with ships, coasters, fishing smacks and distinctive local craft called 'keels'. When Trotter and his new wife arrived to take up residence, Newcastle was still essentially a mediaeval city, though in Georgian times it had begun to spread beyond the limits of its original walls. It still had a castle, but only two of the city gates remained, Newgate to the north-west and Westgate further to the south. The commerce of the town was dominated by the carrying trade, the most important component of which was coal. The district was famous for its mining. The north-east's coalfields were vastly productive and in 1800 accounted for about a third of total national output. Newcastle alone exported 2.5 million tons a year. In times of war, the navy would provide escort for the coal flotillas. The coal industry was a major employer of labour, comprising men, women and small children, and enjoyed the natural advantage of ready access to a river and to the sea. The countryside was cut with wooden wagon-ways along which horses hauled trucks filled with coal to the Tyne, where it was put onto keels and shipped downstream to North and South Shields, to be loaded onto colliers for export. Fleets of these vessels had supplied the hearths and furnaces of London for centuries, and now sailed to other ports at home and abroad carrying this vital commodity.

Apart from the markets and commotion in the riverside areas, Newcastle was an attractive and increasingly genteel city, its northern and western districts set among green fields that often dated back to the time of the monasteries. It had a population of some 29,000. There were factories and workshops producing glass, lead, pottery, leather, linen and beer in the lower town, but the north-east had so far been spared the full impact of the Industrial Revolution. Further south, coal, iron, new technological processes and the ability to move goods in bulk via the new canal system had transformed places like Manchester and Birmingham into noisy landscapes of mills, chimneys and forges that were covered in smoke by day and lit by fires at night. In Newcastle, similar developments were still over the horizon. Steam engines were in their infancy and were static, being used to pump out mines and to power cotton looms. It was with the later development of locomotives, the railway and the iron ship, that Tyneside would come into its own.[1]

Approaching Newcastle by the London mail-coach from the south, Trotter and his wife would have crossed the Tyne from Gateshead over a recently built, elegant nine-arched stone bridge. From this point there was no route by which coaches could go directly into the town. Immediately ahead was a precipitous slope, filled with tenements and cut by alleyways and flights of steps lined with stalls and street vendors. Above towered the bulk of the castle and immediately behind could be seen St Nicholas's church, with its pinnacles and tall spire with delicate supporting buttresses. Occupying the river bank to the right of the bridge lay Quayside. Here were concentrated the warehouses, coal stores and quays that were vital to Newcastle's trade, and the public houses, tenements and narrow alleyways called 'chares', which were the location of the town's red-light district. To the left, close to the river, stretched a long narrow street called The Close. This had once been inhabited by the nobility and gentry. Now, except for the Mansion House that remained as a symbol of its former glory, the area was crowded with warehouses, factories and wharfs.

With direct access to the upper town impossible from the bridge, the Trotters' coach would have ascended a wide incline called the Sandhill. Reaching the top, they would then have gone up a steep narrow street called The Side which led to St Nicholas's church. The Side, like Sandhill, was a picturesque jumble of tall half-timbered, stone or brick houses. It was here that Vice-Admiral Cuthbert Collingwood, Nelson's friend and later second-in-command at Trafalgar, had been born sixty years before.

Newcastle's market area and the more genteel parts of the city stretched northwards from The Side, its eastern edge marked by Pilgrim Street. This was a desirable place of residence. Its upper section featured ranges of newer, well-built terraces with gardens behind, while the lower, though no less genteel, was older and the location of two highly respectable hostelries, the *Queen's Head* and the *George Inn*. The *Queen's Head* was the terminus of the mail coach from London and it was here that the Trotters would have ended their journey.

The Trotters took up residence at 103 Pilgrim Street. This was a convenient location for Thomas Trotter. Indeed, the street already housed the residences of a third of the city's physicians and surgeons. Beyond Bell's Court were ancient almshouses called the Holy Jesus Hospital, and beyond that the hall of the Company of Barber Surgeons. In the opposite direction was a small alley appropriately called Drury Lane since it was the site of the Theatre Royal. This would become familiar to Trotter as the venue at which his play, *The Noble Foundling or the Hermit of the Tweed*, would be presented to the public ten years later.[2]

---

[1] A picture of Newcastle at the turn of the nineteenth century can be obtained from Mitchell's *Newcastle Directory of 1801*; McKenzie and Dent's *Newcastle Directory of 1811*; the detailed individual sections of Aneas Mackenzie's *Historical Account of Newcastle-upon-Tyne* of 1827; William Whellan's *History, Topography and Directory of Northumberland* of 1855; and the city maps of Cole and Roper, 1808, and Beilby, 1788

[2] 'Streets within the walls', in Mackenzie, *Historical Account*, 160–82

Fig. 10. Thomas Trotter aged 37, wearing unofficial naval 'uniform'

The buildings and streets of Newcastle presented a mixture of the old and the new. The same was true of its institutions. Dating from its more distant past were its castle, churches, various almshouses including the Holy Jesus Hospital, and the Free Grammar School. More recently, the city's growing commercial prosperity had been reflected in a wave of building, which had seen the opening of a new customs' house, a bank and branch offices for two leading fire-insurance companies. There had been a parallel expansion of medical, intellectual and cultural institutions.

Fig. 11. Newcastle seen from across the Tyne. Engraving by T Miller after T Allom

Of particular interest to Trotter were the medical facilities. The leading institutions were the Keelmen's Hospital, founded by the boatmen for their own use, and the infirmary for the poor, that was run by public subscription in an airy location beyond the city walls to the west. The infirmary ran the equivalent of an accident and emergency service for all comers, though patients normally entered only on the nomination of one of the subscribers. To plug this gap and offer free medical advice and medicines to all, in 1771 Dr John Clark had inspired the opening of a dispensary, in the vicinity of a newly built lunatic asylum. Also nearby were the public baths, which boasted hot, cold and vapour rooms. When Trotter arrived in Newcastle, the infirmary was being improved and extended. Pressured by the experienced and popular, though impatient, Dr Clark, who was now one of the infirmary's physicians, the trustees were extending and modifying the existing structure so as to increase its capacity to house 140 patients, improve ventilation, and provide consulting rooms and separate medical and surgical wards. The infirmary's only drawback was that when the wind was from the south it was inconvenienced by the smoke from the factories by the river.

There had also been developments on the cultural side. Elegant colonnaded assembly rooms with a ballroom 90 feet in length and illuminated by seven chandeliers had been opened in 1776, and the Theatre Royal twelve years later. A medical society had been established in 1787 and in 1793 Newcastle's famous Literary and Philosophical Society was founded. Eschewing subjects with political sensitivities, its declared purpose was 'the discussion of the several branches of polite literature, inquiry into the situation and property of the mineral products of this neighbourhood, and the elucidation of the sciences applicable to commerce, antiquities, local history, biography, literary intelligence, nautical inquiries etc.'. It immediately began to acquire collections of scientific and botanical specimens, and to purchase books for a library which eventually numbered nine thousand volumes. Most of these institutions were located near the Free Grammar School in Westgate Street, a long and pleasant thoroughfare on the south-western edge of the city.[3]

Trotter would have lacked little in terms of social or intellectual stimulation. He had been associated with the Literary and Philosophical Society since its foundation and, as early as 1792, had been approached by the institution's driving force, the Rev. William Turner, asking for papers and specimens gathered on his travels which might be of interest.[4] He had been too busy to oblige but, now that he was settled in Newcastle, he became an active member. The following year, 1804, he was elected a member of the governing committee. He was thus able to attend lectures such as the Rev. W. Turner's 'General introductory Discourse on the Objects, Advantages, and intended Plan of the New Institution for public Lectures on Natural Philosophy in Newcastle upon Tyne', and William Thomas's 'Observations on the Propriety of introducing Roads on the Principle of Coal-wagon-ways for the general Conveyance of Goods; with a particular Reference to shewing the Practicability of a Road on this Principle

---

[3] 'Literary institutions', in Mackenzie, *Historical Account*, 461–500
[4] Turner to Trotter, 19 January 1792, NMM, MS 62/111

from Newcastle to Hexham'. There were three newspapers to claim Trotter's attention, each with its own political sympathies. There was the reformist but generally independent *Tyne Mercury*, the Whig-oriented *Newcastle Chronicle* and the best established and influential of all, the Tory *Newcastle Courant*.

Tragedy

At first, Trotter seems to have been unsure as to where his future lay. A letter from Dr Jenner in March 1803 suggests that Trotter was hankering after a medical post in London.[5] Jenner's reply was decisively in the negative: Trotter should stay in Newcastle. But first there was unfinished business from the past. Much of 1802 has been spent finalizing the third volume of his *Medicina Nautica*. The book was published the following year. It consisted of a chronological journal detailing the operations and health of the Channel Fleet from 1799 to 1802, extracts from the reports of naval surgeons, and specific sections dealing with the pay and conditions of surgeons, and with contagion, ventilation, typhus, pneumonia, tuberculosis, the malignant ulcer, scurvy and the sick bay. The book was well received and was republished in a second edition within a year.

Trotter was also nursing a grievance. The Admiralty no doubt regarded an award of half-pay at a rate of 10 shillings a day a generous act. There were no existing regulations covering the conditions of fleet physicians and the amount awarded was, after all, the same as had been paid to Dr John Harness and was double that paid to senior naval surgeons on half-pay. Trotter thought differently. To him, the amount was derisory, and evidence of the Admiralty's coldness towards him. In view of the rank Trotter had held and contribution he had made to the health of the navy, his annoyance at the modest amount on offer is understandable.

When Trotter sent complimentary copies of *Medicina Nautica* to his naval patrons and friends, he did not hesitate to air his grievance. Replies expressed gratitude and admiration for the book, but refrained from comment on what was clearly an embarrassing topic. Nelson, for example, provided a handsome tribute to his work and reputation in the service, but expressed ignorance of Trotter's treatment by the Admiralty, and avoided making any judgement.[6] Sir Roger Curtis was full of praise for the book, but expressed regret that Trotter saw himself as ill-used.[7] Admiral Thornborough agreed that he had been shamefully treated.[8]

In May 1803, war with France broke out again. Faced with an invasion scare, all over the country men rushed to join the colours or don the extravagant uniforms of the new volunteer regiments, while half-pay officers returned to their military and naval units. In May, Admiral Collingwood passed through

[5] Jenner to Trotter, March 1803, quoted in Joan Carmichael, 'Thomas Trotter, Physician to the Fleet', in *Medicine in Northumberland* (Newcastle, 1993), 164–72

[6] Nelson to Trotter, 7 January 1803, NMM, MS 62/iii

[7] Curtis to Trotter, 28 June and 5 November 1803, NMM, MS 62/iii

[8] Thornborough to Trotter, 3 January 1803, NMM, MS 62/iii

Newcastle on his way to take up a command, and the city corporation offered an extra bounty of one guinea to any local man who enlisted on his ship.[9] Thomas Trotter, on the other hand, remained aloof and sent no offer of service to the Admiralty. He was, after all, incapacitated by a hernia and had a new medical practice and a now pregnant young wife. His reasons were understandable, but he was demonstrably neither willing nor able to return to the navy. While the Newcastle Loyal Armed Association and the Newcastle Volunteers were mustering on the Town Moor and Collingwood's ships were preparing for sea, Trotter was preoccupied with writing to the *Courant*, announcing that he was preparing a book on drunkenness, and asking medical colleagues for case studies and experience.[10]

Trotter was already in the process of setting up his practice. There was no shortage of medical men in Newcastle to treat the affluent and more seriously ill and the town directory of 1801 includes the names of seven physicians and twenty surgeons. With Trotter's qualifications and experience, he seems to have had little difficulty in getting started. Perhaps the fact that his younger brother, Andrew, had established himself as a surgeon in nearby North Shields helped. As in Wooler, he treated the poor free of change in his house on Tuesday and Saturday, seeing around a hundred patients a year.[11] This appears to be a small number, but the majority of such people would probably have only dared to consult a Latin-speaking physician in extreme circumstances, otherwise preferring self-medication or folk healers. The task of establishing himself as a member of the medical fraternity was not helped when Trotter found himself in disagreement with the doyen of Newcastle physicians, Dr John Clark, over the treatment of a patient. In January 1804, Trotter was summoned to the bedside of the wife of a prominent citizen, who was in the latest stages of pregnancy and was suffering from violent pain under the ribs and a racing pulse. Clark, who was already in attendance, saw the symptoms as the early stages of pleurisy, bled the patient, and administered purgatives. Trotter disagreed. His diagnosis led him to conclude that the reason lay in debility and the patient's nervous state. In his opinion, Clark's treatment was not only harmful, but seemed to have no logic or science to back it. After weeks of diplomatic disagreement with his colleague, Trotter withdrew from the case.[12] Unwisely, he decided that matters should not be allowed to rest there.

Before he could take matters further, Trotter was distracted by a personal shock. First, there had been a happy event. On 20 April 1804 a son was born and named John Everitt Howe Roddam, after Trotter's father-in-law and his major naval patrons. Then came tragedy. His wife Elizabeth failed to recover from the birth and on 1 May she died. She was twenty-nine years old. Left alone with a tiny baby, Trotter was grief-stricken. He expressed his feelings in words carved on Elizabeth's headstone in St Andrew's churchyard:

---

[9] *Newcastle Courant*, 28 May, 1803
[10] Dated 14 Aug 1803, in the *Medical and Physical Journal* 10 (1803), 382–3
[11] Trotter to Editor of the *Medical and Physical Journal* 13 (1806), 213
[12] Trotter to Editor of the *Medical and Physical Journal* 12, (June–December 1804), 1 August 1804

Hail! Task divine, to pour the tender tear
O'er the lov'd wife, companion, partner dear,
And as it ſtreams, thou sainted spirit, see,
Behold the bleeding heart ſtill points to thee:
Yet while it throbs with pangs too ſtrong to feign,
No impious guſts shall Heaven's decrees arraign,
I bow all grateful for those blessings gone,
I heave no murmur, though I weep and moan;
And while with all an anxious father's care
I rear thy babe and plant thy virtue there.[13]

Work and controversy

Trotter dealt with his loss by throwing himself into his work. First, there was the need to get his latest work ready for publication. It was his *Essay on Drunkenness*, which appeared in 1804 and will be discussed in the next chapter. With the book on its way to the printers, Trotter returned to grind his axe on the subject of Dr Clark. On 1 August 1804 he sent a long letter to the *Medical and Physical Journal*. In a tone of laboured patience, with an air of self-righteousness, Trotter gave his version of events. He professed respect and cordiality towards his distinguished colleague, but his opinion of Dr Clark's methods was undisguised. In response to the state of the patient, Trotter wrote,

> Dr C again proposed bleeding; I was now confounded. There did not appear a single symptom to juſtify it. I asked for explanation. He could give none. I begged he would cite any authority for bleeding in such a case. He answered evasively; but added, that his own practice convinced him he was right.

Trotter claimed that he gave Clark his reasons for diagnosing debility and nervous strain, and that he showed the beneficial effects achieved by treating her for that condition. Dr Clark, however, remained immovable. Trotter returned to the attack, asking him

> Do you then mean to contend that there is no appeal to the firſt principles of our art? Are the authority of the learned in our profession, the wisdom and experience of ages, to be overthrown by an opinion of either yours or mine, that reſts on no foundation? Can you support your method of cure by any practical writer on pleurisy such as Sydenham, Huxham or Cleghorn? He [Dr C] offered to appeal to none of these. I quoted the celebrated Aphorism of Hippocrates in defence of my argument '*Qui acidum cruciant non pleuritici sunt.*' ['Those who have a sharp pain are not pleuritic'] . . . He [Dr C] evinced no approbation for the judgment of the Coan Sage; nor did he seem disposed to quit the ground he had taken at the beginning of the conversation.[14]

[13] Printed in 'St Andrew's church', in Mackenzie, *Historical Account*, 342–57. No sign of the headstone now remains.
[14] Trotter to Editor of the *Medical and Physical Journal* 12 (June–December 1804), 1 August 1804

If Trotter had wished to make himself unpopular in Newcastle, he could not have done it more effectively than by taking on the city's most distinguished physician and exposing him in public. Dr Clark was then sixty years old and was at the peak, indeed the end, of his career. Like Trotter, he was a native of Roxburghshire and had obtained his medical qualifications at the University of Edinburgh. While there he had suffered an accident which had left him with a nervous complaint and digestive disorder that was to dog him for the rest of his life – indeed, six months after his encounter with Trotter Clark suffered an attack which caused him to withdraw to Bath in desperate search of a cure. After graduation, he had travelled to India and China and, following further study at St Andrews, had moved to Newcastle. There Clark had been the driving force behind the establishment of the dispensary, and had guided the destinies of the infirmary after being elected a staff physician in 1788. He was variously described as possessing 'great benevolence and intellectual powers . . . sound judgment and unwearied industry', of being 'the greatest benefactor of the afflicted poor' and the possessor of 'an immense collection of medical facts which he applied with the most accurate judgment'.[15]

The publication of Trotter's letter was not well received in Newcastle and seems to have split local medical opinion. Clark's friends rallied to his support and, according to Trotter, his own friends did likewise. In view of the furor, and what he described as the local opinion that 'it was a presumption in Dr Trotter to give an opinion on a disease different from Dr Clark', on 4 December 1804, he thought it necessary to write another letter to the *Medical and Physical Journal* justifying himself and defending his reputation. However, true to the principle that virtue required the airing of truths however unpalatable, he repeated his criticism of both Clark's methods and his refusal to discuss his position openly, writing

> he has it in his power to reply: but by silence it is not given him to treat me with contempt. From being his equal in professional rank, I am secured against that; and as his superior in those gradations of study and education that lead to the fair and regular acquirement of medical honours, I am not afraid of being obscured by his shadow.

According to Trotter, he was not the only one.

> The predicament in which I stand, in relation to Dr Clark is not singular; it is nearly the same with that of all the other physicians here, except one . . . In the only other case, in which I have been joined with him, I also differed widely in opinion. I have since then, followed him in another; and, must confess, that his treatment was equally unaccountable . . . When a physician in consultation appeals to his own experience, it has not been unusual for him to give reasons for preferring particular modes of practice. In the case which I have given, Dr C was either unable or unwilling to do this.[16]

---

[15] Clark biographical note in 'Medical establishments: the infirmary', in Mackenzie, *Historical Account*, 512

[16] Trotter to Editor of the *Medical and Physical Journal* 13 (January–June 1805), 132–5 (4 December 1804)

Dr Clark never replied. By the time the letter was published in the July edition of the *Journal*, poor Clark, in spite of the efforts of his Newcastle friends and confreres, had died. Neither the second letter nor the untimely death of his opponent did Trotter's reputation any good. At some stage in his career, Trotter seems to have considered applying for a post as physician to the infirmary when one of the four was left vacant. It would have been useful for him to have secured such an appointment, which would have provided a small steady income, as well as raising his profile in Newcastle. But he decided against it. The story goes that 'he tendered his services, but finding it expected he should go round and ask for votes, he withdrew the offer'.[17] Perhaps in the aftermath of his quarrel with Clark, it was as well he did.

Controversy was not to stop with the case of Dr Clark. In January 1805, the Admiralty promulgated an order in council which made sweeping improvements in the pay and conditions of naval medical staff. All surgeons at last became eligible for half-pay, and a salary of £2 2s a day was established for physicians with three years service in the post.[18] For the first time, they also introduced a uniform for medical officers. This would have been much to Trotter's taste since, like many of his colleagues, he had previously worn a blue coat with brass buttons and lace trimmings which, although civilian dress, was designed to appear 'naval'. Once again, Trotter's 1801 letter to Lord St Vincent seems to have had an effect, although it was his successor, Charles Middleton, now Lord Barham, who introduced the changes. Trotter immediately wrote to the Admiralty asking that his half-pay of 10 shillings a day should be increased to the new rate of £1 1s.[19] Alas, the order in council had stated firmly that 'those who have not served during the present war if capable are not entitled to the forgoing regulations'. Trotter had not offered his services when the Napoleonic Wars had begun in 1803, and had had no medical examination to show his incapacity. To his dismay, the Sick and Hurt Board accordingly ruled that he was ineligible and rejected his request. Developing a conspiracy theory, Trotter attributed this rejection to annoyance at the barrage of proposals and criticism they had received from him over the last ten years. He was later to write:

> All the usual forms of service were set aside in order to deprive a medical officer, who has filled the higheſt ſtation in the public service of the country, of the fair emoluments which he had earned by a life of virtuous induſtry; and acknowledged by officers of all ranks to have done more for the Navy than any person living.[20]

Meanwhile Trotter had thrown himself into preparing the three pioneering non-naval works for which he is best known – *Essay on Drunkenness*; *A proposal for Destroying the Fire and Choke-Damp of Coal-Mines*, and *A View of the*

---

[17] Trotter biographical note in 'Medical establishments: the infirmary', in Mackenzie, *Historical Account*, 514
[18] *Steel's Navy List* for 1806
[19] Trotter to Admiralty, 20 February, and reply of 1 March 1805, NMM, Adm F/36
[20] Trotter, preface to *Sea Weeds*

Nervous Temperament. The following chapters will be devoted to the genesis and importance of each.

———•———

13

An Essay on Drunkenness

TROTTER'S *Essay on Drunkenness*, or to give the full title *An Essay, Medical, Philosophical and Chemical on Drunkenness and its Effects on the Human Body* was published in 1804.[1] Further British editions appeared in 1807, 1810 and 1812. It was published in the United States, and achieved translations into German and Swedish. Copies of the original 1804 edition are today greatly sought after by collectors of rare books. A facsimile edition was published in 1988, with a useful introduction by the medical historian Roy Porter, and is much more accessible.[2] The 1804 volume derived from, and greatly extended, the Latin dissertation which had won Trotter his Edinburgh MD in 1788.

Why, some two hundred years since its original publication, should the *Essay* be accorded classic status? It was a pioneering text and the first book-length treatise on what is today referred to as 'alcoholism' to appear in any language. But beyond that lies the fact that in several ways it is still a thoroughly modern book, which offers thinking of relevance to understanding the patient who is to be seen in tomorrow's clinic, anywhere. It is modern, but it is also a book which is a product of the Enlightenment, with an insistence that drunkenness is to be understood rather than morally denounced. With the vigour and clarity of the language, its acute observations of human behaviour and its compassion, this is a book which also puts us directly in contact with Thomas Trotter the man.

This chapter will first put the book in context by sketching the long history of British drinking and the way in which the arrival of cheap distilled spirits changed awareness of the nature of the problem. It will go on to describe the drinking culture with which Trotter would have been familiar and the medical views on alcohol that were evolving at the time. We will then see what the *Essay* had to say about drink and the drinking problem with Trotter speaking for himself.

The deep history of British drinking

The history of British drinking can be traced through a number of different interlocking themes.[3] The first relates to what was actually drunk – mead, ale,

---

[1] T. Trotter, *An Essay, Medical, Philosophical and Chemical, on Drunkenness, and its Effects on the Human Body* (London, 1804)

[2] Facsimile edition of Trotter's *Essay on Drunkenness* edited with an introduction by Roy Porter (London, 1988)

[3] G. Edwards, *Alcohol: The Ambiguous Molecule* (London, 2000), published in the USA as

wines, fortified wines or spirits – at any period, and how much. In relation to the latter, official statistics based on the production and sale of alcohol are only available for England and Wales from 1684 and for Scotland from 1718, and the reliability of data for the earlier years is open to question.[4] Another is the way in which drinking was embedded in the culture – the place of alcohol at baptisms, weddings and wakes; the development of the inn and tavern and of drinking in the home; toasts and pledges and feastings. There is also an important story line around who produced the drink and profited from the activity. The shift from home brewing to commercial brewing was one of the triumphs of nineteenth-century capitalism.

In addition to the external features of this long story, subtle questions arise concerning the notions of what was worrying about excessive drinking. In so far as there was a problem with drink, it was perceived in terms of individuals getting drunk, and then engaging in lewdness or profanity. The cause of this lamentable behaviour was sin, and responsibility for dealing with it lay very largely with the church.[5] The definition of the problem as sin, for which the remedy was preaching, prayer and personal repentance, can be found in Britain as early as the eighth century. It was not until 1556 that the civil authorities took a hand in the matter, with public drunkenness becoming a punishable civil offence.

At the end of the seventeenth century and the first half of the eighteenth, the age-old choice of beer as Britain's favourite alcoholic drink was replaced by a taste for distilled spirits and an increase in wine drinking. After the revolution of 1688, the establishment of distilleries was encouraged and the urban poor got a taste for cheap gin. Thus was born an epidemic of drunkenness on a scale never previously experienced in this country. Over the next forty years, the annual consumption of gin went up from 0.5 million gallons to over 5 million gallons.[6] By 1725 one house in seven in London was selling drink, and mass drunkenness had become the order of the day. This is how Lord Lonsdale described the London street scene in a House of Lords debate in 1743:

> In every part of the metropolis, whoever shall pass along the ſtreet, will find wretchedness ſtretched upon the pavement, insensible and motionless and only removed by the charity of passengers from the danger of being crushed by carriages or trampled by horses, or ſtrangled with filth in the common sewers; and others, less helpless perhaps, but more dangerous, who have drunk too much to fear punishment, but not enough to hinder them from provoking it . . . No man can pass a single hour in a public place without meeting such objeᴄts and hearing such expressions as disgrace human nature – such as cannot be looked upon without horror . . . and which there is no possibility of removing or preventing, whilſt this hateful liquor is publicly sold. . . . These liquors not only infatuate the mind, but poison the body, and

Alcohol: The World's Favourite Drug (New York, 2000), 30–46

[4] J. A. Spring and D. H. Buss, 'Three centuries of alcohol in the British diet', *Nature* 270 (1977), 567–72

[5] Edwards, *Alcohol*, 32–4

[6] A. Shadwell, *Drink, Temperance and Legislation* (London, 1902), 24

not only fill our streets with madmen and our prisons with criminals, but our hospitals with cripples.[7]

In that dire situation, a new definition of the problem with drink began to evolve. It was no longer seen as the problem of individuals, but as a population-level issue, or what in today's terminology would be termed an issue of public health. This reformulation found powerful expression in a petition to Parliament made in 1736 by an assembly of Middlesex magistrates:

> That the drinking of geneva, and other distilled liquors, had for some years past greatly increased. That the constant and excessive use thereof had destroyed thousands of his Majesty's subjects. That great numbers of others were by its use rendered unfit for useful labour, debauched in morale and drawn into all manner of vice and wickedness . . . [and] that the public welfare and safety, as well as the trade of the nation, would be greatly affected by it . . . and tended greatly to diminish the labour and industry of his Majesty's subjects.[8]

The government responded to this plea by introducing a restrictive Gin Act. It met with little success. A series of further measures followed, aimed at controlling and licensing sales outlets and imposing heavy excise duties, but drinking was to continue in the eighteenth and throughout the nineteenth century at a destructive level. The drunkenness of the urban poor became entrenched as a feature of the Industrial Revolution, and the ruling classes were not immune. In 1787, Sir Gilbert Elliot commented thus on the drinking of well-known politicians:

> Fox drinks what I should call a great deal; Sheridan [MP and dramatist, and the bosom friend of the Prince of Wales] excessively and Grey more than any of them . . . Pitt, I am told drinks as much as anybody.[9]

Books railing against drunkenness became a popular form of publication. The most declamatory was J. Strenock's 1677 effort, *God's Sword Drawn Forth against Drunkards*. That was followed by William Jole's *A Warning to Drunkards* in 1680, Mathew Hayes's *Against Drunkenness* in 1709, and the Rev Edmund Gibson's *An Earnest Discussion from Intemperance* in 1750.

The escalation in national levels of drinking, and in the widespread social problems which resulted, meant that by Trotter's lifetime doctors had begun to take an interest in the health consequences of drinking, and in the question of why some people got drunk so repeatedly. The stage was thus set for a new kind of professional discourse very different from the age-old assumption that drunkenness was moral failure to be prevented by preaching, and cured by prayer.

---

[7] Edwards, *Alcohol*, 40

[8] *House of Commons Journal*, 20 February 1736; Shadwell, *Drink*, 25–6

[9] Countess of Minto, *The Life and Letters of Sir Gilbert Minto 1751–1796* (London, 1874), 189

Fig. 12. Gin Lane. Hogarth's depiction of the ravages of
drink in the middle of the eighteenth century.
Wellcome Library, London

Drinking and ideas about drunkenness at the turn of the eighteenth century

What then was the contemporary drinking world through which Trotter moved, and what were the evolving professional ideas on drinking that would have been available to him?

Trotter's teachers and the doctors of his generation were witnessing a very different drinking landscape from that of their not so distant forebears. Drink was now a matter of medical concern whether in relation to the care of the desperate poor or the self-indulgent rich.

Trotter's personal introduction to alcohol would have been as a lad growing up in Roxburghshire, and at Edinburgh University. There was therefore a specifically Scottish colouring to this young man's alcohol-awareness. Historical data showing the amount of tax paid on spirits in Scotland confirm that the capacity to distil and consume whisky had been a national tradition for many centuries.[10] As far back as 1617, the Scottish Parliament had legislated against 'the vile and detestable vice of drunkenness daily increasing to the high dishonour of God and the great harm of the whole realm'. Nevertheless, after the Act of Union in 1707, Scotland managed to remain exempt from taxes on spirits for fifty years. By 1829 there were in Scotland 17,371 public houses selling spirits to a population of 2.3 million, or about one such sales outlet for every 130 citizens.[11]

A famous literary Scot of around Trotter's time who left extraordinarily detailed accounts of his own debauches was James Boswell, though his taste seems to have been more for wine than whisky.[12] A British select committee taking evidence in Westminster in 1834 recorded the words of Mr Thomas Roberts, describing the drinking habits of his fellow Scots:

> Drunkenness forms part of their education as much as learning the A B C at school. These drinking schools are the domestic fireside, the parent takes it and gives a little to the child; he gives it as something that is excellent.[13]

Spirits have generally tended to be favoured in northern countries, and a common explanation for the Scottish predilection for whisky was the climate. The national temperament was also offered as an explanation, with dour Scots seen as better able to hold strong drink than more excitable southerners. Dr Norman Kerr, a Glaswegian himself, and an important nineteenth-century authority in the alcohol field, claimed in the 1880s that the palatal affections of most of his acquaintances, whether Highlanders or Lowlanders, 'were about equally divided between whisky and porridge'.[14] That may read like stereotyping, but multiple lines of evidence support the contention that Trotter's Scotland had a heavy drinking culture, with whisky the national beverage and drunkenness a frequent accompaniment.

---

[10]   G. B. Wilson, *Alcohol and the Nation* (London, 1940), 19–20
[11]   Ibid., 385
[12]   J. Boswell, *Life of Samuel Johnson* (Oxford, 1904, originally published 1791); T. B. Gilmore, 'James Boswell's drinking', *Eighteenth Century Studies* 24 (1991), 337–57
[13]   Shadwell, *Drink, Temperance and Legislation*, 39
[14]   N. Kerr, *Inebriety or Narcomania, its Etiology, Pathology, Treatment and Jurisprudence* (London, 2nd edn, 1888), 248

A transitional culture for Trotter between Scotland and England was the British navy, in which he spent, on and off, his years from the age of twenty to forty-two. He himself pictured the officer class as temperate in their drinking. But he viewed the ordinary sailors as likely to engage in heavy drinking and gross drunkenness whenever the opportunity arose. In so far as Trotter's views were shaped by exposure to contemporary English drinking culture, it seems inevitable that he would have been sensitized to the general public concern about drunkenness in a country that had been exposed to cheap imported gin, and where the social consequences of the Industrial Revolution made it possible to be 'drunk for a penny, dead drunk for tuppence, and for threepence to purchase all the straw the drunkard might want for a comatose dossing down'.[15]

In short, one may assume that in 1804, a work which tackled the problem of drunkenness would have been likely to attract attention and be seen as timely.

Early medical opinions on drunkenness

In an article entitled 'The drinking man's disease: the pre-history of alcoholism in Georgian Britain',[16] Roy Porter traced a line of British medical authorities who had spoken of chronic drunkenness constituting some kind of disease state well before Trotter came on the scene. He quoted a respected English physician, John Coakley Lettsom, who wrote in 1787 about the progressive enslavement brought about by alcohol abuse:

> Those of delicate habits who have endeavoured to overcome their nervous debility by the aid of spirits; many of these have begun the use of these poisons from persuasion of their utility, rather than from love of them: the relief however, being temporary, to keep up their effects, frequent access is had to the same delusion, till at length what was taken by compulsion gains attachment, and the little drop of brandy, or gin and water, becomes as necessary as food.[17]

That is a finely observed description of the progressive nature of alcohol dependence from seventeen years before the *Essay on Drunkenness*. However, although a reading of Lettsom's original text shows that the habit of drinking was thoughtfully considered, it is not described at the level of detail to be found in Trotter's analysis. Other British physicians of note who commented that drunkenness was a medical issue included Erasmus Darwin and E. F. Fothergill. Popular encyclopaedias on health also began to deal with drunkenness.

Another and more important authority who deserves attention as an intellectual predecessor to Trotter was the distinguished American physician, Benjamin Rush. Having finished a medical apprenticeship in Philadelphia in 1766, he sailed for Liverpool and spent the next two years attending lectures at Edinburgh Medical School, where Cullen was one of his teachers.[18] His

---

[15] Edwards, *Alcohol*, 39

[16] R. Porter, 'The drinking man's disease: the history of alcoholism in Georgian Britain', *British Journal of Addiction* 80 (1985), 385–96

[17] Ibid., 391

[18] B. Rush, *Travels through Life: An Account of Sundry Incidents and Events in the Life of Benjamin*

experience would have been entirely similar to that of Trotter a decade later. Rush was awarded his MD in June 1768 for a dissertation on the digestion of food in the stomach.[19] On return home, he not only contributed greatly to his profession, but in 1776 became a signatory to the Declaration of Independence. In 1777 he was appointed surgeon general to the United States Army and in 1799 he became treasurer to the Mint.

In the world of alcohol studies, Rush's fame derives from the publication in 1790 of a pamphlet entitled *An Inquiry in the Effects of Ardent Spirits upon the Human Body and Mind with an account of the means of preventing and of the remedies for curing them.*[20] Drunkenness had become a problem in America because of the ready availability of rum. Rush's concern was almost entirely restricted to the evils of drinking spirits, which he lambasted with considerable rhetorical energy:

> A more effecting spectacle cannot be exhibited than a person into whom this infernal spirit, generated by habits or intemperance, has entered. It is more or less effecting according to the station the person fills in a family, or in society, who is possessed by it. Is he a husband? How deep the anguish which rends the bosom of his wife! Is she a wife? Who can measure the shame and aversion which she excites in her husband! Is he a minister of the gospel? Here language fails me – If angels weep – it is such a sight.[21]

In another passage he described the effects of spirits on people living in rural communities:

> Behold their houses with shattered windows, – their barns with leaky roofs, – their garden overrun with weeds, – their fields with broken fences, their hogs without yolks, – their sheep without wool, – their cattle and horses without fat, and their children filthy and half-clad, without manners, principles and morals. . . . The farms and properties thus neglected, and depreciated, are seized and sold for the benefit of a group of creditors. Thus we see poverty and misery, crimes and infamy, diseases and death, are all the natural and usual consequences of the intemperate use of ardent spirits.[22]

In contrast to his ferocious denunciation of spirits, Rush's attitude towards beer and cider was positive and, regarding wine, he wrote:

> These fermented liquors are composed of the same ingredients as cider and are both cordial and nourishing. The peasants of France who drink them in large quantities, are a sober and healthy body of people. Unlike ardent spirits, which render the temper irritable, wines generally inspire cheerfulness and

Rush (Philadelphia, 1825), reproduced in G. W. Corner (ed.), *The Autobiography of Benjamin Rush* (Princeton, 1948), 47

[19]   Ibid., 43

[20]   B. Rush, *An inquiry into the Effects of Ardent Spirits on the Human Body and Mind, with an Account of the Means for Preventing and of the Remedies for Curing them*, 8th edn (Boston, 1823)

[21]   Ibid., 11

[22]   Ibid., 12

good humour. It is to be lamented that the grape has not as yet been sufficiently cultivated in our country.[23]

Rush contrasted with Trotter not only in his emphasis on spirits as the unique evil, but also in the inherent moralism of his approach. Here is a passage as remote in its conclusions from Trotter's thinking as is imaginable:

> Persons under the pressure of debt, disappointments in worldly pursuits, and guilt, have sometimes sought to drown their sorrows in strong drink. The only radical cure for those evils, is to be found in religion; but where its support is not resorted to, wine and opium should always be preferred to ardent spirits.[24]

In another passage Rush referred to fear of 'punishment in a future world' as a possible remedy for drunkenness.

Although Rush and Trotter were thus in some ways poles apart, in others, their thinking was quite close. Trotter nowhere makes any acknowledgement of the influence of Rush's *Pamphlet* on the *Essay*, which seems strange given his proclivity for wide reading.

The 'Essay on Drunkenness'

The work begins with a dedication to Edward Jenner.[25] It was the custom of the time for authors to dedicate their works, usually to an aristocrat or person of political influence from whose patronage the author hoped to receive favours. Trotter, however, acted differently and chose Jenner, the discoverer of smallpox vaccination, who, although he was acknowledged in medical circles to be a benefactor of mankind, was neither rich nor powerful. Jenner readily gave his permission. Trotter had advocated the introduction of Jenner's smallpox vaccination into the Royal Navy, and had established a friendly relationship after presenting Jenner with a gold snuff box in 1801 as an expression of the appreciation of his fellow naval surgeons. Jenner's response to this compliment came in a letter dated 2 July 1804:

> In point of good manners and indeed for feelings of gratitude for your very elegant dedication, I ought sooner than this to have thanked you but I hope you will pardon this seeming neglect. Believe me it is no more for I have the greatest friendship and esteem for you. I sincerely hope that the mirror you have held up may reflect the face of many a drunkard in that hideous shape that may terrify and reform. I think your work will be of great use to young men launching into the vice of ebriety. The habitual drunkard, the man engulfed in alcohol, will scarcely be able to get out. In the course of my life, I have known one instance and I think that is all. Enclosed is some vaccine.[26]

---

23 Ibid.,17
24 Ibid., 24
25 Trotter to Jenner, 26 December 1803, in *An Essay*, v–vi
26 Jenner to Trotter, 2 July 1804, NMM, MS 62/iii

Fig. 13. Dr Edward Jenner, discoverer of vaccination,
to whom Trotter's book on alcohol was dedicated.
Pastel by John Raphael Smith. Wellcome Library, London

In the preface, Trotter explained that the origins of the book lay in the dissertation that had won him the Edinburgh MD in 1788. Other medical authorities had written about drunkenness but to take this issue as the basis for a doctoral thesis was bold. One may suspect that it was Trotter's experience of alcohol problems in the navy which had catalysed his interest in the problem. And it should be remembered how important this thesis was for him, an already mature student who needed the MD degree as ticket for further professional advancement. Trotter's public examination before the professors of the Medical School, with the famous Dr William Cullen presiding, was successful and he left the hall as Dr Thomas Trotter, MD (Edinburgh), the holder of a doctorate from one of the most respected medical schools in Europe.

The choice of 'ebriety' as a topic was in the event a sensible career strategy, but it can also be seen as revealing something about Trotter's character. He showed here a characteristic willingness to break new ground. That this thesis

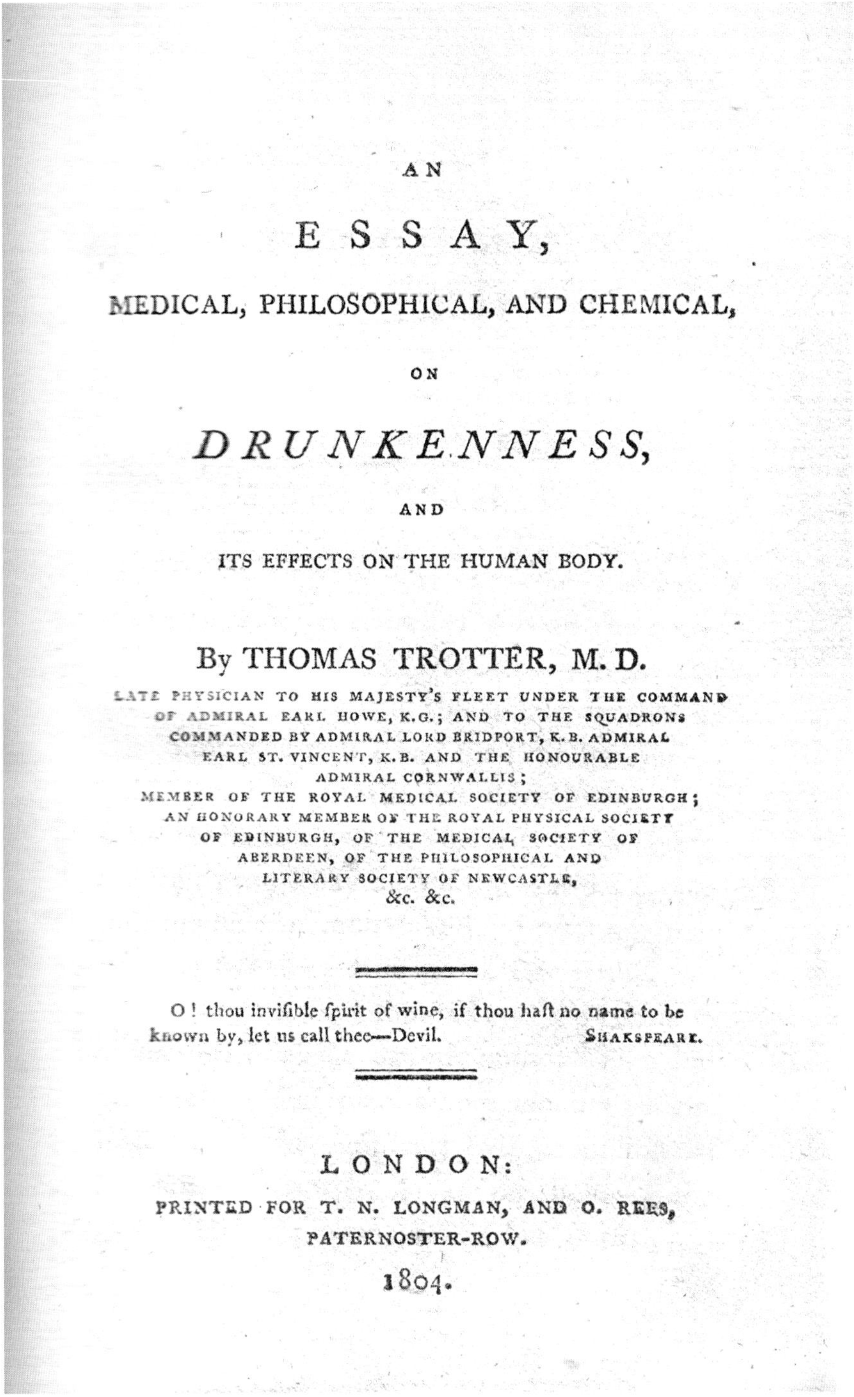

AN

E S S A Y,

MEDICAL, PHILOSOPHICAL, AND CHEMICAL,

ON

D R U N K E N N E S S,

AND

ITS EFFECTS ON THE HUMAN BODY.

By THOMAS TROTTER, M.D.

LATE PHYSICIAN TO HIS MAJESTY'S FLEET UNDER THE COMMAND
OF ADMIRAL EARL HOWE, K.G.; AND TO THE SQUADRONS
COMMANDED BY ADMIRAL LORD BRIDPORT, K.B. ADMIRAL
EARL ST. VINCENT, K.B. AND THE HONOURABLE
ADMIRAL CORNWALLIS;
MEMBER OF THE ROYAL MEDICAL SOCIETY OF EDINBURGH;
AN HONORARY MEMBER OF THE ROYAL PHYSICAL SOCIETY
OF EDINBURGH, OF THE MEDICAL SOCIETY OF
ABERDEEN, OF THE PHILOSOPHICAL AND
LITERARY SOCIETY OF NEWCASTLE,
&c. &c.

O! thou invisible spirit of wine, if thou hast no name to be
known by, let us call thee—Devil.   SHAKSPEARE.

L O N D O N:

PRINTED FOR T. N. LONGMAN, AND O. REES,
PATERNOSTER-ROW.

1804.

Fig. 14. Frontispiece of Trotter's pioneering work on alcohol

was in the judgement of his contemporaries viewed as innovative was confirmed by the letter of congratulation which he received shortly afterwards from the Humane Society: 'The investigation of so important an inquiry, in a regular scientific manner, was never before thought of: it was a subject left, happily left, to be ingeniously executed and amplified by Dr Trotter.'[27] Early in his book Trotter demonstrated that he regarded the consumption of alcoholic beverages as generally acceptable. What concerned him was excessive drinking, its consequences for the individual, and the problems this posed for society. Within the modern formulation, his was a text which developed a public health perspective, as well as embracing clinical concerns. But he was not a proto-prohibitionist or advocate of total abstinence. One can find in his poem *The Origin of Grog* bountiful praise for the British navy's taste for rum mixed with water. He instructed that the song should be sung to the music by Fisher Tench for John Wilmot, earl of Rochester's 'Vulcan contrive me such a cup':[28]

> Gay with a cup Apollo sung,
> The Muses join'd the strain;
> Mars cried 'Encore!' and Vulcan rang –
> Let's drink her o'er again.[29]

To describe a mixture of rum and water as 'cup divine', would not have been the sentiments of Benjamin Rush or any tee-totaller. Furthermore, in the *Essay* Trotter described in adulatory terms the positive psychological impact to be expected of alcohol, provided too much of it was not taken:

> The first effects of wine are, an inexpressible tranquillity of mind, and liveliness of countenance; the powers of imagination become more vivid, and the flow of spirits more spontaneous and easy, giving birth to wit and humour without hesitation . . . Placed, as it were, in a paradise of pleasure, the being only contemplates delightful and agreeable objects; the most prominent of these are love and desire.[30]

Have a few drinks, said Trotter, and the man who is in love 'sees beauties in his mistress that he overlooked before'.

In another passage, he extolled the capacity of alcohol to soothe away anxiety:

> Invigorated with wine, the infirm man becomes strong, and the timid courageous. Even the trembling hypochondriac, unmindful of his fears and ominous dreams, sports and capers like a person in health.[31]

---

[27] Trotter, *An Essay*, viii
[28] The musical notation can be found in 'American Drinking Songs' at www.americanrevolution.org/songs
[29] Trotter, 'The Origins of Grog', *Sea Weeds*, 39–42
[30] Trotter, *An Essay*, 14
[31] Ibid., 17

But beyond those beneficial effects, alcohol consumed in excessive quantities would take the individual into realm of mental 'chaos and madness'. As for what might constitute the safe limit, Trotter saw the answer to that question as age-related:

> I am of the opinion that no man in health can need wine till he arrives at forty. He may then begin with two glasses in the day; at fifty he may add two more; and at sixty he may go to the length of six glasses *per diem* but not to exceed that quantity though he should live to be a hundred . . . The ſtimulus of wine is favourable to advanced age . . . For these reasons, wine has been aptly called '*the milk of old age*'.[32]

Thus, rather than preaching against drink, the *Essay* sought to give a balanced account of the positives and negatives. True to the spirit of the Enlightenment, Trotter insisted that moral condemnation of drunkenness as vice should be replaced by rational analysis of the nature and genesis of the problem:

> The prieſthood hath poured forth anathemas from the pulpit; and the moral-iſt, no less severe hath declaimed againſt it as a vice degrading to our nature. Both have meant well . . . But the physical influence of cuſtom, confirmed into habit, interwoven with the aᶜtions on our sentient ſyſtems, have been entirely forgotten.[33]

With his acceptance of the pleasure to be derived from drink matched by warnings against the social acceptance of drunkenness, Trotter took a position near to that favoured by a seventeenth-century American divine, Increase Mather. While castigating drunkenness Mather felt able to describe alcohol as 'the good creature of God'.[34] Both for Mather and Trotter, it was the abuse of alcohol that was the problem, not alcohol itself.

Drunkenness, said Trotter, was common in all ranks of society. And he pointed to a conflict of interest that can still be seen today between government keenness to maximize the take from the liquor tax and the interests of public health. A government faced with the need to finance the Napoleonic Wars was hardly likely to favour a cut in the nation's drinking.

Trotter was interested in the supply as well as the demand side of the drink problem. He noted that public health benefits had followed a run of poor harvests which had left malt in short supply, and deprived the distillers of their raw material. His commitment to the public health had found expression in his campaign against the proliferation of gin shops in Plymouth in 1800.

Trotter also drew attention to the way in which cultural attitudes put people under pressure to drink:

> It cannot be doubted that the convivial disposition of the inhabitants of Great Britain and Ireland, has a ſtrong tendency to extend the habit of

---

[32] Ibid., 151
[33] Ibid.,147
[34] P. Miller, *The New England Mind in the Seventeenth Century* (Harvard, 1982), 42

ebriety. There is no business of moment transacted in these islands without a libation to Bacchus. It prevails among the peers of the realm down to the parish committee . . . man is an imitative animal and quickly assimilates with his associates.[35]

The *Essay* then moved on to chronicle in detail the dangers and damages that can be the result of excessive drinking for the individual. A curious aspect of modern medical discourse on the harm that can be done by alcohol is the frequency with which drunkenness *per se*, and its consequences, are left out of the reckoning. It is as if the fact that alcohol can produce intoxication is too banal an observation to deserve attention. Not so for Trotter, however: drunkenness was at the front of his listings of the harm that can be done to the drinker.

Trotter described the early stages of intoxication with a nice eye for breaches of etiquette:

> Noisy folly and ribaldry next appear; the song becomes louder, and dancing commences with the rude squeeze and every odd gesticulation; cheerfulness and wit are changed into low humour and obscene jests. . . . The man is now drunk, and whatever he says or does, betrays the errors of the thinking principle.[36]

He warned against the resentments and quarrelling which he saw as a typical outcome of drunkenness – 'these give rise to numerous feuds and animosities which frequently terminate in bloodshed and death'. His analysis also allowed that different people would behave very differently when under the influence of drink:

> The cultivated mind is even seen in drunkenness. It commits no outrage, provokes no quarrel . . . But the ignorant and the illiterate man is to be shunned in proportion to his excess; it is human nature in its vilest garb, and madness in its worst form.[37]

In addition to the feuds and animosities, Trotter was aware that drunkenness resulted in self-neglect, accidental exposure to the elements and death by overdose. He quoted the example of a gentleman who 'after getting very drunk in his own house with some jolly companions, went to take the air in his garden', where he was set upon by his favourite dogs and only saved from death by servants. He said that horses do not like being ridden by a drunkard – 'the generous horse, when mounted by a drunkard, forgets his wonted spirit and dignity of mien, as if ashamed of his burden'.

Beyond the immediate impact of intoxication on the individual's deportment lay the long-term consequences of drinking for physical and mental health. A chapter headed 'The Catalogue of Diseases induced by Drunkenness' dealt with matters within the territory of the average modern text on

[35] Trotter, *An Essay*, 142
[36] Ibid., 21
[37] Ibid., 23

alcoholism. Clearly he did not have today's laboratory science available to underpin discussion, nor the modern epidemiological studies to establish the relative frequency of the various alcohol-related disorders which can affect the heavy drinker. Nevertheless, the chapter still reads as a well-informed catalogue of the harm that alcohol can do. Stroke, brain damage, convulsions, gout, liver disease, dyspepsia, intercurrent infections and 'abolition of the sexual appetite' were in the listing. Trotter also described 'melancholy' as a possible outcome: the relationship between excessive drinking and depression is today well recognized.

Besides the effects on the drinker of alcohol itself, Trotter mentioned the damage which might result from additives nefariously introduced by unscrupulous manufacturers and suppliers. He alleged, for instance, that 'porter brewed in London' might be spiked with opium, and he calculated that four grains of the opiate would 'double the intoxicating power of a gallon of porter'. He also alleged that, on occasion, lead was being put into wine as a sweetener.

Trotter hoped that his catalogue of possible harms might serve as dreadful warning to the potential drunkard. As he graphically put it:

> The thought of a human being rushing into eternity, from a board of gluttony, riot and intemperance, ought to appeal to the most depraved and obdurate of mortals![38]

With the cataloguing of alcohol-related diseases completed, halfway down page 172 of the *Essay* comes a sentence which leaps out in italics:

> *The habit of drunkenness is a disease of the mind.*[39]

That sentence packs into short space a conceptual revolution: but its brilliance needs decoding. *The habit of drunkenness* and a *disease of the mind* are two linked concepts that require separate dissection.

One can understand what Trotter meant by *habit of drunkenness* from a case study which he derived from a lecture given by his revered teacher, William Cullen:

> The late Dr Cullen, in his lectures, used to mention a family, all of whom were in the habit of taking a dram at a certain hour before dinner, about one o'clock. When the Doctor expressed his wonder at the practice, it was acknowledged by all, that if the time passed, or if they were from home, and did not get the usual dram, it was attended by a considerable *sense of consciousness*. In plain English, they had got into a very bad habit, and found themselves low spirited for want of their cordial.[40]

That story identifies what, in the language of modern psychology, would be called the acquisition of a learned habit. A particular time of day had been so

---

[38] Ibid., 103
[39] Ibid., 172
[40] Ibid., 154

often paired with the pleasure of the dram that the arrival of the clock hands at one o'clock cued the craving for a drink. The 'sense of consciousness' would today be called a conditioned response. Long before Pavlov enunciated his ideas on the conditioned reflex, here was Trotter talking about the dram drinkers as prototypes of Pavlov's dogs.

For the psychologist, habits develop in gradations – they are not all-or-nothing phenomena – and the same concept was articulated by Trotter:

> However seducing the love of inordinate drinking may be, like other habits, mankind seldom gets into it at once. There is a gradation in the vice.[41]

'Gradation in the vice' is directly translatable into the modern phrase 'habit strength'.

Trotter's core insight was that behind the catalogue of harmful results of excessive alcohol consumption lay the habit which drove that individual's drinking forward, the strength of that habit being crucial to understanding the individual's negative experience with alcohol. He boldly asserted that it would be useless for a physician to concentrate on the harmful results while ignoring the underlying problem of the acquired habit. As he vividly put it:

> When ebriety has become so far habitual that some disease appears in consequence the physician is for the first time called in . . . Whatever the disease may be, whether stomach complaints, with low spirits, gout, epilepsy, jaundice or any other of the catalogue, it is vain to prescribe for it until the evil genius of the habit has been subdued.[42]

This habit was for Trotter no mere abstract construct but a tangible clinical reality. Once established 'the habit of ebriety' would, he said 'be difficult to overcome whatever causes it began'. To illustrate the destructive force of this habit he gave a story about a friend casually encountered one day in the street:

> A few years ago I met an old and once valued friend in the public walk . . . I observed him more slovenly in his dress than usual, and his face rather bloated; I requested the favour of his company to dinner which he accepted in an embarrassed manner, and came. But alas! . . . At dinner his conversation was all in broken sentences; his fine literary taste was gone, and the feast of reason and the flow of soul had no share in our entertainment. He drank incessantly of sherry, as if insensible why he did, and filled bumpers every time . . . I could trace no cause for the pernicious habit in the accomplished young man but the effect of a proud spirit broken by disappointments in his profession.[43]

That passage offers a wonderfully accurate and live representation of what Trotter meant by 'the habit of drunkenness is a disease of the mind'. He is revealing here the inner meaning of an epigram.

---

[41] Ibid., 170
[42] Ibid., 171
[43] Ibid., 170–1

An Essay on Drunkenness

The pernicious habit made tangible

We need next to look at the second key term in that italicized statement found at page 172 of the *Essay – disease of the mind*. This needs to be interpreted with an awareness that the word 'disease' was being used to indicate a state of discomfort or lack of ease, rather than the modern meaning of a disorder with a unique pathology. To credit Trotter with the discovery of 'the disease concept of alcoholism' as promulgated in the twentieth century by Alcoholics Anonymous would be to misread his intention. . As for 'of the mind', what Trotter was confirming in that phrase was his belief that it was the habit that drove the behaviour, with habit seen as a psychological phenomenon.

Before moving on from the idea of habit to the follow-through in terms of treatment, it is necessary to deal briefly with a few further core aspects of the way Trotter was using words in the *Essay*. To get into Trotter's thinking we need to look a little more closely at the technical terms available to him and how he employed them.

He did not, for instance, have the word 'alcoholism' in his vocabulary. That term only came into use after the publication in 1849 of a book entitled *Alcoholismus Chronicus, eller Chronisk alkoholssjukdom*, written by a Swedish physician, Magnus Huss. Similarly 'addiction' in the modern technical sense was not available to Trotter: at the time it was a word implying that a person was becoming rather too keen on something. It was possible, for instance, to describe an Evangelical parson as 'much addicted to enthusiasm'. Now and then Trotter used the word 'addicted' in a lay sense, and at one point described a 'respectable tradesman' as 'much addicted to the bottle'. 'Dipsomania' was another term yet to be invented. As a consequence, Trotter had to make do with the word 'drunkenness', with 'ebriety' or 'inebriety' as near synonyms; and with no semantic differentiation between common-or-garden drunkenness and the compulsive drinking which characterizes alcohol dependence.[44]

Diagnosing the habit and treating it

Trotter was a hands-on physician. Thus although the *Essay on Drunkenness* gave insights into what lies behind the habit, the theoretical analysis was not offered as abstract intellectual diversion, but as a basis for a rational approach to the treatment of the next alcohol-dependent patient that any physician might encounter.

How to do it started with how to make the diagnosis. The signs and symptoms which Trotter identified included the drinker's experience of early-morning withdrawal:

> The morning hours of a drunkard, when the bottle has been withheld, often exhibit the last degree of dejected spirits, which are apt to bring on hallucination of mind. The habit of ebriety feeds itself. In the absence of stimulus

---

[44] 'The alcohol dependence syndrome' chapter in G. Edwards, E. J. Marshall and C. C. H. Cook, *The Treatment of Drinking Problems* (Cambridge, 2003), 47–69

the ideas have all a gloomy caſt, and every feeling is unpleasant: there is an aching void, that nothing can fill up but a renewal of the cup.[45]

The withdrawal symptoms were thus inevitably followed by the morning relief drink. The mention of 'hallucination of mind' flags up the possibility of withdrawal escalating into delirium tremens. Trotter was also aware that the alcohol-dependent patient would be likely to develop tolerance to the drug-effects of alcohol, and this too could be a diagnostic sign. Trotter encapsulated his views on tolerance when, in another passage, he wrote that a long-term habit might 'enable a man to devour an enormous load'. As illustration, he reported that 'a midshipman of my acquaintance, only 16 years old, drank in the West Indies, three gallons of punch daily'.

With habit-formation viewed as the root cause of the patient's continuing drunkenness, the logical treatment had to use methods which could weaken or eliminate the habit. This chain of reasoning led Trotter to take the following position:

> Studying the patient's temper and charaƈter . . . would lead us to the particular cause, time, and place of his love of the bottle. The danger of continuing his career may be then calmly argued with him, and something proposed that will effeƈtively wean his affeƈtions from it, and ſtrenuously engage his attentions.[46]

The stimuli which provoked the craving were thus to be minutely analysed. Trotter said that it was the job of the physician to 'hold up a mirror' to the patient's conduct. He was aware that a trusting relationship between doctor and patient would be vital to the success of any treatment – without using the latter-day term 'therapeutic alliance' his writing encapsulated that idea as follows:

> When the physician has once gained the full confidence of his patient, he will find little difficulty in beginning his plan of cure . . . This confidence might sometimes be deployed to great advantage when your regimen is in danger of being transgressed.[47]

In general, Trotter was a doctor who believed more in talking and listening than in bleeding, purging and bottles of medicine. As he put it, 'The practice of Physic is sometimes so tightly laced in its technical habiliments that it is incapable of turning around!'

Trotter suggested that a visit to Bath might help a patient to break from the drinking habit. He believed that the waters could be beneficial to the inebriate's physical condition, and he emphasized the value of a polite social environment in encouraging the new habit of abstinence. He repeatedly stressed that the goal of treatment had to be immediate and total abstinence from every

---

[45] Trotter, *An Essay*, 130–1
[46] Ibid., 154–80
[47] Ibid., 173

type of alcoholic drink. He poured scorn on a proposal made by another doctor that the drunkard should be gradually tapered off the drink by adding a dab of sealing wax each day to the wine glass to reduce its size.

Although the primary focus of Trotter's approach was on psychological interaction with the patient and the freeing of that individual from a habit, he also wrote about the need to bring the spouse into the treatment plan. He asserted that 'the good sense and management of an amiable wife, we know, will often accomplish wonders'. In most of his discussion on treatment, Trotter assumed that the patient was a man. He was, however, aware that women also had problems with drink, and perhaps also with laudanum kept in the reticule.

The 'Essay' appraised

Trotter was neither the first nor the last person in the history of medicine to propose that excessive drinking was a 'disease', with the variations in the meaning of that word duly noted. That said, *The Essay on Drunkenness* deserves acknowledgement as the first detailed and rational attempt to understand why some people drink too much rather than indulge in age-old moral condemnation. It sought to make alcohol dependence the business of the physician, and his idea that drinking could lead to a compulsive habit is much in accord with modern thinking on the alcohol-dependence syndrome as defined in the major diagnostic manuals. By any criteria, the *Essay* was an outstandingly clever book written by a recently retired naval physician who was showing that he could write with authority on matters other than the diseases of seaman.

But any expectation that the book would dramatically turn around the medical response to the drinking problem was to be belied by ensuing events. By the end of the nineteenth century, Trotter and the *Essay* had virtually vanished from medical consciousness. The Society for the Study and Cure of Inebriety, which was founded in London in 1884, did not acknowledge Trotter as a founding father. The moving spirit and president of that society was Dr Norman Kerr, who has been briefly quoted earlier in this chapter. His 1888 book *Inebriety, its Etiology, Pathology, Treatment and Jurisprudence*, did not so much as mention Trotter's name. That neglect was general, both in Britain and America.

Why this intellectual amnesia? Perhaps in part the answer lies in the weakness of Trotter's power base. He never held a university position, and was not able to influence a generation of students. And there was no specialized professional movement to which he could relate, or use to advance his cause. Furthermore, there was probably little profit to be made in treating drunks: and there was no emerging entrepreneurial specialism to run with his ideas. It is possible also that the temperance movement, when it began to emerge in the 1830s, looked with disfavour on the positive things he said about drink – for these people, drink, not drunkenness, was the enemy.

Within the flow of ideas in the 1880s and 1890s, a medical movement did, however, emerge on both sides of the Atlantic which took as it marching banner the slogan of inebriety as a disease, and with much claimed underpinning by science. But this later formulation was far more mechanistic than Trotter's.

It favoured genetics, and had lost the subtle psychological thinking on 'habit'. The advised treatment became an inebriates' retreat for the better classes, while long-term compulsory incarceration in an inebriates' reformatory was the favoured response for the working-class drunk.

For the modern reader, the *Essay on Drunkenness* is a book waiting to be rediscovered. With its forward-looking conclusion, its stock of anecdotes, its shrewd analyses and astute clinical observations, the *Essay* is still a good read and seems very adequately to fulfil the author's intention of appealing both to a lay and a professional audience. Trotter noted that he had always had more inclination for study than opportunity to pursue a scholarly life. On reading this book one is left with the feeling that having retired from naval service, he greatly enjoyed its writing. Turn the pages today, and that enjoyment is likely to prove infectious.

$$\sim 14 \sim$$

A War of Pamphlets

O N AN AUTUMN DAY in early November 1805, Trotter found himself in Jarrow, then a small village, some 6 miles from Newcastle on the road to South Shields. As he approached St Paul's church he became aware that the burial ground was filled with a multitude of grim-faced people. He paused to watch, and realized that he was witnessing the results of a mining disaster. A fortnight before, on 21 October, underground gases in the nearby colliery of Hebburn had exploded, killing thirty-five mine workers, the youngest aged only sixteen. The tragedy had left twenty-five widows and eighty-one orphans.[1] Funerals of this kind were not, alas, a rare occurrence. In the mining industry the gases that lurked in the depths of coal mines were a constant threat. Miners could be poisoned by the accumulation of carbon monoxide or carbon dioxide, called 'choke (or choak) damp', or killed – as in this case – by explosions due to methane, known as 'fire damp'. Trotter was deeply affected by the scene in the churchyard and returned home determined to do something about it.[2]

The result was a pamphlet entitled *A Proposal for Destroying the Fire and Choak-Damp of Coal-Mines*. Trotter had originally intended that his ideas should be published as a letter to a newspaper, but he had found that the exposition required a pamphlet-length space. The publication of Trotter's pamphlet was a demonstration of his concern for humanity, but also of his dedication to the Enlightenment principle that science in general should be useful in the public sphere and that chemistry might offer the answer to the recurrent tragedies which were blighting the local coal fields. It was Trotter's misfortune that this well-intentioned publication should once again plunge him into controversy and the eye of a professional storm.

King Coal

Coal-mining has a long history. The Romans had made some small-scale use of coal to warm their villas when they settled in Britain. As a source of domestic heating, however, easily gathered wood was the dominant fuel throughout the Middle Ages until the growth of towns necessitated a more efficient source of

[1] J. Sykes, *Local Records or Historical Register of Remarkable Events . . . in Northumberland and Durham* (Newcastle, 1833), entry for 21 October 1805
[2] T. Trotter, *A Second Address to the Owners and Agents of Coal-Mines on Destroying the Fire and Choke Damp In Confutation of two pamphlets, lately circulated in the neighbourhood of Newcastle* (Newcastle, 1806), 3

energy. By the early 1500s England was well and truly into the burning of coal, and was outstripping the rest of Europe in its keenness for this combustible. It was in the eighteenth century, however, that demand for coal soared; production went up from 2.6 million tons in 1700 to over 10 million tons in 1800. The reason lies in the combination of circumstances that are commonly grouped together under the title 'the Industrial Revolution'. Not all the uses of coal were industrial. Domestic demand was enormous and continued to increase as population and incomes grew and prices fell following improvements in canal and water transport and reductions in taxes. In 1800, for example, London alone used over 2 million tons of coal a year, of which 95 per cent came from Northumberland and Durham.[3] Inevitably, however, as the century progressed and the new manufacturing towns established themselves, the demand for coal for industrial purposes came to dominate, whether to satisfy the normal needs of such things as brewing, tanning and brick-making, or to fuel the increasing number of steam engines and, most notably, to facilitate the smelting of iron.

The north-east of England was in the forefront of this expansion and, by 1800, was responsible for over a quarter of national production. In mediaeval times, coal had been obtained from horizontal tunnels running into the sides of hills. By 1700, these shallow seams had been largely worked out and were slowly being replaced with deeper mines, in which a vertical shaft was connected to horizontal passages shored up with timbers. The increased demand occasioned by the Industrial Revolution could only be achieved by sinking even deeper mines. In 1700, the deepest were about 300 feet. By the 1750s they reached 600 feet and were going deeper.[4] This inevitably caused problems in terms of increased flooding, having to wind coal greater distances to the surface and lack of air. Only dramatic technological advance, notably the invention of the steam engine, enabled the coal industry to find the answers. The use of the Newcomen engine, with later improvements by James Watt, spread rapidly and by the end of the century had transformed the situation as regards mine drainage and haulage.[5] Other advances included improved winding gear, the use of gunpowder in shaft excavation and the invention of Sir Humphrey Davy's famous safety lamp – ironically enough, tested at Hebburn colliery in 1816. The problem of carbon monoxide and the explosive gases, however, remained and, indeed, got worse as mines went deeper.

When Trotter arrived in Newcastle, he was settling into a city which was enjoying boom times, with coal the basis for much of the burgeoning wealth. The downside was that coal-mining constituted an appallingly hazardous occupation. It has been estimated that over a forty-year life of employment, a miner at the turn of the eighteenth century would have had up to a 50 per cent

[3] N. McCord and D. J. Rowe, *Northumberland and Durham: Industry in the Nineteenth Century* (Newcastle, 1971)
[4] J. U. Nef, *The Rise of the British Coal Industry* (Cambridge, 1984), II, 124; S. Jevons, *The Coal Question* (London, 1865), quoted in G. Clark and D. Jacks, 'Coal and the Industrial Revolution', *European Review of Economic History* 11 (2007), 39–72
[5] J. Farey, *An Historical Account of the Steam Engine* (1827), 233–7, quoted in Clark and Jacks, 'Coal and the Industrial Revolution'

chance of being killed in an accident.[6] The toll of injuries is more difficult to estimate but was substantial. The causes of these accidents were various. Many deaths were the result of small-scale mishaps such as a fall of rocks or a lift failing, with just one or two miners killed. The larger tragedies, which might easily kill dozens of miners at a time, tended to be the result of sudden flooding, the explosion of methane or poisoning by the accumulation of choke-damp.

Methane is today widely known to the public as 'natural gas'. It can seep or spurt out of coal seems, and some workings are intrinsically more gassy than others. Methane when mixed with air and coal dust is dangerously explosive, with ignition easily caused by the flame of a miner's candle. The situation must have been made more perilous by the fact that fires were lit in mines to create convection currents that would suck air out of the depths. Here is a contemporary description of such an explosion:

> Enveloping the unhappy miners is quick burning fire – awful and horrible as this situation is, 'tis but the prelude to what still is more dreadful – the equition suddenly attains its height, a momentous silence ensues and an immense volume of highly rarefied air is produced . . . acquires incalculable velocity and force, with the noise of the loudest thunder and sweeps before it into horrible ruin and destruction the unhappy miners with the horses, carriages and working implements, and dashes, mangles and buries them in one common ruin amid the rubbish of timbers carried along this fiery desolating tempest.[7]

One strategy which was employed to prevent these explosions was to send a 'fireman' crawling along a tunnel with a long lit taper in front of him, in the hope of burning off the methane in a controlled sort of way. A contraption which ground a flint against a rotating steel wheel was introduced as a substitute for candle-power, but it probably improved safety not at all. In 1815 the invention of the safety lamp greatly reduced the risk from fire-damp, but that was some years after Trotter's pamphlet had been published.

The second focus of concern was choke-damp, a term sometimes applied to carbon dioxide, and sometimes to carbon monoxide. The last was in particular likely to flood into mines as a result of the explosion caused by fire-damp and incomplete combustion. The result of poisoning by either of these gases was likely to be a quick death. There are accounts of miners falling down as if shot.

When Trotter was starting to think about how science could be applied to prevention of these industrial dangers, he was addressing important questions of safety at work. The solutions, however, remained baffling and mine owners did not want to see the problem discussed in public. Thus, the *Newcastle Journal* in March 1767 concluded a report of yet another disaster with a plea that owners should make adequate provision for widows and orphans, and the comment

---

[6] M. W. Flinn, *The History of the British Coal Industry, 1700–1830: The Industrial Revolution* (Oxford, 1984), II, 419
[7] Ibid., 129

as the catastrophes from foul air become more common than ever: yet, as we have been requested to take no particular notice of these things, which in fact could have very little good tendency, we drop further mention of it.[8]

When in 1805 Trotter entered this arena, he was addressing issues which needed fresh thinking and independence of mind. Not until 1830 did the state take a hand in regulating the safety of mines, and it was mid-century before any formal system was in place to count the fatalities from mining accidents.

Trotter's pamphlet of 1805

A Proposal for Destroying the Fire and Choak-Damp of Coal-Mines[9] was published in 1805. The work was addressed to 'the Owners and Agents of Coal-Works etc.' but was also intended for a wider audience. In a dedication, he explains that his arguments would be rooted in experiment, that he would deploy 'the principles of modern chemistry', and that he would eschew 'specious but fanciful theories'. 'Philosophy' he added, 'can little avail society if confined to the study or the laboratory: it is valuable only as it makes mankind comfortable and happy.'[10] The author identifies himself as 'Thomas Trotter MD, Late Physician to his Majesty's Fleet, etc. etc. etc.' and he further asserts that this essay might be construed as 'the continuation of some former labours in the public service'.

Moving into his main text, Trotter sought further to bolster the legitimacy of his entry into this field by claiming that the safety of mines had 'a great analogy to the ventilation and purification of ships'[11] and launched into an account of 'pneumatology', defined as the science of air – 'the sky, the lake and the cavern are its vast laboratories'.[12] The French chemist Lavoisier's 'fine experiments' on the constitution of water were cited. Trotter then went on erroneously to assert that both choke-damp (which he spelt as choak-damp) and fire-damp derived from coal coming into contact with stagnant water.

With the supposed chemistry which led to the formation of these gases in coal mines expounded at some length, Trotter discussed his proposed science-based preventative strategies. The first response had to be rigorous measures to prevent the accumulation of water, because 'where these is no moisture there can be no foul airs'.[13] It was stagnant water that was the root of the evil but fresh water should be used to wash out accumulated pockets of gas. And any rotting timber and horse dung which had been left lying around should be cleared out.

Trotter went on to discuss what should be done if, despite these measures, gases should seep into mines. If fire-damp was detected, miners should be encouraged to lie 'face flat on the ground': methane was lighter than air and

---

[8] Ibid., 416
[9] Trotter, *A Proposal for Destroying Fire and Choak-Damp*
[10] Ibid., 7
[11] Ibid., 8
[12] Ibid., 9
[13] Ibid., 10

would float upwards. Trotter then went off into a lengthy diversion on the prevention of contagious diseases, with a reaffirmation of his previously stated opposition to fumigation aboard ships, and a follow through with a passage on the worthiness of his ambition to prevent mining disasters.[14]

Returning to the main purpose of the pamphlet, Trotter suggested that vapours from strong acids could be deployed so as to 'seize' the fire-damp and neutralize it – which he thought was the answer.[15] He favoured 'oxygenated muriatic acid' (hydrochloric acid), as an agent of choice. Fumigation with this vapour would be cheap and should be maintained down the pits day and night. How the vapour was to be diffused along the mine shafts in suitable quantity without noxious side effects was not considered.

Attack!

In 1806, a Dr Henry Dewar MD published in London a pamphlet highly critical of Trotter's communication, which had come out the previous year.[16] The attack was not only on Trotter's ideas but was viciously personal, and its target would undoubtedly have been shocked to see it publicly circulated. This 'letter to Thomas Trotter MD' took fifty pages to denounce him, slightly longer than the original pamphlet.

Dewar declared that he had no intention of offering a 'ceremonious apology' for the wounds he was going to inflict:

> The boldness of your pretentions and the freedom with which you scrutinize the pretentions of others, lay your works open to the most unreserved criticism. Your errors, also, are of sufficient magnitude to justify an explicit avowal of disapprobation from any reader who has at heart the interests of humanity and science, and the respectability of our profession.[17]

No quarter was to be given.

Dewar then picked up on Trotter's characterization of the mines as 'winding and tortuous'[18] and suggested that Trotter had no first-hand knowledge of the realities. The mines of Newcastle – as he correctly pointed out – consisted of 'straight and parallel passages'. Trotter had emphasized the difficulty in ventilating deep mines but 'the modern principles of ventilation seem to be wholly unknown to you'[19] Dewar offered a brief note on how such ventilation was effected so that the deepest mines were 'as completely ventilated as any place above ground',[20] which was manifestly untrue.

---

[14] Ibid., 11
[15] Ibid., 13
[16] H. Dewar, *A Letter to Thomas Trotter, M.D., occasioned by his Proposal for Destroying the Fire and Choak Damp of Coal Mines; Containing Chemical and General Strictures on that Work* (Manchester, 1806)
[17] Ibid., 3–4
[18] Ibid., 6
[19] Ibid., 7
[20] Ibid., 8–9

After a few further strictures relating to 'want of information', 'mere conjecture' and 'shallow theory', came the thunder clap:

> But, in investigating the operation of chemical principles in the formation of fire and choke damps, you do not show the smallest care to confirm your opinions by actual observation . . . some of the collateral opinions on chemical subjects intermingled with your explanation of these airs discover a gross inattention to the fact: others are delivered with a culpable vagueness of expression.[21]

Dewar then suggested that Trotter had misinterpreted Lavoisier's high-temperature experiment on decomposition of water by passing steam through a red hot tube packed with charcoal.

The demolition of Trotter's theory on the formation of the noxious gases was followed by development of Dewar's own and equally erroneous theory, namely that water was being broken down by contact with 'native sulphuret of iron', but he accused Trotter of 'gross inattention to fact'.[22]

With Trotter's explanation of how choke-damp and fire-damp came to be present in mines comprehensively rubbished, Dewar proceeded to criticize Trotter's proposals for prevention. He attacked as a dangerous absurdity the idea of washing away the choke-damp with pumped water. And it would be very expensive to install the extra pumps that would be needed to remove this extraneous addition to the all-too-common flooding.

The idea that fumes of hydrochloric acid would be effective in neutralizing fire-damp was mocked as impractical and dangerous:

> The horses as well as the men below ground, if not completely suffocated, would be subject to perpetual coughs of the most convulsive kind, whenever these animals are so unfortunate or the men so imprudent, as to spend much of their time in such infernal regions.[23]

With Trotter's suggested strategies for prevention demolished, Dewar returned once more to a root-and-branch attack on Trotter's credibility:

> I beg leave to observe that your language, with all its pomp and glitter is extremely deficient in the estimable qualities of purity and precision . . . it is somewhat lamentable to find you so little sensible to the disadvantages under which you labour. Your exclamations partake more of the transient ecstasy with which the juvenile mind receives the first dawnings of truth than the calm approbation of an enlarged mind . . .[24]

And on and on, with more of the like over many pages. The final attack related not to any alleged errors in the content and style of the previous pamphlet, but went sideways to sneer at the way in which Trotter had quoted favourable

[21] Ibid., 10
[22] Ibid., 16
[23] Ibid., 28
[24] Ibid., 36–7

statements from various authorities in the preface to his *Essay in Drunkenness* of 1804. The charge here was of self-advertisement. Publication of the letter from Dr Howes of the Humane Society was singled out for particular disapprobation:

> As for the testimony of Dr Howes, which forms the summit of the climax, it would have been considered by many as too complimentary even for a private letter. You might have been excused for valuing it as an effusion of fond and partial friendship: but by publishing it as a preface to one of your books, you discovered how little you were aware of the ridicule with which the world receives from an author such expressions of self- complacency.[25]

By the closing sentences of Dewar's pamphlet his intentions were plain to see. Obviously, he wanted to refute Trotter's proposals for dealing with choke-damp and fire-damp in the mines. But a discussion around those issues was only pretext for the larger and central intent, which was that of damaging Trotter's reputation beyond repair. However justified the technical criticisms made of Trotter's proposals, Dewar's attack went beyond the objectivities. At about the same time that Dewar's assault on Trotter was published, a hostile pamphlet also appeared under the anonymous authorship of 'A Friend to Rational Schemes of Improvement'. It does not seem to have caused Trotter as much distress as did Dewar's animadversion.

Trotter strikes back

If one had at that time been Trotter's good friend, how would one have advised him to deal with the fact of Dewar's attack being out on the bookstalls? Any well-wisher who happened to call on him at 103 Pilgrim Street would have been likely to have found him pacing the room in a state of anger and agitation. The response of a modern-day friend would probably be to advise the victim of such an attack to ignore it entirely, or to write a very short letter of refutation for publication in a local newspaper. Meet malice with cold distain, that's what one would have said. This might have been the temperate advice, but it will come as no surprise that Trotter's response was heated in the extreme. The bookstores were shortly carrying the 36 page *Second Address to the Owners and Agents of Coal Mines . . . in confutation of two pamphlets, lately circulated in the neighbourhood of Newcastle.*[26] The front sheet pointedly carried the motto 'Thou shalt not bear false witness against thy neighbour'.

Trotter began his counterattack by describing how his interest had been stirred by witnessing the burial of miners who had been killed at Hebburn colliery at the church in Jarrow. He pleaded that his motivations were entirely altruistic with no taint of self-interest. He conceded that he had no expertise in the matters he had decided to address, but he had hoped his ideas might excite the attention of others better qualified than himself. And he admitted to some

---

[25] Ibid., 49
[26] Trotter, *A Second Address*, 6

disappointment that his proposals had not so far received attention from the mine owners. If he was guilty of any errors he hoped they were minor and could be corrected. He described his pamphlet as 'an ephemeral production written on the spur of the moment'.[27]

Distress ensued when he discovered that 'two pamphlets of most extraordinary complexion and character'[28] had been circulated that contained attacks on his reputation and character. Regarding the production by the 'Friend to Rational Schemes of Improvement', Trotter deplored the anonymity but largely passed by the publication. The attack to which he gave major attention was Dewar's.

At first, Trotter's response had been moderate. But then his anger burst into the open. He accused 'this malignant *duumvirate* of wilful and deliberate *falsehood*!!!' Following that flurry of exclamation marks, epithets such as 'flagrant', 'vindictive', 'vile', 'palpable sophist', 'hyena-like', 'a soul tormented with jealousy and spleen' and 'unrivalled effrontery' were soon spattered across the pages.

Trotter accused his detractors of attempting to 'despoil me of the rank I hold in my profession'. He sought to counter such defamation by reprinting no less than eight complementary testimonials. Included were letters from Earl Howe and Lord Nelson. The Latin inscription that adorned the silver service presented to him in 1802 by his naval colleagues was reproduced. He furthermore claimed that his books 'had been handsomely received by all that is respectable in medicine in this country, and have been translated into all languages of the continent'.[29] He asserted that his work for the navy constituted 'a permanent good to the nation' and went on to claim that 'it can be demonstrated that ten thousand British seamen have been saved to the state in every year of war, since 1794, by measures and doctrines of health which originated with me'.[30] He concluded by consigning his 'calumniators' to the 'punishment of their own reflections', before signing himself off as 'your devoted humble servant T. Trotter'.

Then came the final shot in this battle, albeit something of a damp squib. The 'Friend of Rational Schemes' struck back with a pamphlet published in London and Newcastle on 26 August 1806.[31] It was a production which attempted self-justification, played injured innocence, objected to the phrase 'hyena-like', and rather surprisingly went sideways to attack a passage in *Medicina Nautica*. It was replete with typographical errors.

What motivated Dewar's attack on Trotter?

Here was an attempt at something near murder of Trotter's reputation. As in all the best crime stories, the reader will want to identify the perpetrator and his motivation.

[27] Ibid., 6
[28] Ibid., 6
[29] Ibid., 32
[30] Ibid., 32
[31] A Friend to Rational Schemes of Improvement (1806), *A Reply to Trotter's Second Pamphlet respecting the means of destroying the Fire-Damp; by the author of 'An address to the proprietors and managers of coal mines* (London and Newcastle, 1806)

First, who was Henry Dewar? His original name was Henry Frazer – in fact the Rev. Henry Frazer since he had been ordained in 1796. That same year, however, he inherited a modest fortune and ownership of the estate in Lossedale, Fife, on condition that he changed his surname. He did so and was known thereafter as Dewar. The change in circumstances led to a change in career. He acquired a medical degree and briefly served as an assistant surgeon in the army, being present during the invasion of Egypt and ejection of the French by a British army under Sir Ralph Abercrombie in 1801. Retirement to civilian life followed first in Manchester, where Dewar claimed to have been briefly a physician in the infirmary and where he was certainly a corresponding member of the city's Literary and Philosophical Society. He then moved to Scotland and became a member of the Royal Society of Edinburgh. From that point until his death in 1823[32] Dewar's life seems to have been that of a scientific dilettante, reading and publishing papers on an assortment of subjects – ophthalmia in Egypt, measures to assess the benefits of foreign trade, the education of a young man who was deaf and blind and the treatment of the sinuous ulcer[33] – not to mention the exchanges with Trotter over chemistry and choke-damp.

It is difficult not to see Dewar's military and scientific career as a mirror image, although a pale shadow, of Trotter's own. Did Dewar's awareness of this, and his envy of Trotter's reputation and success, lie at the root of his animosity? Or was Dewar genuinely annoyed at the sight of a retired naval doctor, only recently moved to the district but willing to pontificate on matters of which, at a practical level, he knew little? A measured rebuke might have been in order. But the fury of Dewar's assault and its personalized nature make this an insufficient explanation for the attack.

Another possibility is that Dewar was a friend of Dr Clark and was incensed by the way he believed Trotter had maligned Clark's reputation. The animus seemed to derive from Trotter's letters to the *Medical and Physical Journal* detailing his differences of opinion with his elderly confrere. Whether or not Dewar perceived accurately Trotter's intentions towards Clark, he believed that wrong had been done to a colleague's memory and that an off-hand remark by Trotter constituted an attack on his 'Collection of Papers on Fever Wards'. But here again the possible provocation does not seem commensurate with the ferocious nature of the response.

Did Dewar have other motivations? Could there have been tensions around Dr Trotter as a newcomer moving in to catch a share of the local demand for private practice? Were the mine owners keen to neutralize a doctor who seemed hell-bent on stimulating public interest in a scandal they did not want exposed? This in sum is a crime story of a rather unusual kind – a mystery without any final answer offered to the waiting audience. As to motivations of that shadowy assailant, the 'Friend to Rational Schemes of Improvement', we are left entirely in the dark

---

[32] *The Edinburgh Annual Register* 16 (1823), 320
[33] *Transactions of the Royal Society of Edinburgh* (1815 and 1816). 'On the education of James Mitchell the young man born deaf and blind' in vol. 6 (1813), 77–87; 'Observations on the theory of language' in vol. 7 (1814), 387–410; 'On the treatment of the sinuous ulcer' in vol. 8 (1816), 477–93

A battle, even when it involves exchange of pamphlets rather than crashing of cannonballs, can, however, reveal much of character. So what light does this engagement throw on Trotter? The decision to publish the initial *Proposal for Destroying the Fire and Choak-Damp of Coal-Mines* was a response to a tragic encounter as Trotter passed a churchyard. He was innately a feeling person and this sort of reaction was in accord with what we otherwise know of his temperament. It also matches with his generally well-developed level of professional self-confidence, and his belief that he was someone who could solve problems, even if in this instance confidence spilled over towards over-confidence.

The reply to Dewar contained in Trotter's second address reveals some other aspects of Trotter's disposition. Here we see him rounding on his assailant in an attack every bit as vitriolic as Dewar's. That may have been the way in which pamphleteers in a robust age were likely to conduct themselves. The characteristic that is shown most vividly in Trotter's reactions to Dewar's assault relates to his willingness to deploy grand testimonials in his defence. Within the expectations of modern manners, to call Howe and Nelson as character witnesses and use an inscription on a silver service as evidence may seem absurdly overdone. What in fact stands out as sharply and painfully revealed is how important the opinions of high authority were for Trotter's self-esteem.

15

A View of the Nervous Temperament

IN 1807, three years after the *Essay on Drunkenness* had reached the book-shops, Trotter published another major text, with the same kind of joint lay and professional readership intended. The full title of the new book was *A View of the Nervous Temperament being a Practical Enquiry into the Increasing Prevalence, Prevention and Treatment of those Diseases commonly called Nervous, Bilious, Stomach and Liver Complaints, Indigestion, Low Spirits, Gout etc.*[1] – a title virtually as synopsis. Further editions appeared in 1807 and 1812. A fac-simile edition appeared in 1976 in an American 'Classics in Psychiatry' series.[2] The choice of James Gregory, then head of the Edinburgh Medical School, as person to whom the book was dedicated, was designed to enhance Trot-ter's credibility with the medical profession, although Gregory was not as well known as Jenner. At various points in the text Trotter stressed the extent of his medical experience, with an insistence that it had encompassed much more than the treatment of the fleet. His views were therefore

the result of a more extensive field of experience than generally falls the lot of every physician: for it has been acquired by attendance on some thousands of cases in both sexes, under all varieties of rank, employment, age, situation, climate etc.[3]

The two sides of Georgian prosperity

Fully to comprehend the significance of Trotter's social critique one needs to be reminded of the magnitude of what was taking place in Britain at the time. The Georgian period was one of unprecedented change and prosperity. By its end, the agricultural scene had been transformed by the enclosure of common land and improvements to soil, crops and livestock. Likewise, industry had been revolutionized by new technological processes, the ingenuity of profit-seeking entrepreneurs, the availability of raw materials like coal and iron and the development of speedy transport systems, notably canals and turnpikes. And in support, trade, backed by the necessary infrastructure of banks, credit, insurance and ships, was flourishing. During Trotter's own lifetime, industrial and

---

[1]   Trotter, *A View of the Nervous Temperament*
[2]   Trotter, *A View of the Nervous Temperament* (facsimile edition), Classics in Psychiatry series, ed. E. T. Carison (New York, 1967)
[3]   Ibid., viii–ix

commercial output doubled and agricultural production went up by a quarter.[4] England had become, in the words of Horace Walpole, 'the capital of the world'.

These economic changes were mirrored in the demographics. Between 1760 and 1800, the population increased by one third to reach 8.5 million, and the number living in towns doubled to 3.5 million. London alone boasted 900,000 inhabitants, while Manchester, Liverpool and Birmingham had over 75,000 each.[5] Economic expansion brought prosperity to some, but it meant disruption and hardship to many. The displacement of the landless from the countryside, the insanitary conditions in the sprawling industrial towns and the naked capitalism of the new factory system left their marks in pauperism, malnutrition and low life expectancy. But for those who had the skills, flair or capital needed to take advantage of the opportunities, the standard of life rose. Employment prospects were good, prices remained steady or fell, and there were plenty of people with enough cash in their pockets to buy the new brick houses that were spreading over Georgian Britain and to equip them with the latest, specially manufactured household goods – crockery made by Josiah Wedgwood, silver-plated dinner services by Matthew Boulton, and furniture by Thomas Sheraton or George Hepplewhite. It was now possible to dress according to fashion rather than comfort, and to indulge in imported tropical luxuries like tea, sugar, chocolate and tobacco. And above all, there was money for leisure and for pleasure. 'Pleasure', said the earl of Chesterfield in a letter to his son, 'is now, and ought to be, your business'. There were theatres to attend, race meetings to gamble at, assemblies to dance at, and fashionable novels by Sterne, Smollet or Fielding to read. For many, Georgian society offered comfort, leisure and luxury.

There were, however, many who found these changes worrying. Thinkers had already abandoned the cold reason and formalism of the previous century for a philosophy which stressed feeling, spontaneity and emotion. The cult of 'the noble savage', rooted in Rousseau's idea that the basic goodness of humanity could only flourish in a simple setting far from the corrupting influence of modern society, was growing in popularity and had apparently been confirmed by Captain Cook's voyages to Polynesia. Georgian urban life seemed the antithesis of this ideal. The lives of country folk, whether hardy peasants, hardened and invigorated by working outside in all weathers, or Squire Weston riding to hounds all day then downing a flagon of ale and a side of beef, seemed infinitely more wholesome than those of urban workers trooping into factories, or the middle classes, whose existence, as portrayed by Jane Austen, consisted of nothing more strenuous than elegant drawing-room conversation over tea followed by a novel, letter writing or the occasional stroll. Some argued that wealth and urban living were undermining the nation's moral fibre and making it go soft.

For practical doctors like Trotter, these concerns were reinforced by an awareness of the stresses and temptations inherent in luxurious, urban life-styles. The subject had been first effectively addressed by a fellow Scot, Dr George Cheyne, in his 1733 book *The English Malady*.[6] Cheyne, speaking from

---

[4] W. A. Cole and P. Deane, *British Economic Growth 1688–1967* (Cambridge, 1967), 78
[5] D. Marshall, *Industrial England 1776–1851* (London, 1973), 229–31
[6] G. Cheyne, *The English Malady*, ed. with introduction by Roy Porter (London, 1991)

first-hand knowledge – his own weight reached a gigantic 450 pounds after one gluttonous binge – had drawn attention to the fact that over-indulgence impaired both physical health and mental well-being. Vastly increased consumption of food and drink was leading to harmful consequences in terms of obesity, gout and drunkenness; and he estimated that one third of the affluent were likely to suffer from nervous disorders – hysteria, vapours, spleen, anxiety and low spirits. Cheyne made it plain, however, that he was only talking about the aristocracy: 'Nervous disorders', he wrote, 'are the diseases of the wealthy.'[7] Others pointed out that another consequence of leisure was that the wealthy had more time to worry about their health and more money to spend on remedies. The result was the burgeoning of what Roy Porter described as 'the sick trade'– highly paid doctors and quacks, the over-prescription of drugs, hypochondria, self-medication and continuous resort to pills and powders.

Medical academics were also aware of the trend. A leading figure was Trotter's former teacher, William Cullen, who invented the term 'neurosis', which he defined as a psychological disorder resulting from a disturbance of the nervous fibres which linked brain to body.[8] Former pupils like Thomas Arnold and Alexander Crichton took these ideas further into studies of lunacy.[9] But although Cullen was coming to the conclusion that insanity and psychological diseases could result from malfunctions of the nervous system alone, he still accepted the general principle that physical problems could cause neurosis and vice versa.

There was also a religious dimension in the denunciation of luxurious lifestyles. The affluence of the Georgian period had coincided with a relaxation of public morals and a sharp retreat from the restrictions of their puritan forebears. The evangelical movement of the late eighteenth century became concerned and readily accepted that moral corruption was implicit in a luxurious lifestyle. The *Evangelical Magazine* of 1800 helpfully published a spiritual barometer chart showing the major milestones which would respectively mark the road to perpetual happiness or eternal damnation. Significantly, the first four indicators of progress towards perdition included in sequence 'levity in conversation', 'luxurious entertainment', 'visits to the theatre' and as the climax of sinfulness, 'the love of novels'.[10]

All these themes are reflected in the pages of *A View of the Nervous Temperament*. Some are expanded. Cheyne's seventy-year-old description of the nervous temperament as being restricted to the aristocracy, for example, is updated by Trotter to cover the middle class created by the new prosperity. His ideas may not therefore be new, but they were influential since, as one authority notes, 'his study pulls together many different strands of Georgian thinking about the nervous patient and rearticulates them in images that would persist throughout the nineteenth century'.[11]

---

[7] Ibid., 158
[8] W. Cullen, *Synopsis Nosologiae Methodicae* (Edinburgh, 1772)
[9] R. Porter, *Flesh in the Age of Reason* (London, 2003), 312
[10] *The Evangelical Magazine*, in R. Porter, *English Society in the 18th Century* (London, 1982), 309
[11] P. M. Logan and P. Melville, *Nerves and Narratives: A Cultural History of Hysteria in 19th Century British Prose* (Berkley, 1997)

The value of Trotter's *View of the Nervous Temperament* is that it gives a comprehensive description of late Georgian thinking on the consequences of luxury and idleness on the nation's health, it discusses the physical and mental problems which result, and it proposes practical measures aimed at preventing or overcoming them. The pages that follow will attempt to analyse these various themes.

Trotter's psychology and the meaning of 'temperament'

Throughout the book there are references to 'habit' as explanation for various types of dysfunctional behaviour, and to that extent the theoretical basis echoes that favoured by Trotter in his *Essay on Drunkenness*. But there is a different perspective here. 'Temperament' is at the centre and, in a key passage, he asserts that the human subject 'however much he may be styled the *creature of habit* is . . . in many respects the creature of his own temperament'. What meaning was Trotter giving to the phrase 'nervous temperament'? It is, he explains a 'predisposition, whether hereditary or acquired . . . which is now to be considered as a permanent state of body, that cannot be easily changed, and will commonly remain for life'.[12]

This nervous temperament, whether acquired or reinforced by exposure to a lifestyle that is sedentary, indulgent and replete with stimulants, manifests itself in 'shades and gradations' that interlock with other aspects of temperament, the key physiological consequence being 'a sensitive, irritable, and mobile condition of nerves: by which different organs of the body from slight causes, are urged into violent and involuntary action'.[13]

A wide range of disorders was identified by Trotter as possible consequences of the nervous temperament. They include disorders of the digestive system, asthma and gout and abuse of alcohol and opiates. The major psychological consequence is manifest in

> *a disposition of mind* . . . beginning with uncommon sensibility to all impressions; peevishness of temper; irresolution of conduct; sudden transitions from sadness to joy, and the contrary; silent or loquacious; officiously busy or extremely indolent; irascible; false perceptions; wavering judgement; melancholy; madness; exhibiting in the whole, signs of deranged sensation.[14]

It is not easy to identify an exact modern equivalent of the idea of 'nervous temperament' as Trotter employed that term. The fact that he seems to have had in mind a condition equivalent to a personality disorder, the criterion of which was a state which will 'commonly remain for life', is in accordance with that interpretation. But Trotter probably envisaged the nervous temperament as more a physical than a psychological disorder. He saw its origin as lying in malfunction of 'the great sympathetic nerve'.

---

[12] Trotter, *A View of the Nervous Temperament*, 197
[13] Ibid., 197
[14] Ibid., 195

Trotter was a general physician, but one with an innate sympathy for a psychological perspective on medicine. That vision of things, he said, had been with him since his early days in the profession:

> I well remember, when I was young in the profession, no disease puzzled me so much as those of the nervous kind. I was everyday committing blunders: in vain I had recourse to books, but books could not supply the deficiency . . . most young men, in beginning their medical career run great hazard of mistaking these complaints as they only become apparent by a concourse of symptoms, that is extremely irregular and equivocal.[15]

He hoped that his book would help familiarize young doctors with the many faces of nervous disorders, and enhance their confidence in treating such conditions.

Noble savages as people who do not have bad nerves

Like Cheyne, Trotter considered that the labouring classes would be immune to the nervous temperament. In true Rousseau style, he sought to persuade his readers that people who did not share in the luxuries of civilized societies would be unaffected. As no contemporary evidence base existed, he attempted to carry the argument by means of rhetoric and by reference to the Roman Tacitus, a source of quasi-anthropological information to which a classically trained eighteenth-century scholar would instinctively have turned. The belief that people living in less-developed societies were free from mental illness continued to hold sway until the middle of the twentieth century, when it was refuted by epidemiological field studies. In truth, dwellers in such societies probably experienced the same rates of psychological problems as Trotter encountered in his contemporary Britain.

In an extended flight of fancy, Trotter asserted that 'few bodily disorders' were to be found among 'our ancestors who dwelt in huts and hovels', were exposed to the elements, and survived by hunting or herding. The primitive Germans of whom Tacitus wrote were known to have drunk 'to the most ferocious degree of ebriety', but their robust constitutions, deriving from hard exercise and simple diet, protected them from adverse alcohol-related consequences that would enfeeble members of civilized society if they had binged in the same way. Trotter also stated that these Germans had, in their state of innocence, been remarkably chaste.[16] Likewise, 'in the woods of Germany . . . such complaints as *bilious and nervous*, must have been unknown because all the causes which render them prevalent in this age, did not then exist'. They are, he concluded 'the progeny of wealth, luxury, indolence and intemperance'.[17]

This confident assertion was drawn from little evidence. Here one seems to be in the presence of an exponent of the new Romanticism, rather than the critical Enlightenment mind that had authored the *Essay on Drunkenness*.

[15] Ibid., ix
[16] Ibid., 21
[17] Ibid., 23

Noble sons of labour

Trotter's contention was that rustics and labourers in contemporary society were less prone to nervous disorders than wealthier citizens. And, like the ancient Germans, the modern labouring classes were able to sink quantities of alcohol without any harm done – their lifestyles conferring a beneficent resistance:

> Indeed it is to be remarked everywhere how much longer the laborious porter and drayman, who get often drunk, will continue their career than the less exercised gentleman: a proof that labour by invigorating and hardening the body, makes it resiſt even the effeéts of debauch. How soon would the morning dram of a Billingsgate fishwife deſtroy one of our high bred women of fashion![18]

In line with thinking at the time, Trotter further suggested that the constitution of 'a labouring and active peasantry . . . exposed to weather in all seasons', was likely to be characterized by

> A vigorous vital power, a rigid fibre, and a florid dense blood: they are a direétly opposite ſtate of the syſtem to what predisposes to nervous diseases. No kind of diet comes wrong to the ſtomach of a hale ruſtic . . . He is also capable of braving fatigue, privation of food and sleep, and every other hardship, in a manner that would soon deſtroy the town inhabitant.[19]

Trotter saw this robust and hardy peasantry as the essential recruiting ground for the army and navy. Indeed, sailors were unlikely to be affected by luxury and softening. Both officers and men entered the navy at a young age 'before they can be acquainted with the softening arts of the day'. This was good news because

> amidſt the general effeminacy of manner, that is rapidly consuming the manly spirit and physical ſtrength of this age, and which may ultimately annihilate all that is great in the charaéter of Britons, it is somewhat consoling to observe, that the seamen of the navy, that bulwark of our liberties, will be the laſt of our community to feel the effeét of those enervating cuſtoms.[20]

The debauching of Britain

Although Trotter's views on the benefits likely to flow from hard labour and the rustic life are unlikely to be persuasive to a modern critic, his observations on the mores of Georgian society were those of an astute witness, and carry much more conviction. Before the phrase 'lifestyle' had come into common usage, he was writing about the health consequences of the changing lifestyles

---

[18]   Ibid., 21
[19]   Ibid., 153
[20]   Ibid., 14

which were the outcomes of the increasing urbanization and prosperity of Georgian Britain. It is interesting to have a physician of any period in history talking about what manner of people he has seen on his house calls.

Trotter's denunciation of the way in which society had gone soft veered at times towards apocalyptic intensity. Society, he cried out, was being debauched by the affectations of modernity – by sedentary, indoor lifestyles, self-indulgence, harmful stimulants and artificial passions. The end result could well be the destruction of the British nation and the triumph of its enemies. The only way to avoid this was

> by returning to simplicity of living and manners, so as to check the increasing prevalence of nervous disorders; which if not reſtrained soon muſt . . . make us an easy conqueſt to our invaders; and ultimately convert us into a nation of slaves and helots.[21]

He warned that

> when wealth and luxury arrive at a certain pitch in any country, mankind cannot remain long ſtationary in mental qualifications or corporeal ſtrength. Domeſtic peace is firſt invaded by asperity of temper and turbulent passions. Vices and diseases are close attendants on riches and high living . . . when polished society may be said to bring on its own *dotage* and to dig its own *grave!*[22]

Trotter's purpose was therefore not limited to offering advice to doctors on the cause and cure of neurosis. Rather, his intention was to put before a wider audience a demand for root-and-branch reform of lifestyles, with no less a price than national survival as the ultimate stake. As with the *Essay on Drunkenness*, he was thinking at the level of national health, rather than that of the individual patient.

Besides asserting that society was in a state of decay and dissipation compared with its original lost innocence, Trotter listed the specific aberrations which he saw as factors predisposing the population to the development of the nervous temperament. Modern life was beset by a plethora of threats to psychological well-being.

Gluttony and the voluptuary

Overeating was high on Trotter's list and, in the footsteps of George Cheyne, he argued 'that temperance as to quality [and] abstemiousness to quantity is one of the golden rules of health'.[23] He warned about the ways in which the fashionable dining table could encourage gluttony, with the desire to eat huge quantities of rich food, ' heightened to the palate by all the arts of cookery'.[24]

---

[21] Ibid., xi
[22] Ibid., 165
[23] Ibid., 68
[24] Ibid., 68

To Trotter, the 'voluptuary' was a feature of the time: a person whose life was one of indolence, luxurious diet and fermented liquors. He would be 'characterized by a florid complexion, sparkling eyes, and unmeaning simper, softness of flesh and fullness of blood' but would not necessarily be obese.[25]

As for the psychological character of this despicable product of high living:

> The mind is light, indolent, and indifferent to everything but pleasure. A person of this description is perpetually in pursuit of some selfish indulgence . . . flatters the weak part of the sisterhood, but shuns the society of sensible women.[26]

The outcome of such a lifestyle could be early decrepitude and nervous debility.

Stimulants and sedatives

Trotter warned against *opium*. This related to an era when laudanum, as an alcoholic tincture of opium, was not only heavily prescribed by doctors but available over the counter from druggists and grocers. In the early decades of the nineteenth century, annual consumption of opium averaged for every man, woman and child in the United Kingdom the equivalent of 120 standard doses of morphine.[27] Small wonder that opium featured in Trotter's list of concerns:

> when opium happens to be soothing to weak nerved people from their quick sensations, it is apt to be the more craved for and converted into habit. The languor and dejection which follow its operation pave the way to the repetition of the dose, till generally debility succeeds.[28]

Midwives, nurses and persons outside the medical profession who dispensed laudanum ought to be 'solemnly warned' against it because it could become addictive.

Trotter commented on the difficulties facing a fee-dependent physician who tried to limit the prescribing regime demanded by a determined patient:

> hard is the task imposed on a medical attendant; he must obey or starve. The *night draft* thus becomes familiar in the family; the servant goes to the apothecary for it with as little ceremony as he buys kitchen salt. He sees the shop boy count the drops into a phial, and when he gets home, narrates the composition of the placebo to the cook and the nursemaid. Not a domestic in the house but soon learns what a fine thing laudanum is.[29]

[25] Ibid., 69
[26] Ibid., 69
[27] V. Berridge and G. Edwards, *Opium and the People: Opiate Use in Nineteenth Century England* (London, 1981)
[28] Trotter, *A View of the Nervous Temperament*, 135; see also R. Porter, *Flesh in the Age of Reason*, 402–4
[29] Ibid., 136

That is a well-observed description of the social transmission of attitudes towards a drug. Trotter had over the previous three years encountered seven young women who had intentionally overdosed with opium, and he suspected that it was responsible for many unexplained causes of sudden death. Trotter's warning on the dangers resulting from the uncontrolled availability of opium was well founded. It was not until 1886 that the first Pharmacy Act was to put the supply of this drug on a different footing from kitchen salt.

Trotter described *tobacco* as a 'narcotic in common use', with the word 'narcotic' employed in a way roughly equivalent to the modern phrase 'mind-acting drug'. Trotter's use of the word is broad, and while he appears to use it in the classical sense of inducing numbness or sleep, he implies, in the modern sense, that the 'narcotic principle' also includes acting as a stimulant. He stated that it 'powerfully acts on the nervous system', and 'those who devour it in great quantities die of apoplexy, palsy and dropsy'. He warned against chewing and snuffing as well as smoking. Amazingly, he alleged that smoke 'injected into the rectum' had frequently proved fatal.[30]

Tea-drinking attracted several pages of warning and denunciation. Tea was consumed in huge quantities throughout Great Britain. It was a 'beverage suited to an indolent and voluptuous age' which dilutes a substantial dinner, and soothes the stomach of drunkards but results in 'debility and nervous diseases'. It is particularly hurtful, he wrote, 'to the female constitution'.[31] Trotter said that he had known a number of men and women who could not take tea in any form without a worsening in their nervous symptoms. He had himself given up tea-drinking because 'it added to my natural shortness of vision'.[32] He reported that the use of tea was increasing among the 'lower orders of the community and the labouring poor', with the consequence that nervous complaints were becoming more common amongst this class. He also believed that the use of tea by this sector of society 'paves the way to habitual dram drinking'. And problems could be caused by money being spent on tea rather than on nourishing food. Erroneously, coffee was said to contain less of the 'narcotic principle' than tea: a cup of coffee has in fact twice the stimulant content of a cup of tea.

Soda water too was included in Trotter's listing of modern evils. Taken increasingly as a regular morning draft after a nightly debauch, he saw it as degenerate and 'humiliating to the physical vigour of Britons to see . . . a medicine converted into a tavern beverage!'[33] He alleges that long-term use of soda water could damage the stomach and cause 'very serious cutaneous diseases'.

The over-prescription of medicines

Trotter was not a doctor who favoured promiscuous prescribing; he preferred talking to the pushing of pills. But he was aware that patients with nervous dispositions found medicines alluring.

[30]   Ibid.,139
[31]   Ibid., 71
[32]   Ibid., 188
[33]   Ibid., 319

All nervous persons are uncommonly fond of drugs; and they are the chief consumers of advertised remedies, which they conceal from their medical friends. Among some well-meaning people, this inordinate desire for medicine has frequently become of itself a disease.[34]

Trotter cautioned against the dangers inherent in the overuse of emetics and purgatives. He also warned against the poisoning which could be caused by popular medicines that contained mercury. To illustrate this he told the story of a physician on a foreign station, who 'took it into his head that all modern diseases originated from syphilis', and insisted on a course of treatment for the sailors which went on for years. The result, said Trotter, was 'some of the most unfortunate stomach affections which ever came under my care; a few valuable men were brought to the grave by it'.[35]

That story serves as a reminder that at the time when Trotter was writing not only were drugs uncontrolled, but medical practice itself was totally unregulated. Any practitioner obsessed by an overvalued idea could do vast harm.

The sedentary life

Trotter viewed the *lack of physical exercise* as an important factor contributing to the ill-health of urban society, whether men of business confined to their offices and the counting houses or the wealthy males lounging in Bond Street. As for thousands of women, their exercise consisted of little more than 'a formal walk before dinner, to call on a few friends or to make some purchase at a shop'. At the slightest fatigue, 'the remainder of the journey is performed in a coach'.[36] As for children, they are coped up in restricted spaces, have little opportunity for exercise and are actually disadvantaged in this regard when compared to the father's hounds and horses.[37]

Special concern was expressed about the situation of girls:

we indulge our boys to yoke their go-carts and ride on long rods, while little miss must have her more delicate limbs crampt by sitting the whole day dressing a doll...All female employments that are performed in the sitting posture injure health; and are hurtful in proportion to the early age in which they are begun.[38]

Lack of exercise is also liable to undermine the ability of a privileged city woman to cope with the *perils of child birth*.[39] This pampered female would still be lying stretched on her postnatal couch and exhibiting some nervous complaint, when her robust countrywoman would be out helping her husband in the fields. Too much refinement might also make a woman prone to miscarriage and diminish her fertility.

---

[34] Ibid., 104–5
[35] Ibid., 128
[36] Ibid., 62–3
[37] Ibid., 62–3
[38] Ibid., 51
[39] Ibid., 356

Trotter also saw *the wearing of inappropriate clothing* as a danger. Anxious to copy the lifestyles of the rich, people of 'the middling sort', such as the wives and daughters of tradesmen, were adopting fashions as unhealthy as one might see in a duchess. 'In the present time', he wrote, 'cloathing or dress is to be found in the extreme: either too much or too little.' Young men swaddled themselves in flannel, while young women would often garb themselves in just 'a few folds of fine muslin'.[40] Tight lacing by women was also decried.

Bad air

That a *pure atmosphere* was of the first importance to good health had been a constant in medical thinking for many years. Trotter graphically described those aspects of the urban environment that contributed to air pollution:

> Narrow lanes, high buildings and houses, filthy kennels, small apartments, huge warehouses, manufacturing establishments, cellars underground, consumption of fuel, and a large population, are so many sources whence the air is contaminated . . . It is familiar to people living in great towns to remark, how imperfectly all the trees and shrubs grow in their little gardens.[41]

He criticized the stuffiness of unventilated children's nurseries, left in the hands of nurses and servants, and seldom visited by fashionable mothers.[42]

Novels and the theatre

The potential threats to nervous good health also included *reading novels*, which is

> one of the great causes of nervous disorders. The mind that can amuse itself with the love-sick trash of most modern compositions of this kind, seeks enjoyment beneath the level of a rational being . . . To the female mind in particular, as being endowed with finer feeling, this species of literary passion has often been fatal; and some of the most unfortunate of the sex have imputed their ruin chiefly to the reading of novels.[43]

Parents should prevent their children from access to romances which were likely to engender 'ardent passions without power to resist or subdue them'.
Likewise, all should be protected from the theatre since

> the *drama* is another hotbed of this disease . . . [and] the sentiments they express cannot be much improved from the mouths of some first-rate actresses, who live openly as kept mistresses.[44]

---

[40] Ibid., 78
[41] Ibid., 56
[42] Ibid., 60
[43] Ibid., 90
[44] Ibid., 90

The prevention and treatment of nervous disorders

Trotter put greater emphasis on prevention than on treatment – the nervous disorders once established were, he argued, largely intractable. In the event, the distinction between what he chose to call 'prevention' and what he designated as 'treatment' was often rather blurred.

Prevention involved bringing about what Trotter called 'a reversed mode of living', designed to bring patients back to a simple regimen of food, air and exercise.[45] After three generations of town dwelling, any family would be likely to become degenerate, so their only hope of salvation was to return to 'the habits and amusements of a country life'. Trotter concluded that there was little that could be done for the health of the woman who stayed in the city. Better schooling for girls, however, provided some prophylaxis: their boarding schools should of course be in the country, and inculcate a fondness for long walks and the study of botany, the latter being a subject peculiarly adapted to the minds of young ladies.[46] As for men, if business prevented their living in the country, they should engage in strenuous outdoor exercise in the city such as horseback riding.

Trotter's view on what the pharmacopoeia could achieve in ameliorating the burgeoning level of nervous disorders was very modest. Reversals in modes of living were the answer, and the cure lay in the patient's own hands. Sadly, however, he conceded that the appetite for luxury was more likely to triumph.[47]

Despite Trotter's aversion to promiscuous prescribing of drugs, he accorded some place to medicaments in the treatment of nervous conditions, with iron his favourite tonic. It might occasionally be appropriate to resort to conventional physical treatments such as bleeding, leeching and purging, but he insisted that a doctor's dominant responsibility was to do no harm. What worked for one patient might not work for another, and there was no panacea available from the apothecary's shop. In a phrase that exactly catches his professional philosophy, Trotter described the practice of medicine as a 'conjectural art'.[48]

What view to take of the book?

This is a considerable difference between Trotter's two major texts. His *Essay on Drunkenness* reflects the mind-set of a rational age in which medicine was seen as a science and in which Trotter avoids moralizing and appears as a seeker after objective understanding. By contrast, *A View of the Nervous Temperament* is a work of 'popular science' about a topic of growing concern, in which medicine is seen as an art. Likewise, both the book's undercurrent and Trotter's condemnation of society as 'wallowing in luxury' are strongly moralistic and emotional.

A View of the Nervous Temperament was the culmination of a series of works on nervous disorders going back as far as George Cheyne. Its significance is not therefore that the views expressed in it were new; rather, they represented

---

[45] Ibid., 280
[46] Ibid., 281
[47] Ibid., 257
[48] Ibid., 142

the culmination of late Georgian ideas about the impact of prosperous life-styles on nervous diseases. Trotter's book was therefore part of an established and ongoing eighteenth-century medical and philosophical tradition.

Although ideas on temperament or character were already commonplace in Trotter's medical world, the use of 'nervous temperament' as an organizing idea was original. He did not, however, use the idea consistently. Sometimes he seemed to forget the 'temperament' and dealt with the multiple physical and psychological consequences of bad nerves, as he conceived them. The idea of 'bilious' disorder, which also features in the book's title, was subsidiary and never well worked out.

Likewise, there is a lurking question in this book as to how Trotter intended to handle the mind–body relationship, and the dualism inherent in the Cartesian dichotomy. At times he seemed to be breaking through that separatism and seeing mind and body as one. More often, he was giving precedence to physical causes of psychological disorder. 'Nervous' for him meant, quite crudely, some kind of physical disorder of the nerves: he was not so much foreshadowing psychosomatic formulations as enunciating a somatic-psychic concept of disorder.

The idea that health was influenced by the conditions of living was already common in Trotter's time. His attempt to identify the factors that had a causal bearing on nervous disorder produced an astonishing list – idleness, gluttony, luxury, tea, soda water, stuffy rooms, stimulants, over prescription of drugs, fashionable clothes, tobacco, novels and the theatre. But even these do not exhaust the issues that attracted his concern. He drew attention to the evils of the slave trade and to the problem of child labour in Britain's industrial cities. He castigated 'the gentlemen of the stock exchange'.[49] Antoine Mesmer was denounced as a fraud. Bonaparte was an object of loathing stigmatized as an arch-tyrant who himself exemplified features of the nervous temperament.[50] Closer to home, Trotter attacked 'over grown farmers' who enclosed land and annihilated 'the middling class of countrymen'.

The origins of Trotter's antipathy to things luxurious are not hard to find. There was already a well-established suspicion of wealth and luxury in the eighteenth century, shared by almost every literary figure.[51] It should be said, however, that not everyone joined in the chorus. Samuel Johnson, for example – whose chances of wallowing in luxury were remote – had a far more relaxed view. In conversation with Oliver Goldsmith in 1773, he is reported as saying 'Luxury, so far as it reaches the poor, will do good to that race of people: it will strengthen and multiply them. Sir, no nation was ever hurt by luxury, for, as I have said before, it can reach but a few.'[52]

It needs a stretch of imagination to understand how this book would have been regarded when copies reached the bookshelves in 1807. Seen through the eyes of a reader taking it home on the day of its publication, its comprehensive

---

[49] Ibid., 158
[50] Ibid., 169
[51] J. Sekora, *Luxury: The Concept in Western Thought* (Baltimore and London, 1977)
[52] Ibid., 103

nature and the passion and insistence with which the message was promulgated would have had a considerable impact. Indeed, it was a book which was intended to confront and startle both its general and specialist readership. The fact that it ran into several editions showed that it provoked general interest even if it passed almost unnoticed in the medical press. This is not surprising. The work did not comprise an objective and tightly argued exposition of a new medical theory; but it had freshness and energy, and addressed a subject that pressed home and was of contemporary interest. To the modern reader Trotter's book is valuable in that it encapsulates late Georgian thinking about the consequences of luxury and idleness on the nation's health. And, of equal importance, it is a mirror to Georgian society held up by a physician with first-hand experience and an unforgiving eye.

16

Physician as Poet and Playwright

As well as his large accomplishments as a medical author, Trotter wrote poetry throughout his life and was the author of a play. He made his debut as a poet when aged only sixteen, with verses published in an Edinburgh newspaper. He continued to write poetry throughout his adult life and in 1829 collected his traceable compositions into a volume called *Sea Weeds*, with the sub-title *Poems written on various occasions, chiefly during a naval life*.[1] The 'M.D.' was as ever put after his name, and Trotter identified himself as 'Physician of the Fleet'. Facing the title page is a portrait of the author 'Aet. 37', reproduced here on page 147. The picture is of a youngish man of direct and commanding manner who is wearing a periwig. There is a high kerchief around his neck and he sports what appears to be the smart uniform jacket with embroidered buttonholes which, although unofficial at the time, he is known to have enjoyed wearing.

Anyone who gives to the public an offering of their poems written over a lifetime is likely to reveal something of himself, his inner life and changing attitudes – and that is certainly the sub-text for examining *Sea Weeds*. In terms of literary merit, his verses include some clever and engaging pieces that are likely to give pleasure to any reader, while others by common reckoning would probably be rated as mundane. His play of 1810, *The Noble Foundling or the Hermit of the Tweed*,[2] is also an interesting document. We will look at these two publications in sequence.

As well as being a personal statement, one would expect Trotter's work to reflect the social and cultural atmosphere in which he lived. He was born at a time of changing literary taste. Poets were reacting against the formality of the Augustan period, with its contrived subjects and carefully controlled style and form. There was now an interest in expressing feeling and emotion, and in using more natural, pastoral settings to induce awe, wonder or nostalgia. The works of Thomas Gray, Oliver Goldsmith, George Crabbe and Robert Burns are good examples. The eighteenth century's interest in the 'noble savage' and the philosophies of Rousseau both contributed to this shift. But it also reflected a desire to evoke the simple virtues of traditional life that economic change and prosperity were destroying.

The new interest in rural subjects led to the emergence of rustic or peasant poets. There was Mary Collier, the washerwoman poet; Robert Dodsley, the

---

[1] Trotter, *Sea Weeds*
[2] T. Trotter, *The Noble Foundling or the Hermit of the Tweed* (Newcastle and London, 1812)

footman poet; Stephen Duck, the thresher poet; Ann Yearsley, the milkmaid poet and, of course, Robert Burns, the ploughman poet.[3] In fact, although they enjoyed a homespun image, none were unlettered versifiers and although of working-class origins, they had all had a good basic education. Nevertheless, the message was that the writing of poetry was now the legitimate province of all, whether milkmaids, ploughmen, parsons or, like Trotter, naval surgeons.

The new literary interest in the emotions, the solitary, the countryside and the simple rustic life of the shepherds, ploughmen and farmers who populated it was popular in Scotland. The trend was first marked by James Thomson's *The Seasons* in the 1720s and was continued by Robert Blair, co-founder of the 'graveyard school' which, in the 1740s, specialized in the melancholy. Writing verse became popular and the number of poets who contributed at least one memorable lyric is large. Three writers, however, were particularly influential in terms of the quality and content of their verse: Allan Ramsay, who saw Scottish ballads as the authentic voice of the countryside and published anthologies and collections of his own verse in the 1720s and 1730s; Robert Fergusson, who wrote of life in Edinburgh before his untimely death in the 1770s; and, of course Robert Burns. Each one built on the achievement of the other and acknowledged the debt.

In Scotland as elsewhere, writers reflected these general changes in literary taste. But there were extra nuances following from the Act of Union of 1707 which created Great Britain but removed Scottish political independence. Although the target of both jokes and envy in the south, individual Scots were fully accepted as citizens and prospered in the new state, just as Scotland itself received enormous economic benefits as a result of access to the growing British Empire. Indeed, some Scottish intellectuals regarded progress and the union as being inseparable.[4] Some, whose number clearly included Trotter, easily embraced the new concept of 'Britishness' and developed a political loyalty to Britain without losing their cultural affinity with their native land.[5]

Scottish intellectuals also seem to have accepted 'Scots English' as part of the progressive package, using it for 'polite' literature while reserving the Scots dialect for rustic themes. Indeed, writing a contribution to the new *Encyclopaedia Britannica* in 1768, William Smellie was enthusiastic about 'the British tongue', describing it as 'a healthy oak planted in rich and vigorous soil'.[6] It is therefore ironic that the current fame of Ramsay, Fergusson and Burns is based on the works they produced in the Scots dialect. Nationalistically orientated critics in the late nineteenth and twentieth centuries thought that these writers could only achieve their full potential by writing in their 'native' tongue, and that any verse in English must necessarily be inferior and imitative. As a result,

[3] S. Kord, *Women Peasant Poets in 18th Century England, Scotland and Germany* (Woodbridge, 2003), 3, 40–4, 51
[4] T. M. Devine, *Scotland and the Union 1707–2007* (Edinburgh, 2008), 2
[5] Ibid., 30
[6] S. Manning, 'Post-Union Scotland and the Scottish idiom of Britishness', in I. Brown, S. Manning and M. G. H. Pittock (eds), *The Edinburgh History of Scottish Literature* (Edinburgh, 2007), 52

their extensive body of work in English was ignored. Whether the occasional choice of the Scots dialect by Ramsay, Fergusson and Burns was an act of resistance to English cultural assimilation or merely the selection of the most appropriate language for the subject is now a matter of academic debate.[7] Trotter, as a Borderer and a proud North Briton, faced no such dilemma. Like many in his position, he wrote exclusively in English.

The desire to maintain a Scottish cultural identity after the Union gave the development of literature a special twist. Thus, while pastoral subjects were chosen as opportunities to extol the simplicity of rural life, they were also used as a way of showing the country's special historical and cultural origins. This was a reflection of the importance of national identity in the early days of the European Romantic movement. After the Napoleonic Wars, this would manifest itself in political forms; but before 1800, the emphasis was on cultural traditions, and the belief that they could be revealed by the study of myths and stories from ancient times. In Scotland, this expressed itself in antiquarianism and a fascination with a legendary mediaeval past. Typical of this were the *Ossian* poems, published during the 1760s by James Macpherson. Whether they were translations of an ancient part-oral and part-written Gaelic epic (as was claimed), or were rather the product of Macpherson's imagination is unimportant. At the time they struck a chord in a nation seeking its past. The theme was repeated in collections of folk poetry, and particularly in historical verse dramas, such as Ramsay's *The Gentle Shepherd* or John Home's *Douglas*, with their casts of hermits, lords and shepherds. One does not have to look far to find the genesis of Trotter's own play, *The Noble Foundling*.

'Sea Weeds'

AN EXTRAORDINARY INTRODUCTION

It is a safe wager that no other volume of poems has ever been published with a dedication to an earl and a lengthy preface, both deployed as vehicles for searing complaints about half-pay arrangements. But that is what Trotter did, along with some self-congratulation on the worthiness of his career. This is a cry of anger and resentment from a man who towards the end of his life needed ferociously to declare that he has been wronged and undervalued. Here are these sad feelings as they are to be found in the Dedication to Earl Spencer, KG. After presuming 'to lay these *Sea Weeds* at your Lordship's feet', the text launches directly into complaint:

> Happy had it been for the Physician [Trotter], had Lord Spencer remained in power, or Earl Howe lived, to the conclusion of the war in 1802; for then he would have been sure of being compensated for the severe personal hurts he had suffered in actual duty: and ultimately not excluded, as he has been, from receiving the same returns with others his juniors in service.

---

[7]   C. E. Andrews, 'Almost the Same but Not Quite: English Poetry by Scots in the 18th Century', *The Eighteenth Century* 47 (2006), 52

There is much of the same kind and 'the Physician' is credited with having 'seen and conversed more than any man living' on the health of the navy.

Trotter uses the opportunity to give an account of the author's public service, and his version of the refusal by the authorities to increase his half-pay of 10 shillings a day. Alas, 'the reputation he had attained as well as the national good he had done' has only served to 'excite the strongest degree of jealousy against him'. Trotter then claims that the measures he introduced to combat scurvy saved no less than 100,000 lives, and that he had made a unique contribution to the improvement of the health of the navy. Under his direction, previous neglect was corrected and every sick sailor 'fed like a babe and attended like a prince'. The admiring inscription on the presentation silver service which Trotter received on his retirement from the navy is quoted as evidence of his distinction. In fact, of course, beneath the self-congratulation lies a strong element of truth.

Nevertheless, however important Trotter's public services may have been, it is difficult to see how the Admiralty could have acted differently. Trotter did not seem to have got himself officially invalided out of the navy as a consequence of the hernia he contracted in 1795, and he did not seek to return to service when war was resumed after the short-lived Peace of Amiens. This made him legally ineligible to receive the increase in half-pay granted in 1805. Trotter failed to understand this and it provided him with a lifelong grievance. Being slightly elastic with the truth, he later attributed his leaving the navy entirely to his injury, and claimed that he was forced to retire from private practice in Newcastle in 1827 because of the service-induced hernia.

The preface concludes with a passage that puts professional responsibilities and poetry in counterpoise:

> Who could condemn a Physician that has seen so large a portion of human misery, and contributed so much to relieve it, for now and then relaxing his mind to compose a sonnet, or cultivating a flower from the beauties of nature, to alleviate a pensive moment!

Set out one after another are the names of twenty-five persons who had supported Trotter during his 'personal calamity'. The list includes seven doctors, four knights of the realm, one minister and two colonels of marines.

PASTORAL AND ROMANTIC POETRY

With calamity proclaimed in the introduction, *Sea Weeds* then offers a selection of poems. Dates are often given with a note on place and circumstances of writing, but there is no strict chronological order. It is no surprise in view of the British literary tradition that fifteen of Trotter's poems have pastoral settings. Thus, there are pieces such as an 'Ode to Winter' written from onboard the *Berwick* in 1781, 'The Falling Leaf' of 1797, 'Eden Streams' of 1800, and the undated 'Willow'. A footnote records that a jingling little piece entitled 'The Hawthorn or the Disconsolate Tar' had been set to music by Mr J. Monro of London.

The contents of these pastoral poems, however, present a surprise. We know from Trotter's *A View of the Nervous Temperament* that he was concerned with the corrupting effect of progress on contemporary society, yet the stylized if well-loved landscapes he describes in his pastoral poetry are empty. The occasional rustic or nymph appears, and there are classical allusions, as when Damon, a shepherd, declares his love to a Chloe, a shepherdess, while a love-sick swain sits by a willow tree lamenting the cruelty of his mistress. But, unlike his contemporaries, Trotter does not dwell on the inhabitants of this rustic landscape nor uses them to draw attention to the virtues of a simple rural life. The exception is 'The Snow Storm: an Elegy'. A footnote reports the circumstances of its composition:

> Written in London, in February, 1799. The author's trunk was forgotten to be sent by the Portsmouth coach, in which he travelled to London; a dreadful snow storm took place, and the fall was so great, that he could not move from his lodgings in Newcastle Street. Having no book to amuse him, his travelling companion Horace being left in the trunk, he had no other resource but poetry; and, inspired by the dreary scene surrounding, his muse produced the Snow Storm.

This poem tells a tragic story of a shepherd and a shepherdess perishing in a snow storm:

> In sorrowful dirge they were borne to their home,
> And many a villager mourn'd at their tomb,
> And wept as they bade it adieu:
> And you who may read the sad tale I relate,
> Should you e'er love like them, may you shun their hard
>   fate;
> But know from their virtues their bliss is complete,
> And learn from a dog to be true.

The dog was Trip, who died faithful unto death.

A dozen of Trotter's earlier verses are concerned with the poet's feelings and involve, or are addressed to, the fair sex. It is not surprising that they are early verses, dating from a time when Trotter was an ardent young man, viewing the world from the masculine confines of a warship. The excuses for their production lie in small domestic incidents – a primrose presented, frost seen on Lucy's ringlets, Hannah grieving for a bird killed by a cat, or a young lady promising the author a bouquet in the month of February, which proved to be a 'Sprig of Furze Blossom'. The strongest emotion evoked is when Miss Curtis, daughter of his friend Captain Sir Roger Curtis, loses her spaniel Guess when he laps up rat poison.

This is all genteel stuff compared with the raw emotional outpourings of Byron and other members of the Romantic movement which was in full swing when Trotter published his volume. Indeed, the 'fair sex' pieces identified above are verses which would have gone well in any scrapbook and would have caused no anxiety to a protective parent. The possible exceptions are a poem dedicated to 'Lovely Sue' and one called 'The Autumnal Rose'. The first is without doubt a love poem. Here it is in full:

> As beams the moon in yonder sphere,
> The cleareſt and the lighteſt,
> So 'midſt the lovely British fair,
> My Susan shines the brighteſt.
>
> The Muses, Loves, and Graces join'd
> Some faultless form to view,
> Each gave a charm – and all combin'd
> Produc'd my lovely Sue.
>
> On her to look, and not to love,
> Scorns all our weak pretences,
> Her meaneſt charms such raptures move,
> As ravish all our senses.
>
> A heedless swain without disguise,
> I met her in the bower;
> One glance from those resiſtless eyes
> Made captive every power.
>
> A cot I'll rear in yonder plain,
> No hoſtile arm shall harm her;
> And if she deigns to bless her swain,
> I'll there conduĉt my charmer.
>
> This faithful heart shall rove no more,
> I live for only you;
> Nor age nor time shall waſte my ſtore,
> While bleſt with lovely Sue.

At the other emotional extreme to the morbid predictions of tragedy and sadness in 'The Autumnal Rose' is 'On presenting a Rose to Mrs T on the 25 September, 1810, being her Wedding Day', with its

> Then as those tints shall die away
> Read in their fate thy own decay

lie well within the Romantic tradition.

POEMS STIRRED BY PATRIOTISM AND EVENTS

The largest proportion of Trotter's poems deal not with compliments to pretty women or pastoral scenes, but with the public events of the time. Almost half of Trotter's work falls into this category, the proportion increasing as he got older. Inevitably, the emotions stimulated by the Revolution in France and the subsequent war loom large. There is a lament for the death of Marie Antoinette; derision for the pretentions of Napoleon on his coronation as emperor; and patriotic tributes to dead heroes like Captain Robert Faulkner, who died in the engagement between *Blanche* and *Pique*, or General Sir John Moore, who died at Corunna. Beyond the limits of the struggle with France, there are verses written in the Ladies'Walk at Liverpool in January 1783, which comprise a stinging condemnation of the slave trade; an ode celebrating the invention of an improved life-boat by Mr Greathead; and poems addressed to the justices and yeomanry on the occasion of the failure of the 'radical heresy', and to the third duke of Northumberland for having done well in Ireland. Appointed viceroy, Northumberland, a high Tory, had resisted the temptation to meet the rising violence of Daniel O'Connell's supporters with force and had chosen the path of moderation while his chief, the duke of Wellington, defused the situation by forcing Catholic emancipation through a reluctant Parliament in London. The most notable of these public poems is the 'A Monody on the Death of Richard Earl Howe K.G.'. This was written in 1800 at Cawsand Bay and it runs to a full twenty pages. An extract from this poem was given in Chapter 8, but it is worth a further short quotation to exemplify the kind of public virtue Trotter esteemed:

> If matchless worth, that never courted fame;
> If Truth and Faith were ever mortal aim;
> A heart prepar'd to fear no earthly foe,
> Yet mov'd to pity at the tale of woe;
> Unsullied honour; faultless, tho' severe;
> That knew no fashion but to be sincere;
> Rich from desert, victorious by his sword;
> Tho' bred in Courts, yet never broke his word:
> Firm to his purpose, 'bove all factious zeal;
> Friend to no party but the public weal:
> While changeling patriots sway'd as interests move,
> His wish was England, and his Sov'reign's love!
> Such were thy virtues; this thy honors shone;
> And long shall grace thy monumental stone.

'The Noble Foundling'

TROTTER AS PLAYWRIGHT

Most busy doctors are unlikely to be found writing a play in their leisure hours. However, besides his achievements as author of medical books, Trotter found time to write a five-act tragedy entitled *The Noble Foundling or the Hermit of the Tweed*. This drama was published in 1812, and a stage production took place in 1813 at the Theatre Royal, Newcastle. In the advertisement or preface to this work, Trotter revealed how it came to be written, in a statement which wonderfully captures a moment in his early life:

When I was about ten years of age, at the school of Melrose, I went with a party of schoolboys to see a stag that had been caught in the neighbourhood. We were disappointed in seeing the hunt: and in our ramble over the country, sat down to rest ourselves at the side of a wall in the ancient village of Holydean. This turned the talk to other times and one of our companions entertained us with anecdotes of Habbie Ker of Cessford once the owner of the spot which we now saw in ruins. Habbie was a Boarder Chief of great wealth, and infamous for his cruelties. It was said that his corpse was stuck full of pins in order to show detestation to his memory. This horrid tale could never be erased from my mind. Part of my education was afterwards offered at Kelso – where I became more familiarized to the scenery where this play is laid. On revisiting Tweedside, after many years of absence in the service of my country, early feelings naturally returned in my remembrance and gave birth to the following drama.

Trotter gives his address as House Byre Tower, Roxburghshire, with the date of 12 August 1810.

The printed version of the play was obviously intended to be a professional production rather than a mere amateur diversion. It runs to 129 pages. Each of the acts into which it is divided has within it six scenes, except for Act Five, which runs to a prodigious nine scenes. The work is in blank verse with interspersed choruses delivered by Moss Troopers, singing women and various other performers. A fair bit of thunder and lightning punctuates the action, and there is much sounding of trumpets. It is a gothic drama with a tortuous plot, duels, dungeons, a beautiful maiden, a virtuous hero and plenty of villainy.

THE TALE OF *THE NOBLE FOUNDLING*

The backdrop to the story is a castle set in the border country, a terrain ravaged by bloody warfare between quarrelling chieftains. The owner of the castle, Lord Roxdale, has succeeded to this fiefdom after the much-loved Lord Fordale had been lost at sea when returning from a crusade. As the play opens, lights blaze from the castle while drunken merriment mixes with plotting as Roxdale, seconded by his evil familiar, Sir John Cessford, tries to persuade the chiefs to join in an attack on the neighbouring Lord Douglas.

Meanwhile, Matilda (Roxdale's beautiful daughter) slips out of the castle to pray at her mother's grave. Matilda is in love with Oswald, a foundling of humble origin but princely demeanour who is part of Roxdale's entourage.

Later that night an aged shepherd, Albert, strays into the castle grounds by mistake whilst on his way to seek counsel from the local wise man, Orlando, the hermit of the Tweed, who dwells in a nearby cave. He is arrested and interrogated by Cessford, who accuses him of being Douglas's spy.

The next day, Roxdale tells Matilda that she is to marry Oliver, a Norman knight attached to the castle. Matilda rejects the proposal. Cessford and Roxdale are then found in council, when they are interrupted by the news that Douglas and his men are advancing on the castle.

With Douglas every moment drawing closer, Oswald visits the hermitage to talk with Orlando, and learns that Lord Fordale, having successfully liberated Christian captives held by the Turks, has been drowned on the homeward voyage. His wife dies of grief, and the fate of his infant son is a mystery. There was suspicion that Roxdale had killed him and usurped his heritage. Oswald, outraged, decides to go over to Douglas's side.

Albert has meanwhile been rescued from his dungeon by two old soldiers and taken to the hermitage. There he describes how, years before, he had been surprised by the sight of two armed men engaged in mortal combat. Near to where they both fell dead was a crying baby. He adopted this child who, tragically, was snatched from him by bandits.

With Douglas virtually on the doorstep, Roxdale is quaking with terror and guilt. Oswald and Matilda are saying their farewells when the Norman, Oliver, bursts in, challenges Oswald to a duel and is killed.

Back in the dungeon, we meet a mysterious prisoner who has languished there for years. The two old soldiers carry him off to Douglas's camp, where the poor man is shocked to discover that he had been a prisoner all these years in his own castle – it is not difficult to guess his identity. Douglas invites his opponents to surrender honourably but Cessford rejects such clemency. Much killing seems inevitable. But Oswald forces the castle gate with an elite band of followers and scales the tower. Within fifteen minutes a bloodless victory is won.

In the finale, Oswald disarms and arrests Cessford; Orlando recognizes the freed prisoner of the tower as the long-lost Lord Fordale; Roxdale confesses his sins and expires; and Oswald is identified as Fordale's long-lost son. Fordale confers his blessing on the marriage of Matilda and Oswald and all is rejoicing as the final curtain falls.

Trotter as playwright and poet

Why then did Trotter write and publish poetry over most of his adult life, and why in 1812 did he have a play produced on the Newcastle stage? It is not unknown for busy professionals to have a literary side to their lives and Trotter might be seen simply as an exemplar of a not uncommon kind of human urge.

Beyond this general truth, it seems reasonable to suggest that Trotter's particular motivation consisted of three interconnected strands. First, there is the fact that in the leisure moments of a medical life dealing often with intense suffering, he needed escape and respite. So much he tells us, and who should blame him if he chose this 'to alleviate a pensive moment'. Second, one may surmise that Trotter had a liking for acclaim. He collected letters of esteem from famous persons who had nice things to say about him, cited the flattering inscription from his presentation silver service on more than one occasion, and was proud of his qualifications and professional eminence. Thus, he did not leave his poems scattered in newspapers but put them together in a volume furnished with a handsome portrait, and staged his play with the patronage of the city's mayor. Last, one might also see the motivation for this venture as deriving from Trotter's desire to express his own deep personal beliefs and values. His play in particular lacks any great psychological subtlety but it enshrines strong beliefs in the contrast between virtue and evil, between heroism and cowardice and with an emphasis on the worth of noble causes.

Trotter's poetry and the play have the same starting points. The choices of subject reflect his developing interests and the historical events which unfolded during his lifetime. They also hint at the cultural traditions and the challenges felt by a Scotsmen in the Great Britain created by the Act of Union. Politically Trotter was a 'North Briton', loyal to the new political arrangements and glorying in their success in war. Culturally, he was a Lowland Scot who shared the same literary roots as fellow countrymen such as James Thompson, Allan Ramsay, John Home and Sir Walter Scott – indeed Scott's estate at Abbotsford was only a stone's throw from Trotter's more modest holding at Housebyres. *The Noble Foundling* fitted well into tradition, and so do the pastoral settings of his poems, even if some were set in the south of England with cadences reminiscent of Thomas Gray.

Trotter's collection of verses attracted no critical comment at the time. Scottish reviewers were uninterested in any work not written in dialect, and to the English, he was probably just one more scribbling Scotsman. Likewise by 1829, Trotter's slightly stilted language and his polite and narrow range of theme must have seemed old-fashioned to those familiar with the raw force of the Romantic movement as exemplified by Keats, Byron and even Wordsworth. As for his play, the only recorded comment is that of a contemporary diarist, who described it as a 'the most wonderful farrago of nonsense ever exhibited on the stage'.[8]

Fortunately, no one is likely to argue that Trotter's fame rests on the merits of his literary endeavours. They do, however, confirm that he was a person with a strong structure of beliefs who esteemed virtue, nobility, loyalty and patriotism, but could grieve for a lost cage bird or a dead spaniel, glory in a landscape, and compose flirtatious love poems for a pretty girl. The poetic writings do reveal the human side to the public figure.

---

[8] E. Hughes, *The Diary of James Losh*, Surtees Society (Durham, 1962), 19

17

Thomas Trotter
and the Great Theatre of Life

> All the world's a stage
> And all the men and women merely players;
> They have their exits and their entrances:
> And one man in his time plays many parts.

Shakespeare, As You Like It

Final years

TROTTER WAS BUSY while he lived in Newcastle. The production of a succession of medical works, their preparation for republication in numerous
editions and the demands of private practice took up all his time. He was
a member of the Literary and Philosophical Society and opened his door
regularly to offer free treatment to the poor, but he did not occupy any official
position in the locality. He did, however, write occasionally on medical matters
to the newspapers, as in 1816 when Newcastle was smitten with smallpox. In
July and September, the *Courant* published open letters from him to the mayor,
urging the introduction of compulsory vaccination against the disease.

One reason that Trotter did not try to find an official position in Newcastle
was that he was still keenly interested in the welfare of the navy, with which
he still felt a strong affinity. As is reflected in his works, his admiration for its
officers and men knew no bounds, and it was in the navy that he had exercised
his greatest influence and achieved distinction. He frequently harked back
to those happy times and, in his writings and letters to the press, invariably
described himself as a former physician to the fleet and quoted extensively
from his naval experience.

He also kept up a correspondence with previous colleagues, notably Sir
Roger Curtis, through whom he was able to advance further the naval career of
his nephew Robert, whose feet he had first placed on the promotion ladder in
1789.[1] In 1808, he raised again the question of his half-pay with the Admiralty,
but got nowhere. In 1818, he applied to be physician to Greenwich Hospital
in succession to the distinguished Dr Robertson. Alas, to get a post of this
eminence required 'influence' which Trotter no longer had. The First Lord,
Melville, kept such appointments firmly in his control, and Trotter's friends in

---

[1] Curtis to Trotter, 28 June 1803 and 11 October 1805, NMM, Ms 62/III

high places had long since retired.[2] Then in 1819 he produced the last of his naval works, *A Practicable Plan for Manning the Navy without Impressment*, dedicated to Lord Exmouth, the former Sir Edward Pellew. It was, as the name implied, a reasoned argument in favour of voluntary enlistment, backed by numerous examples of the disadvantages to health and morale of forced recruitment and the press gang. Trotter's proposal was to abolish impressment altogether and make an improved version of the 1795 Quota Acts a permanent feature of naval recruitment. The changes he proposed comprised basing the system on a rational calculation of the navy's annual manpower needs in time of war (he himself estimated 113,000 men), limiting the period of service required of recruits to five years, 'equalizing' the number of men each parish or port was required to supply by tying it to the tonnage of shipping operating from each place, and offering bounties of such generosity that volunteers would flock to join. In its essentials it was an Enlightenment document designed to apply logic and system to naval recruitment.

Well established now in Newcastle, Trotter prospered. He may have regarded his half-pay of 10 shillings a day as derisory, but it provided a comfortable basic income and was, after all, the same half-pay as was received by a full captain in the Royal Navy. When supplemented by the receipts of private medical practice, he seems to have done well. So much so, that in 1808 he was able to buy two properties at Wester Housebyres and Easter Housebyres, situated in a valley which ran down into the Tweed just to the north of Melrose. The land included commercial plantations containing 120,000 trees.[3]

Well known and reasonably prosperous, Trotter married again, this time to Isabella Agnes Dixon. It was a good match, for Isabella was a member of the local gentry whose family owned estates in Hawkwell, to the west of Newcastle. They were married on 25 September 1810 at St John's church. He made sure that the wedding was announced in the *Naval Chronicle*, a periodical specializing in naval news, ship movements and promotions, which was read avidly by all members of the service. His son, six-year-old John Everitt Howe Roddam, soon had siblings – William Curtis, born in 1812, Thomas Marr in 1815 and Agnes Allison in 1816. Trotter was now able to move his family to a more salubrious and spacious residence in Percy Street, on the northern suburbs of Newcastle beyond Newgate, and to educate his children appropriately. Curiously for a family which was replete with medical men, none became doctors. John chose accountancy and Thomas became a solicitor.

The 1820s were years of political turmoil in Newcastle as elsewhere in the country as pressure for parliamentary reform gathered momentum. There were demonstrations and counter-demonstrations by friends of reform and of the constitution alike. The mob occasionally joined in to smash a few windows, with the yeomanry standing by to prevent real trouble. Trotter's brother Andrew, in North Shields, had by this time become a prominent citizen. He was not only listed as a subscriber to Aneas MacKenzie's encyclopaedic *Historical Account of Newcastle-upon-Tyne, including the Borough of Gateshead*, but featured as the

[2] More to Trotter, 16 November 1818, NMM, Ms 62/III
[3] Curtis to Trotter, 10 December 1808, NMM, Ms 62/III

chairman of the various committees which nominated candidates for the new reformed Parliament. Thomas Trotter kept aloof from all this. Now in his sixties, he was perhaps too tired and incapacitated to become involved, apart from composing a few poems, which on the one hand supported the duke of Newcastle's liberal treatment of Catholics in Ireland while on the other praising 'British Liberty' and the suppression of 'the radical conspiracy' hatched in Cato Street to assassinate the cabinet. In 1827, Trotter left Newcastle, gave up his practice and retired to live in the rural seclusion of Easter Housebyres. While Andrew was involving himself in reform meetings, Thomas was planting the 'Howe Oak' to commemorate the anniversary of his old patron's victory at the Glorious First of June.

The actor and the play

In the preface to this book, a letter was quoted which had a fellow luncheon guest imploring Trotter to put pen to paper, and write his memoirs. That correspondent employed a theatrical image. Trotter, he said, 'has seen so much of the great theatre of life and the great deep'. Who, reading the account of Trotter's career as told in this book, could doubt the justice of that assertion or the aptness of the image?

Trotter's life was acted out in a play of extraordinarily multifarious, varied and contrasting scenes. At age 17 we see him arriving for his year's preliminary medical training at Edinburgh and tasting the atmosphere of the Enlightenment. At 19 he is a surgeon's mate in the Royal Navy. We see him then on board *Berwick*, voyaging to the West Indies, caught up in a hurricane, and at age 21 he is commended for his services amid the carnage of the Battle of the Dogger Bank. Changing scene, at age 23 he sails with the Liverpool slaving ship *Brookes* to West Africa and makes the fearful middle passage to the Carribean: later we hear him give his evidence on the cruelty of the slave trade before the House of Commons select committee. Aged 24, he is experiencing civilian practice as a surgeon and apothecary at Wooler in Northumberland, while working for his Edinburgh MD. Recalled again to the colours, he makes a further voyage to the Caribbean. At the age of 33, he becomes second physician of the celebrated naval hospital at Haslar, with a move from onboard medical service to the exercise of administrative responsibilities. A year later, in 1794, he is centre stage with his appointment as physician to the Channel Fleet, a fighting force which was in the vanguard of the war with revolutionary France. In that role he is a close witness to the battle of the Glorious First of June, and will ever remember the *Queen Charlotte* in full sail making straight for the French line. At the same time, he is making a practical contribution to the health of seamen, and is a major player in the conquest of scurvy, the control of typhus and the elimination of smallpox from the fleet. Incapacitated with a hernia whilst on duty, the coming of peace in 1802 gives him the opportunity to make his exit from naval service and, at the age of 42, he sets up a successful practice as a physician in Newcastle, also treating the sick and the poor for no fee. His first book, *Observations on the Scurvy*, is published when he is aged 26, and thereafter he is a prolific author. The Newcastle years are highly productive in terms of further professional writing as well as seeing the publication of *The Noble Foundling* and the *Sea Weeds* anthology. Then, a brief return to his roots in Scotland and to enjoy the fruits of his labours at Housebyres. Finally, in 1830 declining health makes him move briefly to Edinburgh, then back to Newcastle. There, on 5 September 1832, he dies at 15 Leas Terrace at the age of 72.

Put together all those experiences and achievements, view these scenes in their evolving sequence, and the image of a theatre seems extraordinarily appropriate. 'Theatre' is a metaphor deeply embedded in English literature. Most memorable is the quotation from Shakespeare's *As You Like It* quoted at the beginning of this chapter. A similar image was contained in a popular work authored by Trotter's near contemporaries, Julius Charles Hare and Augustus William Hare:

> Everybody has his own theatre in which he is manager, actor, prompter, playwright, scene shifter, box keeper, door keeper, and audience into the bargain.[4]

Literary tradition seems amply to approve that metaphor of 'great theatre of life'. The awareness carried by that phrase is of the merging, multiple roles played out in chameleon fashion by the one person. Trotter's career gives exactly that sense of life moving across a stage of multiple scenes.

How are we to understand the actor in this particular play? What aspects of character dictated Trotter's movement across his stage? Researchers have over the last several decades put much effort into understanding the determinants of life course for normal people – why some succeed and others fail, why many enjoy happiness and fulfilment while others taste only discontent. A leading example of that kind of enquiry is the remarkable thirty-five-year follow up study of a cohort of Harvard freshman carried out by George Vaillant, professor of psychiatry at Harvard Medical School, and reported in his *Adaptation to Life*.[5] In similar mode, let us take as our starting point the assumption that all life is indeed a play, and look at Trotter's life against an awareness of what science and research tell about the likely shaping of each person's individual drama.

Trotter and the conflict in self-image

The question to be explored here is how Trotter defined the essence of himself, and the consequences of such definition.

A salient aspect of Trotter's self-image is the absence of much evidence of intimate or personal identity, in contrast to definition by qualification, worldly success, rank, important people known, and generally by externals. In Trotter's poetry there are no references to his family or to childhood scenes, and in none of his writings does he once mention his parents, or refer to the fact that he had a brother who was a surgeon. His relatively humble origins thus seemingly

[4] J. C. Hare and A. W. C. Hare, *Guesses at Truth* (London, 1855), 192
[5] G. Vaillant, *Adaptation to Life* (Boston, 1977)

needed to be concealed rather than celebrated. The only glimpse of childhood experience he fleetingly gives us is in the preface to *The Noble Foundling*, and that consists of just a few lines about one early cross-country outing with his school mates. In the context of the times, this reticence about social origin was probably typical of men who achieved distinction in their chosen professions, but who lacked the wealth and aristocratic connections normally necessary for success in the late eighteenth century.

Turn to the converse and there are repeated examples to be found of Trotter seeking to create himself as the successful figure moving across the public stage. His usually extensive recitation of professional positions held and of his Edinburgh MD, as proclaimed on the title pages of his books, was probably no more than accepted practice at the time for men whose status was based on merit rather than birth. Indeed, Nelson's notorious vanity and his propensity to appear in public festooned with decorations was probably rooted in the same cause. For Trotter to have cited the Humane Society's approbation of the *Essay on Drunkenness* was understandable and innocent enough, even if it attracted the critical attention of Dr Henry Dewar. The reproduction of the honorific inscription from the presentation silver tea service was not outrageous self-advertisement. But there are other instances where his self-congratulation veered towards the pretentious. In the preface to *Sea Weeds*, for example, Trotter says that the improvements he had achieved in the health of the navy had received the praise of every officer; that he had been responsible for saving the lives of 100,000 sailors, and that he done more for the navy than any person living.

Trotter liked to see himself as the British patriot he undoubtedly was, loyal to the Union and glorying in its triumphs. That is evident in the tone of his patriotic poems but the cultural roots that formed him were Lowland Scottish. The pastoral settings of some of his verse and the attempt to deal with feelings were typical of much late-eighteenth-century pre-Romantic British verse, but the mediaeval wrappings of *The Noble Foundling* are rooted firmly in the Scottish search for cultural identity.

Trotter's relationship with powerful persons speaks in large measure of the pervasive importance of patronage as a feature of Georgian society. With no family connection available to promote his career, he needed to secure patrons. It is not therefore at all surprising that Trotter's first son had Howe and Roddam among his names, or that *Sea Weeds* should be dedicated to Lord Spencer. Among the senior figures in his firmament, Admiral Roddam played a key role in renewing his career, though it was Lord Howe whom he most revered. The intensity of feeling expressed in Trotter's lengthy 'Monody' on the *Death of Admiral Lord Howe K.G.* might be seen as pointing to very personal grief rather than only the loss of a patron, and one is left wondering whether Howe was in a psychological sense a father surrogate. On the other hand, all Howe's subordinates venerated him as the naval giant of the late eighteenth century, and Trotter's service as physician of the fleet under him marked the high point of his career and influence. It was no wonder that he looked back on Howe with admiration and respect for the rest of his life, long after the time when the great admiral's deeds had been eclipsed in the public mind by those of Lord Nelson.

In his dealings with ordinary working people, Trotter was highly sensitive to the hardships and problems of their lives. When in practice in Newcastle, he provided free treatment for the poor and unfortunate. He spoke with unbounded admiration of the toil and dedication of coal miners and sailors, but had no illusions about their fecklessness and human weaknesses, particularly when faced with the temptations of the bottle. But however sympathetic he was to the plight of working people, Trotter in no way identified with them, seeing himself as a professional man of 'the middling sort'.

Did religion play any part in Trotter's inner life? References to religion of a formal kind are scant in his writing. The sharp rejection in the *Essay on Drunkenness* of the view of inebriety as sin with the substituting of 'disease of the mind' might suggest that Trotter's alignment with the Enlightenment was leading him away from the church and even towards David Hume's atheism. Such was probably not the case. The final poem in *Sea Weeds* is entitled 'The Universal Hymn to Providence', and expresses simple and uncloying piety. The view of himself at the intellectual level as a product of Edinburgh's Enlightenment tradition was, however, an important facet of his self-definition.

It appears reasonable to conclude that Trotter's definition of self, the way in which he daily saw and felt about himself and his achievements, had within it the makings of a lifelong tension. He wanted externally to be not a little grand, while the internal person was distinctly vulnerable. Evidence of such tensions can be seen written across the script of his life story.

Tensions and achievement

Trotter was creative, compassionate, energetic, and vastly competent, and those qualities speak of psychological good health. In contrast he could also be contentious, aggressive and resentful to a degree which was unhealthy and handicapping.

Among the positives in Trotter's personality, what most stands out is his creative energy. This is most evident in his long-term and varied commitment to bettering the health of seaman and strengthening the navy's medical service. His consistent emphasis on preventative health significantly helped reduce the damage being done by smallpox, typhus and other infectious diseases and, although the existence of a powerful patron in the form of Lord Howe was crucial in getting the authorities to act on his ideas, his success in this arena was rooted in his capacity to make persuasive representations and his determination to get things done. His role in the conquest of scurvy is particularly notable. Other medical men with practical experience had written books demonstrating the efficacy of fresh vegetables in keeping the disease at bay and of lemon juice in curing it. But it had been Trotter, in his role as physician to the Channel Fleet, who had done something about it. True, sentiment within the navy in favour of lemon juice meant that he was pushing on a half-open door; but his official efforts at forcing it wide open laid the foundation for the extraordinary improvements in health which took place in the Royal Navy alone between 1794 and 1801.

As an administrator, Trotter's effectiveness in achieving change bears witness to his gifts as much as do his books. In the tradition of the Enlightenment he valued understanding and the practical application of knowledge, and as a working naval doctor he was concerned with results, even if the reason for the success of certain treatments was uncertain. Consequently, as physician to the Channel Fleet, he not only analysed the nature of the major maritime diseases of the times, but secured programmes of action that led to the improvements that played a major part in the navy's victories. This, plus his seniority and the scope and utility of his writings, gave him enormous prestige within the naval medical service.

In his reading and the breadth of his medical interests, Trotter was insatiable. In regard to his written contributions, it is the scope as well as the quality of his technical work which so impresses. No other British medical writer of his generation covered so broad a spectrum – scurvy, maritime diseases, the organization of hospitals, recruitment and the press gang, the administration of naval medicine, the conditions and pay of surgeons, neurosis, the safety of mines and alcoholism. All his writing was innovative, but with *The Essay on Drunkenness* he achieved a work of outstanding creativity and lasting importance. Trotter's poetry and his play speak of a further aspect of his creative drive and imagination, even if they were never likely to constitute the centre of his canvas.

Creativity is one edge to Trotter's character. But the tension within him manifestly shaped and sharpened that other, negative, edge. When he wrote 'I have never been accused of flattery; but I have often suffered for telling the truth',[6] he was being somewhat self-deceiving. He had in fact a nicely polished line in flattery when he chose. For instance, in the dedication which fronted his *View of the Nervous Temperament*, he lauded the less-than-distinguished Professor James Gregory on his 'estimable talents . . . manly spirit and dignified independence'.[7] Within the spirit of the age in which 'influence' and connections counted so powerfully, such obeisance may have been the order of the day, but this is not the only instance where Trotter came uncomfortably close to sycophancy. With little to be said about Gregory's professional distinction he for the most part restricted himself to a congratulatory profiling of Gregory's personality.

As for the claim that Trotter 'had often suffered for telling the truth', truth-telling is here being used by him as a euphemism for a tendency towards a cantankerous or even at times a flagrantly aggressive mode of dealing with those who disagreed with his views. This kind of incident was too frequent to be dismissed as mere accident. Indeed, the older he got, the more opinionated he seemed to become.

There were numerous examples of this trait. One was his reaction to Dr Smyth's ideas on fumigation. To describe the practice as useless and ineffective was a legitimate professional judgement even if it was likely to offend the champions of nitrous gas. But in a later comment Trotter went further

---

[6] Trotter, *Medicina Nautica*, III, 74–6
[7] Trotter, *A View of the Nervous Temperament*, dedication

and described fumigation as mischievous chicanery, and indulged in an *ad hominem* attack unusual in rational scientific discourse. In 1801 there was the incident where Trotter's officious and interfering behaviour resulted in him being banned from the naval hospital of Plymouth. In the judgement of his colleagues, he had engaged in 'scandalous calumnies' against them.

During civilian life, the most flagrant example of interpersonal ineptitude and needless aggression in Trotter's conduct was his dispute with Dr John Clark in 1804, where he argued publicly with this respected Newcastle physician over the management of a patient. When with good sense Dr Clark tried to pull out of further confrontation, Trotter chose to interpret this as insult. In 1806 there was the row over choke-damp with Trotter's remarkable description of his adversary as 'hyena-like'.

This attitude did Trotter no good, as in the confrontation in July 1800 following Lord St Vincent's allegation that he had kept ships unnecessarily in port. The admiral's letter of reprimand was certainly peremptory but was typical of his robust, often brutal style of command. Trotter's sulky response to the criticism made matters worse and his consequent removal to the side lines was very much a self-inflicted wound. It may be that St Vincent's words were offensive and ill-judged. But for Trotter to have reacted to this banality in terms of public contention with so powerful a figure as St Vincent was not politic, nor did it show any understanding of the admiral's well-known style.

That the fire of Trotter's resentment did not over time burn low is manifested by the tone and content of the preface written in 1820 to *Sea Weeds* with its catalogue of grievances, and self-justifications. Much of the complaint was directed at the alleged failure to give him an adequate pension. But he also took this as occasion to attack what he deemed to be the very general and institutionalized incompetence of the navy's administrative machinery, accusing it of 'the sloath and insolence of office'.[8] Perhaps all bureaucracies appear slothful and insolent to outsiders who have to treat with them. But there were in fact numerous instances during his active career when the same naval bureaucracy showed itself totally supportive of Trotter's representations. Indeed, the promptness with which it accepted his proposals on naval hospitals, on surgeons' pay and on scurvy was remarkable, indeed flattering.

This aspect of Trotter's character must over time have needlessly won him many enemies. He showed sustained creativity of the highest order, yes, but this handicapping streak was witness of a tension within him. In middle age, his visible loss of influence within the navy and the discomfort resulting from the hernia may have exacerbated the irritable side of his character.

The play in the round

Standing back from the detail, what is one to make of the play which Trotter acted out over his richly eventful life with its background of contextual shifting of scenery, and with so many other actors crossing that stage? Cullen, Nelson, Howe, St Vincent, Blane, Jenner, Wilberforce – these are some of the stars

---

[8] Trotter, *Sea Weeds*, xvi

who made appearances in the drama. But there was an enormous supporting cast including seamen, surgeons, drunks, voluptuaries, sellers of green apples, the publicans of Plymouth, the iniquitous Captain Noble and Lovely Sue. But what review should we be giving of Trotter as actor, producer, script-writer, seller of programmes, writer of his own theatrical reviews and fulfiller of so many other roles, as the curtain now comes down?

Our conclusion must be that Trotter was an outstanding and creative person, albeit a vulnerable one, who greatly cared about the betterment of health and who contributed energetically and successfully to his central cause, the improvement of the navy's medical services. With the *Essay on Drunkenness* he produced a book of great originality and lasting importance. In a more minor way, he was a poet and playwright. Taken in the round, this was a performance in the Great Theatre of Life, worthy of loud, even tumultuous, ovation.

Bibliography

Andrews, C. E., 'Almost the same but not quite: English poetry by Scots in the 18th century', *The Eighteenth Century* 47 (2006), 59–79

Anstey, R., *The Atlantic Slave Trade and British Abolition* (London, 1975)

Armstrong's Map of Northumberland, 1796

Aubrey, T., *The Sea Surgeon, Or the Guinea Man's Vade Mecum In Which is laid down The Method of Curing such Diseases as usually happen Abroad especially on the Coast of Guinea; with the best way of treating Negroes both in Heath and in Sickness* (London, 1729)

Bailey J., and G. Culley, *A General View of the Agriculture of the County of Northumberland* (London, 1794)

Barnes, G. R., and J. H. Owen (eds), *The Private Papers of John, Earl of Sandwich*, Navy Records Society 78 (London and Colchester, 1938)

Barrow, Sir John, *Life of Richard Earl Howe* (London, 1838)

Bartholomew, M., 'James Lind and scurvy: a revaluation', *Journal for Maritime Research* (January, 2002), www.jmr.nmm.ac.uk

Baugh, D. A., *British Naval Administration in the Age of Walpole* (Princeton, 1965)

Berridge, V., and G. Edwards, *Opium and the People: Opiate Use in Nineteenth Century England* (London, 1981)

Blake, R., *Evangelicals in the Royal Navy 1775–1815* (Woodbridge, 2008)

Blane, Sir Gilbert, *Observation on the Diseases of Seamen* (London, 1789)

—— *Select Dissertations* (London, 1822)

Boswell, J., *Life of Samuel Johnson* (Oxford, 1904; orig. publ. London, 1791)

Bown, S. R., *Scurvy: How a Surgeon, a Mariner and a Gentleman Solved the Greatest Medical Mystery of the Age of Sail* (New York, 2003)

Boyes, J., 'Medicine and dentistry in Newcastle-upon-Tyne in the eighteenth century', *Proceedings of the Royal Society of Medicine* 50 (1956), 229–35

Broadie, A., *The Cambridge Companion to the Scottish Enlightenment* (Cambridge, 2003)

Brockliss, L., and J. Cardwell, *Nelson's Surgeon: William Beatty, Naval Medicine and the Battle of Trafalgar* (Oxford, 2005)

Brogan, T. V. F., A. Preminger and F. J. Warnke (eds), *The New Princeton Encyclopaedia of Poetry and Poetics* (Princeton, 1993)

Bromley, J. S. (ed.), *Manning the Royal Navy: Selected Public Pamphlets 1693–1872*, Navy Records Society 119 (London and Colchester, 1976)

Bryson, G., *Man and Society: The Scottish Inquiry of the Eighteenth Century* (Princeton, 1945)

Burnett, J., *Plenty and Want* (London, 1966)

Campbell, R., *The London Tradesman* (London, 1749)

Cardwell, J., 'The Royal Navy and Malaria, 1756–1815', *Trafalgar Chronicle* (2007), 84–96

Carmichael, J., 'Thomas Trotter, Physician to the Fleet', in D. Gardner-Medwin, A. Hargreaves and E. Lazenby (eds), *Medicine in Northumberland* (Newcastle-upon-Tyne 1993), 164–92

Carpenter, K. J., *The History of Scurvy and Vitamin C* (Cambridge, 1986)

Cecil, R., in Rouse, M.(ed.), *The Life of John Newton* (Fearn, 2000)

Chambers, R., *A Biographical Dictionary of Eminent Scotsmen* (Glasgow, 1835)

Cheyne, G., *The English Malady*, facsimile edition with introduction by Roy Porter (London, 1991; orig. publ. London, 1733)

Childers, S. (ed.), *A Mariner of England: An Account of the Career of William Richardson from Cabin Boy in the Merchant Service to Warrant Officer in the Royal Navy (1780–1819) as Told by Himself* (London, 1904)

Christopher, E., *Slave Ship Sailors and their Captive Cargoes 1730–1807* (Cambridge, 2006)

Cockburn, A., 'Biographical sketch of the late Dr Thomas Trotter Physician to the Channel Fleet', *Edinburgh Medical Surgical Journal* 64 (1845), 430–41

Cole, W. A., and P. Deane, *British Economic Growth 1688–1967* (Cambridge, 1967)

Cook, G. C., 'Influence of diarrhoeal disease on military and naval campaigns', *Journal of the Royal Society of Medicine* 94 (2001), 95–7

Corbett, J. S. (ed.), *Fighting Instructions, 1530–1816*, Navy Records Society 29 (London and Colchester, 1905)

Crimmin, P. K., 'The Sick and Hurt Board and the health of seamen', *Journal for Maritime Research* (December 1999), www.jmr.nmm.ac.uk

—— 'John Jervis, Earl of St Vincent, 1739–1823', in P. Le Fevre and R. Harding (eds), *Precursors of Nelson, British Admirals of the Eighteenth Century* (London, 2000), 325–50

Cullen, W., *Lectures on the Materia Medica as Delivered by William Cullen* (London, 1773)

—— *Synopsis Nosologiae Methodicae* (Edinburgh, 1772)

Curtin, P., *The Atlantic Slave Trade: A Census* (Madison, 1969)

Curtis, R., *The Means used to Eradicate a Malignant Fever which Raged aboard HMS Brunswick at Spithead in the Spring of the Year 1791, with some Observations on the Most Probable Means of Preserving the Health of a Ship's Company* (1791)

Daiches, D. E., P. Jones and J. Jones (eds), *A Hotbed of Genius: The Scottish Enlightenment 1730–1790* (Edinburgh, 1986)

Davies, D., *Slavery in the Age of Revolution* (London, 1975)

Denby, D., *Northern Lights* (New York, 2004)

Devine, T. M. (ed), *Scotland and the Union 1707–2007* (Edinburgh, 2008)

Dewar, H., *A Letter to Thomas Trotter, M.D., occasioned by his Proposal for Destroying the Fire and Choak Damps of Coal Mines; Containing Chemical and General Strictures on that Work* (Manchester and London, 1806)

—— 'On the education of James Mitchell the young man born deaf and blind', *Transactions of the Royal Society of Edinburgh* 6 (Edinburgh, 1813), 77–87; 'Observations on the Theory of Language', ibid. 7 (1814), 387–410; 'On the treatment of the Sinuous Ulcer', ibid. 8 (1816), 477–93

Duffy, M., 'Samuel Hood, 1st Viscount Hood 1724–1816', in P. Le Fevre and R. Harding (eds), *Precursors of Nelson, British Admirals of the Eighteenth Century* (London, 2000), 249–77

Duffy, M., *Soldiers, Sugar and Seapower: The British Experience in the West Indies against Revolutionary France* (Oxford, 1987)

—— and R. Morris, *The Glorious 1st of June: A Naval Battle and its Aftermath* (Exeter, 2001)

Edwards, G., *Alcohol: The Ambiguous Molecule* (London, 2000), published in the USA as *Alcohol: The World's Favorite Drug* (New York, 2000)

——, E. J. Marshall and C. C. H. Cook, *The Treatment of Drinking Problems* (Cambridge, 2003)

——, E. Oppenheimer and C. Taylor, 'Hearing the noise in the system: exploration of textual analysis as a method for studying change in drinking behaviour', *British Journal of Addiction* 87 (1992), 73–81

Fisher, R. B., *Edward Jenner 1749–1823* (London, 1991)

Flinn, M. W., *The History of the British Coal Industry vol. 2, 1700–1830: The Industrial Revolution* (Oxford, 1984)

A Friend to Rational Schemes of Improvement, *A reply to Trotter's Second Pamphlet respecting the means of destroying the Fire-Damp; by the author of 'An address to the proprietors and managers of coal mines'* (London and Newcastle-upon-Tyne, 1806)

Fulford, T., and D. Lee, 'The Jenneration of disease: vaccination, romanticism and revolution', in M. O'Neill and M. Sanders (eds), *Romanticism* (Abingdon, 2006)

Galvin, R. W., *America's Founding Secret: What the Enlightenment Taught our Founding Fathers* (Oxford, 2002)

Gardner, J. A., *Above and below Hatches* (London, 1955)

General Assembly of the Church of Scotland, *The New Statistical Account of Scotland* (Edinburgh and London, 1845)

Gillespie, L., 'Observations on the putrid ulcer', *London Medical Journal* 9 (1785), 373–410

—— *Advice to the Commanders and Officers of HM Fleet serving in the West Indies on the Preservation and Health of Seamen* (London, 1798)

—— *Observations on the Diseases which Prevailed in HM Squadron in the Leeward Islands* (London, 1792)

Gilmore, T. B., 'James Boswell's drinking', *Eighteenth Century Studies* 24 (1991), 337–57

Goddard, J. C., 'The surgeon's chest: surgical instruments of the Royal Navy during the Napoleonic War', *Journal of the Royal Society of Medicine* 97 (2004), 191–7

Goodwin, P., *Nelson's Ships* (London, 2002)

—— *The Construction and Fitting of the Sailing Man of War, 1650–1850* (London, 1987)

—— *The Ships of Trafalgar* (London, 2005)

Goslings, W. R. O., 'Leiden and Edinburgh: The Seed, the Soil and the Climate' in R. W. Anderson and A. D. C. Simpson (eds) *The Early Years of Edinburgh Medical School* (Edinburgh, 1976)

Gray, J. H., *Autobiography of a Country Gentleman* (privately printed, 1868)

Haycock, D. B., and S. Archer (eds), *Health and Medicine at Sea* (Woodbridge, 2009)

—— 'Extermination of the bloody flux', *Journal for Maritime Research* (January 2002), www.jmr.nmm.ac.uk

Hughes, E. (ed.), *Correspondence of Lord Collingwood*, Navy Records Society 98 (London and Colchester, 1957)

Huss, M., *Alcoholismus Chronicus, eller Chronisk alkoholssjukdom* (Stockholm, 1849)

Ismay, T., 'Letter of Thomas Ismay to his Father', *University of Edinburgh Journal* 8 (1936–7), 57–61

James, W., *Naval History of Great Britain* (London, 1826), vols I and II

Kemp, P. K., *The British Sailor: A Social History of the Lower Deck* (London, 1970)

Kerr, N., *Inebriety or Narcomania, its Etiology, Pathology, Treatment and Jurisprudence*, 2nd edn (London, 1888)

Knight, R., 'Richard, Earl Howe, 1726–1799', in P. Le Fevre and R. Harding (eds), *Precursors of Nelson, British Admirals of the Eighteenth Century* (London, 2000), 279–99

—— *The Pursuit of Victory: The Life and Achievements of Horatio Nelson* (London, 2000)

Kord, S., *Women Peasant Poets in 18th Century England, Scotland and Germany* (Woodbridge, 2003)

Laughton, Sir J. (ed.), *Barham Papers*, Navy Records Society 32 (London and Colchester, 1906)

Lavery, B. (ed.), *Shipboard Life and Organization*, Navy Records Society 138 (Aldershot, 1998)

—— 'George Keith Elphinstone, Lord Keith, 1746–1823', in P. Le Fevre and R. Harding (eds), *Precursors of Nelson, British Admirals of the Eighteenth Century* (London, 2000), 377–99

—— *The Ship of the Line* (London, 1984), 2 vols

Le Fevre, P., and R. Harding (eds), *Precursors of Nelson, British Admirals of the Eighteenth Century* (London, 2000)

Leff, J., 'Transcultural psychiatry', in M. G. Gelder, J. J. Lopez-Ibor and N. C. Anderson (eds), *New Oxford Textbook of Psychiatry* (Oxford, 2000), 13–16

Lewis, M., *A Social History of the Navy 1793–1815* (London, 1960)

—— (ed.), *Sir William Dillon's Narrative of Professional Adventures*, Navy Records Society 93 (London and Colchester, 1953)

Lind, J., *A Treatise on the Scurvy* (Edinburgh, 1753)

Lloyd, C. (ed.), *Naval Miscellany*, Navy Records Society 92 (London and Colchester, 1952)

—— (ed.), *The Health of Seamen*, Navy Records Society 107 (London and Colchester, 1965)

—— (ed.), *The Keith Papers*, Navy Records Society 90 (London and Colchester, 1950)

—— *The British Seaman* (London, 1968)

—— and L. Coulter, *Medicine and the Navy* (Edinburgh, 1961), vol. III

Logan, P. M., and P. Melville, *Nerves and Narratives: A Cultural History of Hysteria in 19th Century British Prose* (Berkley, 1997)

MacDonald, S., 'The diffusion of knowledge among Northumberland farmers 1780–1815', *The Agricultural History Review* 27 (Welwyn Garden City, 1979), 30–9

Mackenzie, E., *Historical Account of Newcastle-upon-Tyne, including the Borough of Gateshead* (Newcastle-upon-Tyne, 1827)

Mackenzie and Dent's *Newcastle Directory* (Newcastle-upon-Tyne, 1811)

Manning, S., 'Post-Union Scotland and the Scottish idiom of Britishness', in I. Brown, S. Manning and M. G. H. Pittock (eds), *The Edinburgh History of Scottish Literature* (Edinburgh, 2007), ll, 45–56

Marshall, D., *Industrial England 1776–1851* (London, 1973)

Martin, B., and R. Spurrell (eds), *The Journal of a Slave Trader, John Newton, 1764* (London, 1962)

McCord, N., and D. J. Rowe, *Northumberland and Durham: Industry in the Nineteenth Century* (Newcastle-upon-Tyne, 1971)

Medical and Physical Journal (London), 3 (January–June 1800), 245–7, 429–33, 526–8; 10 (June–December 1803), 382–3; 12 (June–December 1804), 289–97; 13 (January–June 1805), 132–5

Miller, P., *The New England Mind in the 17th Century* (Harvard, 1982)

Minto, Countess of, *The Life and Letters of Sir Gilbert Minto 1751–1896* (London, 1874)

Mitchell's *Newcastle Directory of 1801* (Newcastle-upon-Tyne 1801)

Monthly Review or Literary Journal (London) , R. Griffiths (ed.), 74 (January–March 1786), 316–17; 44 (May–August 1804), 193–5

Morris, R. (ed.), *The Channel Fleet and the Blockade of Brest*, Navy Records Society 141 (Aldershot, 2001)

—— 'Charles Middleton, Lord Barham, 1726–1813', in P. Le Fevre and R. Harding (eds), *Precursors of Nelson, British Admirals of the Eighteenth Century* (London, 2000), 301–23

Mossner, E. L., and I. S. Ross (eds), *The Correspondence of Adam Smith* (Oxford, 1987)

Nef, J. U., *The Rise of the British Coal Industry* (Cambridge, 1984), vol. II

Nicholas, N. H., *The Dispatches and Letters of Vice-Admiral Lord Viscount Nelson* (London, 1846)

O'Byne, W., *Royal Naval Biography* (London, 1849)

Oldfield, J. R., *Popular Politics and British Anti-Slavery* (Manchester, 1995)

Paterson, Lt Colonel, *A New Description of All the Direct and Principal Cross Roads in England and Wales and Part of Scotland*, 15th edn (London, 1811)

Porter, D. and R., *Patient's Progress: Doctors and Doctoring in Eighteenth Century England* (Stanford, 1989)

Porter, I. A., 'Thomas Trotter MD, naval physician', *Medical History* 7 (1963), 155–64

Porter, R., 'The drinking man's disease: the history of alcoholism in Georgian Britain', *British Journal of Addiction* 80 (1985), 385–96

—— *English Society in the Eighteenth Century* (London, 1982)

—— *Enlightenment: Britain and the Creation of the Modern World* (London, 2000)

—— *Flesh in the Age of Reason* (London, 2003)

Ralfe, J., *The Naval Biography of Great Britain, consisting of historical memoirs of those officers of the British Navy who distinguished themselves during the reign of George III* (London, 1828), 4 vols

Rediker, M., *The Slave Ship: A Human History* (London, 2007)

Regulations and Instructions Relating to His Majesty's Service at Sea, 13 editions issued by Order in Council (London, 1734–90)

Rendall, J., *Origins of the Scottish Enlightenment* (London, 1978)

Risse, G. B., 'Britannia rules the seas: the health of seamen, Edinburgh, 1791–1800', *Journal of the History of Medicine and Allied Sciences* 43 (1988), 426–46

—— *Hospital Life in Enlightenment Scotland* (New York and Cambridge, 1986)

Robertson, Robert, *Observations on Fevers and other Diseases, which Occur on Voyages to Africa and the West Indies* (London, 1792)

Roddis, L. H., *James Lind, Founder of Nautical Medicine* (New York, 1950)

Rodger, N. A. M. (ed.), *William Spaven's Memoirs of a Seafaring Life* (London, 2000)

—— 'Commissioned officers' careers in the Royal Navy', *Journal of Maritime Research* (July 2001), www.jmr.nmm.ac.uk

—— 'Medicine and science in the British Navy in the eighteenth century', in C. Bucher (ed.), *L'Homme, la santé et la mer* (Paris, 1997), 333–44

—— *The Command of the Ocean, 1649–1815* (London, 2004)

—— *The Insatiable Earl: Life of John Montague, 4th Earl of Sandwich* (London and New York, 1994)

—— *The Wooden World: An Anatomy of the Georgian Navy* (London, 1986)

Rolleston, H. D., 'Thomas Trotter MD', *The Journal of the Royal Navy Medical Services* 5 (1919), 153–65

Rosner, L., *Medical Education in the Age of Improvement: Edinburgh Students and Apprentices 1760 to 1826* (Edinburgh, 1991)

Rush, B., *Travels through Life: An Account of Sundry Incidents and Events in the Life of Benjamin Rush* (Philadelphia 1825), reproduced in G. W. Corner (ed.), *The Autobiography of Benjamin Rush* (Princeton, 1948)

—— *An inquiry into the Effects of Ardent Spirits on the Human Body and Mind, with an Account of the Means for Preventing and of the Remedies for Curing them*, 8th edn (Boston, 1823). Reprinted in *Quarterly Journal of Studies on Alcohol* 4 (1943–4), 325–41

Saxby, R., 'The blockade of Brest in the French Revolutionary War', *Mariner's Mirror* 78 (1992), 25–35

Schomberg, Capt I., *Naval Chronology* (London, 1802), 5 vols

Scott, Sir Walter, *Memoirs of Sir Walter Scott Bart.* (Edinburgh, 1837)

Sekora, J., *Luxury: The Concept in Western Thought* (Baltimore and London, 1977)

Shadwell, A., *Drink, Temperance and Legislation* (London, 1902)

Sheridan, R. B., 'The Guinea surgeons on the middle passage: the provision of medical services in the British slave trade', *The International Journal of African Historical Studies* 14 (1981), 601–25

Smellie, W., *Literary and Characteristic Lives of Gregory, Kaines, Hume and Smith* (Edinburgh, 1800)

Smout, T. C., 'Scotland as North Britain', in I. Brown, S. Manning and M. G. H. Pittock (eds), *The Edinburgh History of Scottish Literature; Enlightenment, Britain and Empire* (Edinburgh, 2007), II, 1–11

Spring, J. A., and D. H. Buss, 'Three centuries of alcohol in the British diet', *Nature* 270 (1977), 567–72

Steel, D., *Original and Correct List of the Royal Navy* (London Quarterly 1795 to 1806)

Steer, D. M., 'The blockade of Brest and the victualling of the Western squadron, 1793–1805', *Mariner's Mirror* 76 (1990), 307–16

Stewart, C. P., and D. Guthrie (eds), *Lind's Treatise on the Scurvy* (Edinburgh, 1953)

Stubbs, B. J., 'Captain Cook's beer: the anti-scorbutic effects of malt and beer in late eighteenth century sea voyages', *Asia and Pacific Journal of Clinical Nutrition* 12 (2003), 129–37

Sykes, J., *Local Records or Historical Register of Remarkable Events . . . in Northumberland and Durham* (Newcastle, 1833)

Syrett, D., *Admiral Lord Howe* (Staplehurst, 2006)

—— and R. L. DiNardo, *The Commissioned Officers of the Royal Navy 1660–1815*, Navy Records Society Occasional Publications (Aldershot, 1994)

Talbott, John C., *The Pen and Ink Sailor: Charles Middleton and the King's Navy, 1778–1813* (London, 1998)

Tegg, T., *The London Encyclopaedia or Universal Dictionary of Science, Art, Literature and Practical Mechanics* (London, 1829)

The Edinburgh Annual Register (Edinburgh, 1823)

The Hampshire Directory (Winchester, 1784)

Thomas, H., *The Slave Trade: The History of the Atlantic Slave Trade 1440–1870* (London, 2006)

Thomas, R., *The Modern Practice of Physic* (London, 1821)

Thompson, F., *An Essay on the Scurvy showing Effectual and Practical Means for its Prevention at Sea* (London, 1790)

Thomson, J., *An Account of the Life, Lectures and Writings of William Cullen, MD* (Edinburgh, 1859), 2 vols

Thursfield, H. G. (ed.), 'Peter Cullen 1789–1802', in H. G. Thursfield (ed.), *Five Naval Journals, 1787–1817*, Navy Records Society 91 (London and Colchester, 1951), 41–119

Topham, E., *Edinburgh Life in the Eighteenth Century* (Edinburgh, 1994)

Tröhler, U., 'James Lind and scurvy', *Journal of the Royal Society of Medicine* 98 (2005), 519–22

Trotter, T., 'De ebriatate eiusque effectibus in corpus humanum' (MD thesis, Edinburgh, 1788)

—— *Essay on Drunkenness*, facsimile edition, edited with an introduction by Roy Porter (London, 1988; orig. publ. London, 1804)

—— *An Essay, Medical, Philosophical and Chemical, on Drunkenness, and its Effects on the Human Body* (London, 1804)

—— *Medicina Nautica: an Essay on the Diseases of Seamen* (London, 1797–1803), 3 vols

—— *Observations on the Scurvy: with a review of the opinions lately advanced on that disease and a new theory defended* (London, 1787 and 1792)

—— *A Practicable Plan for Manning the Royal Navy* (Newcastle and London, 1819)

—— *A Proposal for Destroying Fire and Choak-Damps of Coal Mines; and their Production Explained in the Principles of Modern Chemistry: addressed to the owners and Agents of Coal-Works etc.* (Newcastle, 1805)

—— *Remarks on the Establishment of Naval Hospitals and Sick Quarters with HINTS for their improvement* (1795)

—— *A Review of the Medical Services of the British Navy with a Method of Reform Proposed* (London, 1790)

—— *Sea Weeds: Poems, Written on Various Oceans, Chiefly during a Naval Life* (London, 1829)

—— *A Second Address to the Owners and Agents of Coal-Mines on Destroying the Fire and Choke Damp in Confutation of two pamphlets, lately circulated in the neighbourhood of Newcastle* (Newcastle, 1806)

Trotter, T., *A View of the Nervous Temperament being a Practical Enquiry into the Increasing Prevalence, Prevention and Treatment of those Diseases commonly called Nervous, Bilious, Stomach and Liver Complaints, Indigestion, Low Spirits, Gout etc.* (London, 1807), facsimile edition, Classics in Psychiatry, ed E. T. Carison (New York, 1967)

Tucker, J. S., *Memoir of Admiral the Rt Hon. the Earl of St Vincent* (London, 1844), 2 vols

Tunstall, B., *Naval Warfare in the Age of Sail: The Evolution of Fighting Tactics* (London, 1990)

Turner, E. H., 'Naval medical services 1793–1815', *Mariner's Mirror* 46 (1960), 119–33

Vaillant, G., *Adaptation to Life* (Boston, 1977)

Vale, B., 'The conquest of scurvy in the Royal Navy 1793–1800: a challenge to current orthodoxy', *Mariner's Mirror* 94 (2008), 160–75

Warner, J. F., 'The naturalization of beer and gin in early modern England', *Contemporary Drug Problems* 24 (1997), 373–402

Warner, O., *The Glorious First of June* (London, 1961)

Watt, Surgeon Admiral Sir James, 'Naval surgery in the time of Nelson', in N. Tracy (ed), *The Age of Sail* (London, 2002–3), 25–33

—— 'Some consequences of nutritional disorders in eighteenth century British circumnavigation', in J. Watt, E. J. Freeman and W. F. Bynu (eds), *Starving Sailors* (London, 1981), 51–71

Webb, P., 'The rebuilding and repair of the British fleet 1783–93', *Bulletin of the Institute of Historical Research* 50 (1977), 194–209

Whellan, W., *History, Topography and Directory of Northumberland comprising a General Survey of the County* (London and Manchester, 1855)

White, W., *Northumberland and the Border* (London, 1856)

Williams, G., *History of the Liverpool Privateers and Letters of Marque with an Account of the Liverpool Slave Trade* (London, 1897)

Wilson, G. B., *Alcohol and the Nation* (London, 1941)

Wilson, M., *Imperial Gazeteer of Scotland* (London and Edinburgh, 1868), vol. II

Wyatt, H. V., 'James Lind and the prevention of scurvy', *Medical History* 20 (1976), 433–8

Index

Index